POWERPRO S

MW00561125

CHEVROLET
Small-Block V-8
ID GUIDE

Covers All Chevy Small-Block Engines Since 1955

Pierre Lafontaine

MBI Publishing Company

First published in 1996 by MBI Publishing Company, PO Box 1, 729 Prospect Avenue, Osceola, WI 54020-0001 USA.

MBI Publishing Company books are also available at discounts in bulk quantity for industrial or sales-promotional use. For details write to Special Sales Manager at Motorbooks International Wholesalers & Distributors, 729 Prospect Avenue, PO Box 1, Osceola, WI 54020-0001 USA.

Library of Congress Cataloging-in-Publication Data Available

0-7603-0175-1

On the front cover: The classic 283ci V-8, introduced in 1957, is basically a larger version of the original 265ci small-block. This engine, installed in a 1957 Bel Air convertible, produces 220hp and features 9.5:1 compression. The car is owned by Bruce and Linda Finley of Lakeland, Florida. *Mike Mueller*

Printed in the United States of America

Contents

Acknowledgments

To my father, who is no longer of this world. I am sure he would be proud. To my wife, Laura, for all of her patience. She took care of the children, Samantha and Zachary, while I was writing this book.

I thank all the people who have taught me about engines and the rebuilding business: Howe Cunningham at R&B Automotive for igniting my passion for the racing engine in the late 70s; Rick Gregoire, my senior machinist throughout my apprenticeship, who taught me a pile of tricks; and Mr. David Vizard. He has a way of explaining things in the clearest fashion. I highly recommend his latest books in the "POWERPRO SERIES" that deal with the small-block Chevy. They are most informative and extremely well researched.

I thank Cesar Da Silva at Mississauga Engines in Ontario, Canada, for letting me use his shop with all the cores he has available. For a Ford guy, he sure has a lot of Chevy bits.

Last, but not least, I thank Michael Dapper at Motorbooks International for his trust and belief in me. He has supported me but still left me alone enough to finish this project.

Introduction

As of 1995, the small-block Chevrolet V-8 engine will have forty years of production under its belt. I would like to thank the Chevrolet Division of General Motors for supplying us with this outstanding little V-8 for so many years. Its popularity is unsurpassed. Not only has it been installed in most of GM's chassis over the years, but it also has been installed by marine, taxi, and other manufacturers as original equipment. The engine also has been used in innumerable other situations, from the grocery getter to the hot rod to racing vehicles of all sorts. In 1994, it propelled Dale Earnhardt to his seventh championship on the NASCAR circuit.

The powers that be have seen fit to keep the small-block within the confines of its original design. Bore spacing, bell housing flange, mounts, balancer location, flywheel flange, and most all external physical properties have remained constant allowing complete interchangeability. This is to the engineers' disdain. For years they wanted to alter the basic configuration of the small-block to eliminate the shortcomings. Finally in the mid-80s, they were allowed to change the rocker cover rail and rear main seal, both of which were prone to leakage. By the 90s, the designers were finally cut loose to flex their creative muscles. This means the overhead cam, multi-valve, port-

The Chevrolet small-block V-8 engine has remained within these original confines throughout its entire existence.

injected LT5 and the new LT1 are still the same old pushrod V-8, but with a few twists. Reverse cooling, front-mounted ignition, and a new intake plenum make this the best small-block yet.

Why write this book? Well, over the years, I have been asked regularly to identify engines for customers. The most common situation occurs when somebody buys a muscle car and would like to know if the seller is truthful in saying, "This is a numbers match car." The answer is very simple: Go to a shop manual and verify the numbers. If they do match, then the numbers jive and it's over. But if the numbers don't match, then the next question I get is, "Well, if it's not the original engine, what is it, what year is it, what did it come out of, and how much horsepower does it make?" For me to determine its exact origin is a time-consuming effort. To this day I have yet to find a complete, sorted, and comprehensive publication catering to this problem. Most all that is written on the subject is usually

sorted by years, just as GM handed it out. If you have only a range of years from which you suspect this engine to be from, then you must go through the whole list to find it; you will probably miss it the first time around. This is not the right way to do this. I don't know about you, but I don't have time to waste. So, in the early 80s I started making a list of all pertinent numbers relating to the small-block Chevy. It really didn't occur to me that this information could be valuable as a publication until a friend suggested it to me a few years ago. This is how this book came about.

Through my research, reading all that I could find, I have noticed that there are an enormous amount of mistakes in all that is already published. Some people mistake part numbers for casting numbers, others mistake block numbers for cylinder head numbers, and one machinist reference manual was simply "out to lunch." I suspect that many of these books were written by

clerical people that have never set a finger on a small-block. I, on the other hand, have the experience of rebuilding exclsively routinely Chevrolet small-blocks; there are enough racers out there to keep a guy like me busy. I have attempted to weed out all erroneous information from this manual. Unfortunately, I still expect that some will creep into the book. Nonetheless, I have left out any questionable bits of information, physically verified as many conflicting situations as possible, and cross-referenced with my stack of notes taken from cores over the years. I welcome any documented corrections and exceptions to the information that I am presenting.

I hope that anybody reading this book will gain the knowledge they seek on this wonderful engine. I dare say, since I feel I have researched this subject so intensively, that even the pros may pick up a tidbit or two. Please enjoy you're journey through this book.

Engine Data Summary

year	cid	carb	comp	hp/ghp	@ rpm	net trq	@ rpm	bore	stroke	models	RPO
1955	265	2	8	162	4400	257	2200	3.7502	3	pass	-
1955	265	4	8	180	4600	260	2800	3.7502	3	pass	-
1955	265	4	8	195	5000	-	-	3.7502	3	Vette	-
1956	265	2	8	162	4400	257	2200	3.7502	3	pass	-
1956	265	2	8	170	4400	257	2400	3.7502	3	pass	-
1956	265	4	9.2506	205	4600	268	3000	3.7502	3	pass	-
1956	265	4	9.2506	210	5200	268	3000	3.7502	3	Vette	-
1956	265	8	9.2506	225	5200	270	3600	3.7502	3	-	-
1957	265	2	8	162	4400	257	2400	3.7502	3	pass	-
1957	283	2	8.5005	185	4600	275	4600	3.8752	3	pass	-
1957	283	4	9.5006	220	4800	300	4800	3.8752	3	-	-
1957	283	8	9.5006	245	5000	300	3800	3.8752	3	-	-
1957	283	FI	9.5006	250	5000	305	3800	3.8752	3	pass	-
1957	283	4	9.5006	270	6000	285	4200	3.8752	3	pass	-
1957	283	FI	10.501	283	6200	290	4400	3.8752	3	pass	-
1958	283	2	8.5005	185	4600	275	2400	3.8752	3	pass	-
1958	283	4	9.5006	230	4800	300	3000	3.8752	3	-	-
1958	283	8	9.5006	245	5000	300	3800	3.8752	3	Vette	-
1958	283	FI	10.501	250	5000	305	3800	3.8752	3	-	-
1958	283	8	10.501	270	6000	305	3800	3.8752	3	Vette	-
1959	283	2	8.5005	185	4600	275	2400	3.8752	3	pass	-
1959	283	4	9.5006	230	4800	300	3000	3.8752	3	pass	-
1959	283	8	9.5006	245	5000	300	3800	3.8752	3	-	-
1959	283	FI	9.5006	250	5000	305	3800	3.8752	3	-	-

year	cid	carb	comp	hp/ghp	@ rpm	net trq	@ rpm	bore	stroke	models	RPO
1959	283	8	9.5006	270	6000	300	3800	3.8752	3	Vette	-
1959	283	FI	10.501	290	6200	290	4400	3.8752	3	-	-
1960	283	2	8.5005	170	4200	275	2200	3.8752	3	pass	-
1960	283	4	9.5006	230	4800	300	3000	3.8752	3	-	-
1960	283	8	9.5006	245	5000	300	3000	3.8752	3	Vette	-
1960	283	8	9.5006	270	6000	300	3600	3.8752	3	Vette	-
1960	283	FI	11	275	5200	305	3800	3.8752	3	Vette	-
1960	283	FI	10.501	315	6200	-	-	3.8752	3	Vette	-
1961	283	2	8.5005	170	4200	275	2200	3.8752	3	pass	-
1961	283	4	8.5005	230	4800	300	3000	3.8752	3	-	-
1961	283	8	9.5006	245	5000	300	3000	3.8752	3	Vette	-
1961	283	8	10.501	270	6000	300	3600	3.8752	3	Vette	-
1961	283	FI	9.5006	275	5200	305	3800	3.8752	3	Vette	-
1961	283	FI	9.5006	315	6200	-	-	3.8752	3	Vette	-
1962	283	2	8.5005	170	4200	275	2200	3.8752	3	pass	STD
1962	327	4	10.501	250	4400	350	2800	4	3.2502	-	-
1962	327	4	10.501	300	5000	360	3200	4	3.2502	pass	-
1962	327	4	11.251	340	6000	-	-	4	3.2502	Vette	-
1962	327	FI	11.251	360	6000	-	-	4	3.2502	Vette	-
1963	283	R 2	8.5005	195	4800	285	2400	3.8752	3	pass	STD
1963	327	R 4	10.501	250	4400	350	2800	4	3.2502	pass	L30
1963	327	R 4	10.501	250	4400	210	4400	4	3.2502	Vette	-
1963	327	R 4	10.501	300	5000	360	3200	4	3.2502	pass	L74
1963	327	H 4	11.251	340	6000	-	-	4	3.2502	Vette	-
1963	327	FI	11.251	360	6000	-	-	4	3.2502	Vette	-
1964	283	R 2	9.2506	195	4800	285	2400	3.8752	3	pass	STD
1964	283	R 4	9.2506	220	4800	295	3200	3.8752	3	Chevelle	L77
1964	327	R 4	10.501	250	4400	210	4400	4	3.2502	Vette	-
1964	327	R 4	10.501	250	4400	350	2800	4	3.2502	pass	L30
1964	327	R 4	10.501	300	5000	360	3200	4	3.2502	pass	L74
1964	327	H 4	11.251	365	5400	-	-	4	3.2502	Vette	-
1964	327	FI	11.251	375	5800	352	5000	4	3.2502	Vette	-
1965	283	R 2	9.2506	195	4800	285	2400	3.8752	3	pass	-
1965	283	R 4	9.2506	220	4800	-	-	3.8752	3	pass	-
1965	327	R 4	10.501	250	4400	350	2800	4	3.2502	-	-
1965	327	R 4	10.501	300	5000	360	3200	4	3.2502	-	-
1965	327	H 4	10.501	350	5800	360	3600	4	3.2502	Chevelle	-
1965	327	H 4	11	365	6200	350	4000	4	3.2502	Vette	-
1965	327	FI	11	375	6200	350	4600	4	3.2502	Vette	-
1966	283	R 2	9.2506	195	4800	285	2400	3.8752	3	full size,	
-	-	-	-	-	-	-	-	-	-	Chevelle,	
-	-	-	-	-	-	-	-	-	-	Nova	-
1966	283	R 4	9.2506	220	4800	295	3200	3.8752	3	full size,	
-	-	-	-	-	-	-	-	-	-	Chevelle,	
-	-	-	-	-	-	-	-	-	-	Nova	-
1966	327	R 4	10.501	250	4800	-	-	4	3.2502	Chevelle,	
-	-	-	-	-	-	-	-	-	-	Nova	-
1966	327	R 4	10.501	275	4800	355	3200	4	3.2502	full size	-
1966	327	R 4	10.501	300	5000	360	3200	4	3.2502	Vette	-
1966	327	H 4	11	350	5800	360	3600	4	3.2502	-	-
1967	283	R 2	9.2506	195	4800	285	2400	3.8752	3	-	-
1967	327	R 2	9	210	4800	325	3200	4	3.2502	-	-
1967	327	R 4	10.501	275	4800	355	2200	4	3.2502	-	-
1967	327	R 4	10.251	300	5000	360	3400	4	3.2502	-	-
1967	327	H 4	11	350	5800	360	3600	4	3.2502	-	-
1967	350	R 4	10.501	295	4800	380	3200	4	3.48	-	-
1968	302	H 4	11	290	5800	290	4200	4	3	Z-28	-
1968	307	R 2	9	200	4600	300	2400	3.8752	3.2502	full size,	
-	-	-	-	-	-	-	-	-	-	Chevelle,	
-	-	-	-	-	-	-	-	-	-	Chevy II	-

year	cid	carb	comp	hp/ghp	@ rpm	net trq	@ rpm	bore	stroke	models	RPO
1968	327	R 2	8.7506	210	4600	320	2400	4	3.2502	Camaro	-
1968	327	R 4	10	275	4800	355	3200	4	3.2502	-	-
1968	327	R 4	10	300	5000	360	3400	4	3.2502	-	-
1968	327	H 4	11	325	5600	355	3600	4	3.2502	-	-
1968	327	H 4	11	350	5600	360	3600	4	3.2502	-	-
1968	350	R 4	10.251	295	4800	380	3200	4	3.2502	-	-
1969	302	H 4	11	290	5800	290	4200	4	3	-	-
1969	307	R 2	9	200	4600	300	2400	3.8752	3.2502	-	-
1969	327	R 2	9	210	4600	320	2400	4	3.2502	-	-
1969	327	R 2	9	235	4800	325	2800	4	3.2502	-	-
1969	350	R 4	9	255	4800	365	3200	4	3.48	-	-
1969	350	R 4	10.251	300	4800	380	3200	4	3.48	-	-
1969	350	H 4	11	350	5600	380	3600	4	3.48	-	-
1970	307	R 2	9	200	4600	300	2400	3.8752	3.2502	-	-
1970	350	R 2	9	250	4800	345	2800	4	3.48	-	-
1970	350	R 4	10.251	300	4800	380	3200	4	3.48	-	-
1970	350	H 4	11	350	5600	380	3600	4	3.48	Z-28	-
1970	350	H 4	11	370	6000	380	3200	4	3.48	Vette	-
1970	400	R 2	9	265	4400	400	2400	4.1253	3.7502	-	-
1971	307	R 2	8.5005	200	4600	300	2400	3.8752	3.2502	-	-
1971	350	R 2	8.5005	245	4800	350	2800	4	3.48	-	-
1971	350	R 4	8.5005	270	4800	360	3200	4	3.48	-	-
1971	350	H 4	9	330	5600	360	4000	4	3.48	-	-
1971	400	R 2	8.5005	255	4400	390	2400	4.1253	3.7502	-	-
1972	307	R 2	8.5005	115	4000	-	-	3.8752	3.2502	-	-
1972	350	R 2	8.5005	165	4000	280	2400	4	3.48	-	-
1972	350	R 4	8.5005	200	4400	300	2800	4	3.48	-	-
1972	350	H 4	9	255	5600	280	4000	4	3.48	-	-
1972	400	R 2	9	170	3800	325	2000	4.1253	3.7502	-	-
1973	307	R 2	8.5005	115	4000	-	-	3.8752	3.2502	-	-
1973	350	R 2	8.5005	145	4000	255	2400	4.001	3.48	-	-
1973	350	R 4	8.5005	175	4000	260	2800	4.001	3.48	-	-
1973	350	R 4	8.5005	190	4400	270	2800	4.001	3.48	-	-
1973	350	R 4	9	245	5200	285	4000	4.001	3.48	-	-
1973	350	R 4	9	250	5200	285	4000	4.001	3.48	-	-
1973	400	R 2	8.5005	150	3200	295	2000	4.1253	3.7502	-	-
1974	350	R 2	8.5005	145	3600	250	2200	4.001	3.48	-	-
1974	350	R 4	8.5005	160	3800	245	2400	4.001	3.48	-	-
1974	350	R 4	8.5005	185	4000	265	2600	4.001	3.48	-	-
1974	350	R 4	8.5005	195	4400	285	2800	4.001	3.48	-	-
1974	350	R 4	9	245	5200	285	4000	4.001	3.48	-	-
1974	350	R 4	9	250	5200	285	4000	4.001	3.48	-	-
1974	400	R 2	8.5005	150	3200	295	2000	4.1253	3.7502	-	-
1974	400	R 4	8.5005	180	3800	290	2400	4.1253	3.7502	-	-
1975	262	R 2	8.5005	110	3500	200	2000	3.671	3.1	-	-
1975	350	R 2	8.5005	145	3800	250	2200	4.001	3.48	-	-
1975	350	R 4	8.5005	155	3800	250	2400	4.001	3.48	-	-
1975	350	R 4	8.5005	165	3800	255	2400	4.001	3.48	-	-
1975	350	R 4	9	205	4800	255	3600	4.001	3.48	-	-
1975	400	R 4	8.5005	175	3600	305	2000	4.1253	3.7502	M 3500	-
1976	305	R 2	8.5005	140	3800	240	2200	3.736	3.48	-	-
1976	350	R 2	8.5005	145	3800	250	2200	4.001	3.48	-	-
1976	350	R 4	8.5005	165	3800	260	2400	4.001	3.48	-	-
1976	350	R 4	8.5005	185	4000	270	2400	4.001	3.48	-	-
1976	350	R 4	9	210	5200	255	3600	4.001	3.48	-	-
1976	400	R 4	8.5005	175	3600	305	2000	4.1253	3.7502	M 3500	-
1977	305	R 2	8.5005	145	3800	245	2400	3.736	3.48	-	-
1977	350	R 4	8.5005	170	3800	270	2400	4.001	3.48	-	-
1977	350	R 4	8.5005	180	4000	270	2400	4.001	3.48	-	-
1977	350	R 4	9	210	5500	255	3600	4.001	3.48	-	-

year	cid	carb	comp	hp/ghp	@ rpm	net trq	@ rpm	bore	stroke	models	RPO
1977	400	R 4	8.5005	175	3600	305	2000	4.1253	3.7502	M 3500	-
1978	305	R 2	8.5005	135	3800	235	2000	3.736	3.48	-	-
1978	305	R 2	8.5005	145	3800	245	2400	3.736	3.48	-	-
1978	350	R 4	8.2	160	3800	260	2400	4.001	3.48	-	-
1978	350	R 4	8.2	170	3800	270	2400	4.001	3.48	-	-
1978	350	R 4	8.2	175	3800	270	2400	4.001	3.48	-	-
1978	350	R 4	8.2	185	4000	270	2400	4.001	3.48	-	-
1978	350	R 4	9	220	5200	260	3600	4.001	3.48	L82 Vette	-
1978	400	R 4	8.5005	175	3600	305	2000	4.1253	3.7502	M 3500	-
1979	267	R 2	8.2	125	3800	215	2000	3.5002	3.48	L39	-
1979	305	R 2	8.4	130	3200	235	2000	3.736	3.48	-	-
1979	305	R 4	8.4	155	4000	250	2500	3.736	3.48	-	-
1979	305	R 4	8.4	160	4000	250	2600	3.736	3.48	-	-
1979	350	R 4	8.2	165	3800	270	2400	4.001	3.48	-	-
1979	350	R 4	8.2	170	4000	270	2400	4.001	3.48	-	-
1979	350	R 4	8.2	175	4000	270	2400	4.001	3.48	-	-
1979	350	R 4	8.9	195	4000	280	2400	4.001	3.48	-	-
1979	350	R 4	8.9	225	5200	270	3600	4.001	3.48	Vette	-
1979	400	R 4	8.5005	175	3600	305	2000	4.1253	3.7502	M 3500	-
1980	267	R 2	8.3	120	3600	215	2000	3.5002	3.48	L39	-
1980	305	R 4	8.6	155	4000	240	1600	3.736	3.48	-	-
1980	305	R 4	8.5005	180	4200	245	2400	3.736	3.48	-	-
1980	350	R 4	8.2	190	4200	280	4200	4.001	3.48	-	-
1980	350	R 4	9	230	5200	270	3600	4.001	3.48	-	-
1980	400	R 4	8.5005	175	3600	305	2000	4.1253	3.7502	M 3500	-
1981	267	R 2	8.3	115	4000	200	2400	3.5002	3.48	L39 code J	-
1981	305	R 4	8.6	150	3800	240	2400	3.736	3.48	LG4, code H	-
1981	305	R 4	8.6	165	4000	245	2400	3.736	3.48	-	-
1981	350	R 4	8.2	175	4000	270	2400	4.001	3.48	-	-
1981	350	R 4	8.2	190	4000	270	2400	4.001	3.48	LM1	-
1982	267	R 2	8.3	110	4000	200	2400	3.5002	3.48	L39 code J	-
1982	305	R 4	8.6	145	4000	240	2400	3.736	3.48	LG4, code H	-
1982	305	TBI	9.5006	165	4200	-	-	3.736	3.48	LU5	-
1982	350	R 4	8.2	190	4000	-	-	4.001	3.48	LM1	-
1982	350	TBI	9	200	4200	-	-	4.001	3.48	Vette L83	-
1983	305	R 4	8.6	150	3800	240	2400	3.736	3.48	LG4, code H	-
1983	305	TBI	9.5006	165	4200	-	-	3.736	3.48	LU5	-
1983	350	R 4	8.2	190	4000	-	-	4.001	3.48	LM1	-
1984	305	R 4	8.6	150	3800	240	2400	3.736	3.48	LG4, code H	-
1984	305	R 4	9.5006	190	4800	-	-	3.736	3.48	L69	-
1984	350	R 4	8.2	190	4000	-	-	4.001	3.48	LM1	-
1984	350	TBI	9	205	4300	-	-	4.001	3.48	L83	-
1985	305	R 4	8.6	165	4000	240	2400	3.736	3.48	code H	-
1985	305	R 4	9.5006	165	4400	-	-	3.736	3.48	-	-
1985	305	R 4	9.5006	180	4800	-	-	3.736	3.48	L69	-
1985	305	TPI	9.5006	190	4800	-	-	3.736	3.48	LB9	-
1985	350	R 4	8.2	190	4000	-	-	4.001	3.48	LM1	-
1985	350	R 4	8.2	205	4200	290	4200	4.001	3.48	code 6	-
1985	350	TPI	9	230	4000	-	-	4.001	3.48	L98	-
1986	305	R 4	9.5006	165	4400	245	2400	3.736	3.48	code H	-
1986	305	R 4	9.5006	180	4800	-	-	3.736	3.48	L69	-
1986	305	TPI	9.5006	190	4800	-	-	3.736	3.48	LB9	-
1986	350	R 4	8.5005	205	4200	290	4200	4.001	3.48	code 6	-
1986	350	TPI	9	230	4000	-	-	4.001	3.48	L98	-
1987	305	R 4	8.6	150	4000	240	2400	3.736	3.48	code H	-
1987	305	TBI	9.3	150	4000	-	-	3.736	3.48	-	-

year	cid	carb	comp	hp/ghp	@ rpm	net trq	@ rpm	bore	stroke	models	RPO
1987	305	TPI	9.5006	190	4000	-	-	3.736	3.48	LB9	-
1987	350	R 4	8.5005	205	4200	290	4200	4.001	3.48	code 6	-
1987	350	TPI	9	230	4400	-	-	4.001	3.48	L98	-
1987	350	TPI	9.5006	240	4000			4.001	3.48	L98	
1988	305	TBI	9.3	150	4000	-	-	3.736	3.48	-	-
1988	305	TPI	9.5006	190	4000	-	-	3.736	3.48	LB9	-
1988	350	R 4	8.5005	205	4200	290	4200	4.001	3.48	code 6	-
1988	350	TPI	9	230	4400	-	-	4.001	3.48	L98	-
1988	350	TPI	9.5006	245	4300	340	3200	4.001	3.48	L98 code 8	Vette
1989	305	TBI	9.3	165	4000	-	-	3.736	3.48	-	-
1989	305	TBI	9.3	170	4400	255	2400	3.736	3.48	code E	-
1989	305	TPI	9.5006	190	4000	-	-	3.736	3.48	LB9	-
1989	350	TBI	9.8	195	4200	295	2400	3.736	3.48	code 7	-
1989	350	TPI	9	230	4400	-	-	4.001	3.48	L98	-
1989	350	TPI	9.5006	240	4000	-	-	4.001	3.48	L98	-
1989	350	TPI	9.5006	245	4000	340	3200	4.001	3.48	L98 code 8	Vette
1990	305	TBI	9.3	170	4400	255	2400	3.736	3.48	code E	-
1990	305	TPI	9.5006	190	4000	-	-	3.736	3.48	LB9	-
1990	350	TBI	9.3	185	3800	300	2400	4.001	3.48	code 7	-
1990	350	TPI	9	230	4400	-	-	4.001	3.48	L98	-
1990	350	TPI	9.5006	245	4000	345	3200	4.001	3.48	L98 code 8	Vette
1990	350	TPI	11	375	5800	370	5600	3.897	3.66	ZR1 code J	-
1991	305	TBI	9.3	170	4200	255	2400	3.736	3.48	code E	-
1991	305	TPI	9.3	230	4400	300	3200	3.736	3.48	code F	-
1991	350	TBI	9.3	185	3800	300	2400	4.001	3.48	code 7	-
1991	350	TPI	9.7506	240	4400	345	3200	4.001	3.48	L98 code 8	-
1991	350	TPI	10	250	4200	-	-	4.001	3.48	L98	-
1992	305	TBI	9.3	170	4400	255	2400	3.736	3.48	code E	-
1992	305	TPI	9.3	205	4400	285	3200	3.736	3.48	code F	-
1992	350	TBI	9.3	195	4200	300	2400	4.001	3.48	code 7	-
1992	350	TPI	9.7506	240	4400	345	3200	4.001	3.48	L98 code 8	-
1992	350	TPI	10.501	300	4400	340	4000	4.001	3.48	LT1	-
1993	305	TBI	9.8	180	4100	255	2400	3.736	3.48	code E	-
1993	350	TBI	9.8	185	3800	300	2400	4.001	3.48	code 7	-
1993	350	mfi	10.501	275	5000	325	2400	4.001	3.48	LT1	-
-	-	-	-	-	-	-	-	-	-	code P	-
1993	350	mfi	10.501	300	5000	340	4000	4.001	3.48	LTI	-
-	-	-	-	-	-	-	-	-	-	code P	-
1993	350	TPI	11	375	5800	370	4800	3.9	3.66	ZR1 code J	Vette
1994	350	mfi	10.501	260	4800	330	3200	4.001	3.48	code P	-
1994	350	mfi	10.501	300	5000	340	4000	4.001	3.48	LTI code P	-
1994	350	TPI	11	375	5800	370	4800	3.9	3.66	ZR1 code J	Vette
1995	350	mfi	10	260	4800	330	3200	4.001	3.48	code P	-
1995	350	mfi	10.501	300	5000	330	4000	4.001	3.48	LTI code P	-
1995	350	TPI	11	405	5800	385	5200	3.9	3.66	ZR1 code J	Vette
1996	350	mfi	10	260	4800	330	3200	4.001	3.48	code P	-
1996	350	mfi	10.4	300	5000	340	4000	4.001	3.48	LTI code P	-
1996	350	mfi	10.6	330	5800	340	4500	4.001	3.48	LTI code 5	Vette

Chapter 1

History

At the time of the initial designs of the engine, the theoretical size was around 230ci. Upon discussion it became apparent that more displacement was required, for it would need to supply power to several accessories, power steering and air conditioning to name two. The ever-increasing frontal area and weight of the vehicles raised the size to 250ci. The engineers were well aware that the larger the engine, more torque and crisper performance would result. They finally settled on 265ci. This configuration was

achieved by combining a 3.75in bore with a 3in stroke. The compression ratio was set at 8:1.

With the vital characteristics established, a very compact, lightweight design emerged from the drawing room. The design was produced by working from the inside out. The length of the engine being determined by the length of the crankshaft, and a minimal amount of cast material was added to complete it.

All this could have been lost if it wasn't for Ed Cole, who was transferred from the Cadillac Di-

vision. He brought with him a version of the current V-8. It was slated for deletion at Cadillac as it was seen as an inferior design. Several new approaches were included in this design that were not considered adequate in the ways of reliability and durability.

The first being that the crank's center line was not deep into the block casting but was only 1/8in higher than the oil pan rail. That was required for the main cap registers. Many thought the design was destined for failure. Another new concept was the individual, ball pivot rocker arms. This was at a time when most everything had rocker shafts. They were thought to be too "flimsy" and were not expected to live very long. Time has certainly proven that if there is anything about the stock small-block Chevy that never needs attention, it's the rocker arms. Only absolute lack of maintenance will make them fail.

The block casting, being short, is inherently very stiff, so very little was needed to be added in the way of ribs and other reinforcements. The coring designers made up a set with only nine major and three minor cores. The industry standards of the time required at least 20 casting cores to produce a V-8 block. This decreased the chance of poor casting by core shift; it was also cheaper to make.

The cylinder head was designed with the same requirements as the cylinder block. It had to be light and compact. Other considerations included high turbulence in the combustion chamber and low heat rejection to coolant. The wedge type was selected for its good combus-

This is the small-block engine in its infancy. The 265ci engine quickly grew to 283ci.

tion control of the pressure rises in the cylinder. All this translated into good power and fuel efficiency. The chamber was cast into its final shape, and only valve seat machining was required. Another advantage of the wedge-type combustion chamber is that when it is used with an easily produced flat-top piston, it would yield a satisfactory compression ratio.

Another new approach was to use smaller fasteners to secure the cylinder head to the block. The 7/16in stud size was selected over the standard 1/2in. Of course, more of them had to be used. This allowed the designers to have five bolts surrounding each cylinder as opposed to four. No reinforcing ribbing had to be used on the cylinder head to support the bolt bosses. The smaller fasteners also required less torque applied to them, thus reducing localized distortion around the bolt holes in the block. This, as it turns out, is far more important than the engineers may have considered it to be at the time. Today, most any serious engine shop, preparing blocks for racing, uses a torque plate when doing the bore work. I have seen blocks distort up to four thousandths of an inch in those areas. All this out-of-round can greatly affect the ring seal.

It seems that everything was well thought out in the first place. That is why General Motors has been able to keep the small-block relatively unchanged for so many years.

The cooling system included some ideas that eliminated the need for other components. For example, the cooling cores included a water bypass within the engine to allow circulation until the thermostat would open; it did this without external piping.

The crank which was the basis for the whole design was of a very short stroke. This was during an era when it was com-

This is the Turbo-Fire 300hp 350ci engine as installed in 1970 Camaros.

mon to overstroke the bores for good torque. The crank throws and counterweights were made as small and thin as possible, and the short stroke allowed for that. The material used at the time was forged steel because of its availability, high modulus of elasticity, and high specific weight. This allowed the designers to reduce the counterweights to an absolute minimum.

The balancing technique used then was, again, another advancement in engine production. All relevant components were balanced to a specific standard prior to assembly, and then the short block was spun up and checked. The required amount of material was then drilled out of the two end counterweights. The engine was then finish-assembled.

The oiling system is probably the most impressive part of the engine. Even today it is adequate for most any application. The bearings used were only half grooved on the mains. The crank drilling for oil supply was timed to the rod journals. The basic oil pump and block passages have been the envy of many other

brands. The design of the rocker arms was such that there was no need for a pressure vessel to reach the top of the deck as all upper lubrication is supplied by the pushrod.

In 1955, the 265ci was the first configuration offered by Chevrolet. It was a long-awaited entry into the performance market. The new body for that year, along with the sports car, the Corvette, were screaming for more power than the venerable old Blue Flame six-cylinder could muster. The highly effective over-square design, meaning less piston travel and therefore less internal friction losses, was rated at 162hp. It could be boosted to 180hp, however, with the Power Pack option, which consisted of a four-barrel carburetor and dual exhaust. As expected, the little engine wasn't without some teething pains. The original design of the main oil passages was so that the rear main journal of the camshaft was notched to allow pressure to reach the valve lifters. This turned out to be a problem, as overall valvetrain performance and durability suffered. Many skeptics of the individual ball pivot rocker arms were quick to condemn them when the problems arose. The problem was quickly addressed when the block was cast with an annular groove behind the cam bearings. This allowed direct oil flow to the lifter gallery, thereby ending most of the problems. The original design called for solid lifters on manual transmission cars and hydraulic lifters on Powerglide cars. This was soon discontinued in favor of hydraulics all around. The solid lifter-equipped engines were getting noise complaints.

As you will notice throughout this book, the Corvette has always had the best performance versions of the small-block. The year 1955 is no different. The 265ci in the Corvette was rated at 195hp. Zora Arkus Duntov

probably had a lot to do with this. Being at the head of Corvette development, he had a vested interest in making America's sports car as fast as possible. The first place to start is with the powertrain. There are several reasons why the car always got the highest power ratings. In many cases, the Corvettes were fitted with superior exhaust manifolds and piping. A second reason is that this was, and still is, Chevrolet's flagship. What better place to showcase the latest hardware available? Another reason is that in many cases the prospective owner was more willing to put up with the inconvenience of a truly high-performance engine. They usually need high-test gasoline, use more of it, require more intensive maintenance, and are generally noisier. This would be unacceptable for a

luxury sedan, but almost mandatory for a true sports car.

The original 265ci design did not include provisions for an oil filter. This certainly affected durability, and Chevrolet soon included the upgrade into the design. In 1956, the 265's output was pushed to 225hp with the help of a dual four-barrel intake manifold and an increased compression ratio of 9.25:1.

In 1957, the engineers upped the ante to 283ci. The 265ci was to be offered for the last time this year and only in stock 162hp trim. Ford may have built the first overhead valve V-8, but Chevy was the first to produce one horsepower per cubic inch. This was accomplished with the new Rochester mechanical fuel-injection intake system. The compression ratio of that engine was now as high as 10.5:1. This is when the small-block Chevy became the legend that it is today.

Until 1962, very little changed. There were some changes in the block casting of the 283ci—thicker cylinder walls and the addition of mounting bosses to the side of the block on top of the front mount bosses. The power rating of the Corvette's fuel-injection engine had reached 315hp in 1960. This was accomplished with the help of a newly designed Duntov solid high-lift cam and a higher compression ratio of 11:1. With the ever-increasing size and weight of the cars, an increase in engine size was mandated. The 283ci was bored to 4in, and the stroke went from 3 to 3.25in. This yielded 327ci. In the Corvette, equipped with the Ram Jet fuel injection, it was rated at 360hp. No longer was the dual four-barrel offered in any chassis. Another reason for the 327 is that the W engine of 348ci was replaced in favor of the 409ci. Chevrolet needed something to fill the gap. The 327ci became the only engine offered in the Corvette. In 1964, the power rating of the Ram Jet 327

In 1982, a new intake system was introduced—the Cross-Fire fuel injection. The design was very close to the cross-ram manifold used in the early 302ci-powered Z-28. This particular example is from the L83 version installed in the Corvette.

installed in the Corvette was upped to 375hp. In that year, the 350hp version of the 327ci was offered in the lightweight Nova. This combination was, in many cases, faster than anything else produced by Chevrolet—even the famed Corvette.

By now, a new engine was born from the mystery engine designed for NASCAR—the 396ci. This, along with Ram Jet servicing problems, signaled the end of the Ram Jet fuel injection in 1965. In 1966, the highest power rating from the 327ci was 350hp.

The Camaro sparked several engine changes in 1967. The newly designed 350ci was installed in a limited amount of Camaros. This engine was meant to be introduced in 1968, but production, being ahead of schedule, allowed some to be shipped to the plant for early installation. Another configuration arose from the need to fit into a 305ci rule for Trans Am racing. Hot rodders had been boring 283ci engines 1/8 of an inch to a 4in bore for almost ten years now, and it was an obvious high rpm combination for road racing. I don't think that GM expected the Z-28 option to cause such a stir among enthusiasts as it did—they only produced 602 of the Z-28 Camaros the first year. Before the 302ci was to be superseded by the LT1 350ci in 1970-1/2, Chevy sold almost 20,000 Z-28 302s in 1969.

The 302ci was offered in two different configurations. The original design used the small-journal configuration; the 1968 and 1969 design used the new large-journal block crank and connecting rods.

Now that I mentioned it, let's consider the first major change affected onto the small-block Chevrolet. In 1968, Chevy engineers felt that the surface area of the crankshaft journals was inadequate to support another increase in stroke. By that time they, again, were looking to get more cubes out of the small-block. They increased the sizes across the board. This would necessitate a complete overhaul of the engine's bottom end. The main journals went from 2.3in to 2.45in; the throws from 2in to 2.1in. Obviously, the connecting

In 1984, the all-new Corvette got a new look under the hood with this unique cover on top of the Cross-Fire fuel injection.

rods did not escape this upgrade. The center-to-center length did not change, but the bearing housing bore increased accordingly, along with a rod bolt size change from 11/32in to 3/8in. At this point, the venerable little 283ci was replaced with a new configuration—the large-journal 307ci. This one was designed with fuel economy and low emissions in mind. It was a case of mixing and matching parts out of stock to create something to suit the purpose. Although the block had to be cast special using the 283ci bore size, the crank was out of the redesigned large-journal 327ci. The larger stroke provided good bottom-end torque.

This, combined with a small bore, made for low emissions.

In 1970, several displacement configurations were dropped from the lineup. With the Trans Am racing series over, the 302ci was replaced by the LT1 in the Z-28. The 327ci was also dropped in favor of the 350ci. The latter became the bread-and-butter engine, as it has been installed in everything including trucks and vans. That year, the engineers increased the bore and stroke of the small-block one more time to achieve an enormous 400ci. To remain within the stock bore spacing originally set in 1955, the cylinders of the 400ci had to be

siamesed. This means that there is no space in between the cylinders. This has certainly created some cooling problems, and many have stayed away from this engine in fear of those problems. This engine was created to motivate the ever-fattening full-size models being produced. It was installed in relatively low-horsepower cars such as the Caprice, Monte Carlo, and Chevelle.

One source claims that the original intent for this torque monster was for the cube vans that would not accommodate a large-block engine but were in serious need of more power. This engine still remains my favorite. It lends itself to modifications just as well as all the other small-blocks, but somehow it seems to produce phenomenal power outputs. I have stroked several to 430+ci without too much trouble, and these engines have made a lot of big-blocks look sick.

The main difference between the 400ci and 350ci, beyond bore and stroke, is in the main bearing journal size. It went from 2.45in to 2.65in. The rod journals remain the same as a large-journal crank. The connecting rod is modified to clear the camshaft. It is made shorter from the bolt seat at the head to the cap or big end parting line. This reduced the overall center-to-center length from 5.703in to 5.565in.

The end of the high-compression era came in 1971. Government mandated lower emissions, and the cost and unavailability of fuel was getting out of hand. Most all closed combustion chambers were replaced with open chamber design. The lower combustion temperatures reduced NO_2 and CO_2 emissions. In 1972, the horsepower rating was changed from gross to net so a drop in power was noted across the board. Gone are the 11:1 compression ratios, the solid cams, and performance Holley carburetors. A 9:1 compression

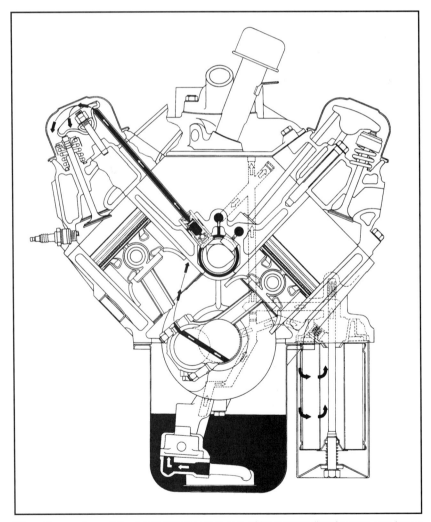

The oiling system of the small-block V-8 is one of its outstanding features and may be partly responsible for the engine's success.

ratio was the highest available—in the LT1. The LT1 was rated at 255hp in the Corvette.

The year 1973 saw even more performance parts removed from the lineup. This was in preparation for 1974 when all automotive applications would have to use a lower-octane unleaded fuel. The year 1974 also notes the end of the 307ci. The same year, GM designed an all-new, small-displacement engine to power its new Monza; it was also installed in the Nova. It was only produced in the 1975 model year.

One unleaded fuel change included the modification of the exhaust seats in the cylinder heads. The reason for this is that exhaust temperatures were on the way up, and the lead which protected the seats from erosion had been fazed out. The solution was to flame-harden the seats. This does make them tougher and more durable, but it also makes them brittle. This type of head seems more prone to cracking. The exhaust port itself was redesigned, but unfortunately at the cost of airflow capacity.

The 305ci was introduced in 1976, to fill the gap left by the 307ci and the 262ci. The need for fuel-efficient and clean-burning engines mandated this one. It probably is the most popular configuration next to the 350ci. It uses the same 3.48in stroke but a much smaller 3.736in bore.

In 1978, GM went on a lightening binge. The cylinder heads and blocks were substantially lightened as improved casting techniques allowed for closer tolerances. The relocation of the dipstick tube to the passenger side allowed for some new, more compact exhaust manifolds to be used.

At this point I would like to mention that the highest performance engine available was the L-82. It replaced the LT1 in 1973 and was carried until 1982 in the Corvette. It was rated at 245hp for most of its life.

In 1979, Chevrolet, in search

Though the small-block engine has been used in many applications, only three different water pumps were used. The first (left) was used until the late 1960s. The middle one was used on Corvettes of the 1970s. The tallest one has been used since 1969.

of yet better fuel economy, came out with the 267ci. This engine has the dubious honor of sporting the smallest bore of all small-blocks ever produced—3.5in. It was only produced until 1982. This was definitely not a powerhouse. I suspect that this was its demise. It does, however, seem to be very durable. The year 1980 marks the last year of production for the 400ci. This one had only been used in vans since 1976.

The next major overhaul of the lineup came in 1982. The all new Z-28, along with a limited amount of Corvettes, got a twin throttle body intake system called Cross-Fire Fuel Injection. This option was not very popular as it was not only expensive but did not yield the improved performance to justify it. It was, however, a hint of things to come. Today, most all small-blocks use some sort of electronic fuel injection. The twin throttle body was dropped after 1983.

In 1984, the Corvette got an all-new injection system: the tuned port induction. The following year, the IROC got the same induction system, but this one calibrated to fit onto a 305ci. Other versions of the 305ci were offered with carburetors, including an HO version using an electronically controlled Rochester four-barrel carburetor. With 9.5:1 compression, it was rated at 180hp.

The year 1986 was the second time GM changed the small-

block significantly. I call them the EFI motors. Although electronic fuel injection had been used before, these engines have several crucial elements redesigned. The most obvious, because of its location, is the rocker cover. Chevrolet engineers were well aware of the shortcomings of the as-cast seating arrangement of the rocker cover rail, and more precisely, the rocker cover gasket. This has always been prone to oil leaks. The designers raised the cast rail and machined it flat. They also relocated the four fasteners from the outside of the cover, where it would distort if overtorqued to the center of the cover. They also added some backup tubes in which the bolts sit; this prevented damage from overtorquing. The other changes occurred with both shafts. The cam now could use roller lifters as there were provisions made for a thrust plate at the front. Towers were cast in the lifter valley to support the alignment plates required for the roller lifters. The crankshaft and block were redesigned to accept a separate one-piece rear main seal and its own housing. The bolt pattern in the crank-to-flywheel area had to be reduced in diameter to accommodate the change.

To date, few other changes have affected these engine configurations, except for annual minor cylinder head changes on the

Corvette. There are several versions of the aluminum head. The early ones have been modified to rectify some rocker stud problems and to increase the airflow potential by raising port locations.

In 1992, Mr. Sperry, head of engine development at Chevrolet Division, was finally allowed to change the small-block to the point where most parts will no longer interchange. Reverse cooling, integral front-mounted distributor, and an all-new intake plenum are a few highlights. This engine is redefining the small-block Chevy.

I hesitate to mention the LT5 as a small-block of the same nature. Although it is based on the same block, the top end is akin to the Ilmoor Indy V-8. With its 32 valves and sophisticated twin runner intake system, it deviates too much from the standard 16-valve single cam, overhead valve design. It also seems that the engine is almost without a reason, since the much cheaper to produce LT1 nearly equals it in the way of performance. I am certain that if it were allowed to be produced in a not so detuned state, it would be an awesome powerplant.

Chapter 2
Vehicle Identification Number Breakdown

In the interest of identifying engines located within their original confines, or simply determining what powerplant should be residing in a specific application, I will cover all the applicable years involved. This includes all GM cars and trucks ever powered by the small-block.

1955

If the car is equipped with a V-8, the first letter of the serial number should be a V. This is used as a prefix; if the car is a six-cylinder model, then the A, B, C, or E letters will be first. This series of numbers determines the model type of the car. If the car is V-8 equipped then, the second letter will be the model number. Following this will be 55, denoting the year 1955. After that will be another letter; this one determines the assembly plant in which the vehicle was built. The last series of numbers will have six digits. This determines the number in the production run of the unit.

Let's consider the following typical VIN as an example.

VC55F001490

The first letter being a V, this car was originally equipped with a 265ci V-8.

The second letter refers to the model of the car.

A: model # 150, B: model # 210, C: Bel Air, E: Corvette.

Digits three and four are the year.

Digit five refers to the plant.

T: Tarrytown NY, F: Flint MI, S: St Louis MO, K: Kansas City MO, O: Oakland CA, W: Willow Run MI, A: Atlanta GA, N: Norwood OH, B: Baltimore MD, L: Los Angeles CA, J: Janesville WI, 1: Oshawa CDN, 2: St Therese CDN, R: Arlington, G: Farmingham, Y: Wilmington, Z: Fremont, C: Southgate, D: Doraville.

From digit six on is the serial part of the number. When GM numbered its cars, it always started the numbers at 001001. This would make this car the 489th of the production run.

As for the trucks for that year, there were two series produced. Only the second series had the V-8 engine offered as an option. Most all rules applying to the cars are still in effect here with some exceptions. Let's use an example to explain the numbers.

VJ255A1020101

If the truck was originally equipped with a V-8 engine, then the first digit of the VIN will be a V. If originally equipped with a six-cylinder engine, then the first digit showing will be the model number letter code. D: 1500 series, H: 3100 series, M: 3200 series, J: 3600 series L: 3800 series.

Looking at the second digit of our example, we can determine that this truck is a 3600 series model.

The third digit in this case refers to the production run. This is unique to 1955 as far as trucks are concerned, because in 1955 GM produced two distinct runs of vehicles. The first run did not have the V-8 engine available, but I must mention them as they are differentiated by the digit immediately following the model digit. In the example, it is the third digit. This refers to the second series of production. In the case of the first series, there would be no mention of one or first. Instead, the following digit in this case would be the first 5 in 55, for 1955.

Getting back to our example, the rest of the number follows the same rule as the cars. After the year designation comes the assembly plant and the serial part of the number. The only exception is that the first number of the series starts at 000001, as opposed to 001001 for the cars. This would make our example the 20101th to come off the line that year and in the second series.

1956

For the cars, the 1956 VIN remains exactly the same as 1955. For the trucks, VIN breakdown changes somewhat. The main difference is with the model number. Following the V prefix on V-8-equipped trucks, the model numbers are as such: D: 1500 series, 3A: 3100 series, 3B: 3200 series, 3E: 3600 series, and 3G: 3800 series.

1957

Most all 1956 car rules apply to the 1957 car VIN breakdown, with two exceptions. The Corvette, or body code E, no longer has a six-cylinder engine available; therefore, the V prefix signifying an optional V-8 engine is dropped, and the first letter of the serial number is always an E. The second exception pertains to the serial part of the VIN. The count now starts at 100001, as opposed to 001001.

As for the trucks, the 1500 model now becomes a 1508 model; otherwise, there are no changes for the trucks from 1956 to 1957.

17

1958

For the cars, the V prefix is no longer used as the model code specifying the engine used in the application. To show this, let's have another example:

F58L100001

With the V prefix no longer used in the cars, the first digit always determines the model type. A: Del Ray 6 cyl., 1100 series; B: Del Ray V-8, 1200 series; C: Biscayne 6 cyl., 1500 series; D: Biscayne V-8, 1600 series; E: Bel Air 6 cyl., 1700 series; F: Bel Air V-8, 1800 series; J: Corvette, all V-8.

The year follows, in this case 58 for 1958. The assembly plant comes after and finally the serial part of the VIN.

As for the trucks, only some model designation letter changes occur. Unlike the cars, the V prefix signifying V-8 is still used in 1958. The new model letters are: G: 1171 series, H: 1271 series, 3A: 3100 series, 3B: 3200 series, 3E: 3600 series, and 3G: 3800 series.

The rest of the VIN breakdown remains the same.

1959

The VIN breakdown for cars remains the same as 1958.

The trucks, however, get model letter changes again. The new letters for 59 are: G: 1100 series and H: 1200 series. 3A, 3B, 3E, and 3G remain the same as 1958.

1960

For 1960, GM completely rethought the method of organizing the VIN numbers for both cars and trucks. To better explain the VIN, it seems an example is definitely in order. Here is an example for cars.

01700S100001

As you may have noticed, the first digit of the VIN is now a number. This one identifies the year of the car. It is the last digit of the year, with this example being

1960. Digits two through five represent the model number of the vehicle's body style. It also implies which engine was used in that model, as the following list shows:

0867: Corvette Convertible 2 dr, all V-8
1111: Biscayne 6 cyl., Sedan 2 dr, 1100 series
1115: Brookwood 6 cyl., Station Wagon 2 dr, 1100 series
1119: Biscayne 6 cyl., Sedan 4 dr, 1100 series
1121: Biscayne 6 cyl., Sedan 2 dr utility, 1100 series
1135: Brookwood 6 cyl., Station Wagon 4 dr, 1100 series
1211: Biscayne V-8, Sedan 2 dr, 1200 series
1215: Brookwood V-8, Station Wagon 2 dr, 1200 series
1219: Biscayne V-8, Sedan 4 dr, 1200 series
1221: Biscayne V-8, Sedan 2 dr utility, 1200 series
1235: Brookwood V-8, Station Wagon 4 dr, 1200 series
1311: Biscayne Fleetmaster 6 cyl., Sedan 2 dr, 1300 series
1319: Biscayne Fleetmaster 6 cyl., Sedan 4 dr, 1300 series
1411: Biscayne Fleetmaster V-8, Sedan 2 dr, 1400 series
1419: Biscayne Fleetmaster V-8, Sedan 4 dr, 1400 series
1511: Bel Air 6 cyl., Sedan 2 dr, 1500 series
1519: Bel Air 6 cyl., Sedan 4 dr, 1500 series
1535: Parkwood 6 cyl., Station Wagon 4 dr, 1500 series
1537: Bel Air 6 cyl., Hardtop sports coupe 2 dr, 1500 series
1539: Bel Air 6 cyl., Hardtop sports sedan 4 dr, 1500 series
1545: Kingswood 6 cyl., Station Wagon 4 dr, 1500 series
1611: Bel Air V-8, Sedan 2 dr, 1600 series
1619: Bel Air V-8, Sedan 4 dr, 1600 series
1635: Parkwood V-8, Station Wagon 4 dr, 1600 series
1637: Bel Air V-8, Hardtop sports coupe 2 dr, 1600 series
1639: Bel Air V-8, Hardtop sports sedan 4 dr, 1600 series

1645: Kingswood V-8, Station Wagon 4 dr, 1600 series
1719: Impala 6 cyl., Sedan 4 dr, 1700 series
1735: Nomad 6 cyl., 4 dr, 1700 series
1737: Impala 6 cyl., Hardtop sports coupe 2 dr, 1700 series
1739: Impala 6 cyl., Hardtop sports sedan 4 dr, 1700 series
1767: Impala 6 cyl., Convertible 2 dr, 1700 series
1819: Impala V-8, Sedan 4 dr, 1800 series
1835: Nomad V-8, 4 dr, 1800 series
1837: Impala V-8, Hardtop sports coupe 2 dr, 1800 series
1839: Impala V-8, Hardtop sports sedan 4 dr, 1800 series
1867: Impala V-8, Convertible 2 dr, 1800 series

The sixth digit represents the assembly plant, and the last six digits are the serial part of the VIN, starting with 100001.

The VIN for trucks also got a revamp for 1960. The basic configuration of the number is along the same pattern as the cars, but with the various model series differences. Here is a truck example.

0K1004S000001

The first digit is still the last number of the year, and the V prefix signifying the V-8 option is dropped as of 1960. The second digit is a letter indicating the chassis type: C: Conventional, K: Four Wheel Drive, G: Sedan and Pickup Delivery with 6 cyl., and H: Sedan and Pickup Delivery with V-8.

The example would be a four wheel drive.

Digits three through six determine the series of the truck. Instead of breaking down this code into explanations of the different numbers, listing all possible combinations will avoid a lot of confusion.

1170: Sedan Delivery, 6 cyl., car chassis, 119in w/b

1270: Sedan Delivery, V-8, car chassis
1180: El Camino, car chassis
1280: El Camino, car chassis
1402: Chassis and cowl, short box, 1/2 ton, 115in w/b
1403: Chassis and cab, short box, 1/2 ton
1404: Stepside pickup, short box, 1/2 ton
1405: Panel delivery, short box, 1/2 ton
1406: Suburban carryall with rear doors, short box, 1/2 ton
1412: Chassis and cowl, short box, 1/2 ton
1416: Suburban carryall with end gate, short box, 1/2 ton
1434: Fleetside pickup, short box, 1/2 ton
1503: Chassis and cab, long box, 1/2 ton
1504: Stepside, long box, 1/2 ton
1534: Fleetside, long box, 1/2 ton
2502: Chassis and cowl, long box, 3/4 ton, 127in w/b
2503: Chassis and cab, long box, 3/4 ton
2504: Stepside, long box, 3/4 ton
2509: Stake bed, long box, 3/4 ton
2534: Fleetside, long box, 3/4 ton
2512: Chassis and cowl (windshield), long box, 3/4 ton
3602: Chassis and cowl, 1 ton, extra long box, 133in w/b
3603: Chassis and cab, 1 ton, extra long box
3604: Stepside pickup, 1 ton, extra long box
3605: Panel, 1 ton, extra long box
3609: Stake bed, 1 ton, extra long box
3612: Chassis and cowl (windshield), 1 ton, extra long box

The following digit represents the assembly plant, and the last six digits represent the serial part of the VIN, starting with 000001.

1961

Both car and truck VIN breakdowns remain the same as 1960, with the exception of the Sedan Delivery and the El Camino. They were discontinued.

A new model was introduced to fill the gap. The Corvair 95 Loadside and Rampside, new for that year, were never equipped with V-8s and were eventually phased out with the return of the El Camino in 1964.

1962

For 1962, the car model numbers were altered somewhat, and in the interest of clarity, I will list the relevant numbers again. Let's recap. The first digit of the serial number is the last digit of the year, in this case 2. The following four digits determine the model number. The list is:

0867: Corvette V-8, Convertible
1111: Biscayne 6 cyl , Sedan 2 dr, 1100 series
1135: Biscayne 6 cyl., Station Wagon 4 dr, 1100 series
1169: Biscayne 6 cyl., Sedan 4 dr, 1100 series
1211: Biscayne V-8, Sedan 2 dr, 1200 series
1235: Biscayne V-8, Station Wagon 4 dr, 1200 series
1269: Biscayne V-8, Sedan 4 dr, 1200 series
1511: Bel Air 6 cyl., Sedan 2 dr, 1500 series
1535: Bel Air 6 cyl., Station Wagon 4 dr, 1500 series
1537: Bel Air 6 cyl., Hardtop sports coupe 2 dr, 1500 series
1545: Bel Air 6 cyl., Station Wagon 4 dr, 9 pass., 1500 series
1569: Bel Air 6 cyl., Sedan 4 dr, 1500 series
1611: Bel Air V-8, Sedan 2 dr, 1600 series
1635: Bel Air V-8, Station Wagon 4 dr, 1600 series
1637: Bel Air V-8, Hardtop sports coupe 2 dr, 1600 series
1645: Bel Air V-8, Station Wagon 4 dr, 9 pass., 1600 series
1669: Bel Air V-8, Sedan 4 dr, 1600 series
1735: Impala 6 cyl., Station wagon 4 dr, 1700 series
1739: Impala 6 cyl., Hardtop sports sedan 4 dr, 1700 series
1745: Impala 6 cyl., Station Wagon 4 dr, 9 pass., 1700 series
1747: Impala 6 cyl., Hardtop sports sedan 2 dr, 1700 series
1767: Impala 6 cyl., Convertible 2 dr, 1700 series
1769: Impala 6 cyl., Sedan 4 dr, 1700 series
1835: Impala V-8, Station Wagon 4 dr, 1800 series
1839: Impala V-8, Hardtop sports sedan 4 dr, 1800 series
1845: Impala V-8, Station Wagon 4 dr, 9 pass., 1800 series
1847: Impala V-8, Hardtop sports sedan 2 dr, 1800 series
1867: Impala V-8, Convertible 2 dr, 1800 series
1869: Impala V-8, Sedan 4 dr, 1800 series.

The rest of the serial number remains the same as 1962.

No changes to the truck line for 1962.

1963

As far as the cars go, the only change is with the Corvette. A new Hardtop sports coupe is added to the lineup, and it carries the 0837 model number. Trucks remain the same as 1961.

1964

The car lineup gets a new model, the Chevelle, and the Nova finally gets the V-8. The VIN breakdown remains the same as before. The Biscayne, Bel Air, Impala, and Corvette model numbers go unchanged. The Nova's model number never reflected if the car was six- or eight-cylinder equipped as other model numbers did, so I have left it out of the list, since it is of no benefit in identifying the original powerplant. The Chevelle's model numbers are very simple to break down relative to models equipped with V-8 engines: the series is in the 5000s. The 5300, 5500, and 5700 series cars were equipped with the six-cylinder engines. The 5400, 5600, and 5800 models were equipped with V-8s.

The only other exception in the car line model numbers is for the Impala SS, which uses the 1300 and 1400 series. The 1400 models are equipped with a V-8.

The truck line sees the return of the El Camino. The 5380 and 5580 models have six-cylinder power, and the 5480 and 5680 have the V-8. The rest of the truck line VIN breakdown remains unchanged.

1965

This year marks a considerable change in the VIN breakdown. In the years past, the serial number had a total of twelve digits. In 1965, one more digit is added to the car line's VIN.

194375N100001

In the case of this example, The first digit (1) represents the division, Chevrolet. Digits two through four (9437) signify a Hardtop Corvette.

The sixth digit determines the year, the last digit of 1965. The seventh digit designates the plant, and the last six numbers are the sequential number assigned at the plant. Here is a list of model series for 1965.

3100: Chevelle 300, 6 cyl.
3200: Chevelle 300, V-8
3300: Chevelle 300 deluxe, 6 cyl.
3400: Chevelle 300 deluxe, V-8
3500: Chevelle Malibu, 6 cyl.
3600: Chevelle Malibu, V-8
3700: Chevelle Malibu SS, 6 cyl.
3800: Chevelle Malibu SS, V-8
5300: Biscayne, 6 cyl.
5400: Biscayne, V-8
5500: Bel Air, 6 cyl.
5600: Bel Air, V-8
6300: Impala, 6 cyl.
6400: Impala, V-8
6500: Impala SS, 6 Cyl.
6600: Impala SS, V-8
9400: Corvette, V-8

From 1965 on, the model numbers and other VIN criteria for the El Camino follow the Chevelle codes. Although it has been sold as a truck, the El Camino is based on the Chevelle chassis, and the serial numbers clearly reflect that.

The truck VIN breakdown remains the same as 1964 with the exception of the sequential number at the end of the VIN. Instead of the numeral count starting at 000001, it now starts at 100001 like the cars.

1966

The full size line gets a new upper scale model—the Caprice. The VIN breakdown for cars remains the same as 1965 with some minor model changes.
6600: Now becomes the Caprice line all with V-8
6700: Impala SS, 6 cyl.
6800: Impala SS, V-8

The truck line remains the same as 1965.

1967

The only new addition to the 1967 model line is the Camaro. The model numbers are:

2300: Camaro, 6 cyl.
2400: Camaro, V-8

The truck line gets a new VIN breakdown with the addition of extra digits.

CE107047A100001

The first digit, being a letter, designates the chassis type.
C: Conventional
K: Four wheel drive

The second digit describes the powerplant.
S: six cylinder
E: V-8

The third digit indicates the GVW range of the truck.
1: 3600-5600lb (1/2 ton)
2: 5500-8100lb (3/4 ton)
3: 3700-10,000lb (1 ton)

The fourth and fifth digits determine the wheelbase of the truck.

07: 115in wheelbase
09: 127in wheelbase
10: 133in wheelbase
14: 157in wheelbase

The sixth and seventh digits determine the cab configuration.

02: Chassis and cowl
03: Chassis and cab
04: Stepside pickup
05: Panel
06: Suburban (rear doors)
09: Platform stake
12: Chassis and cowl (windshield)
13: Chassis and cab (air brakes)
16: Suburban (rear liftgate)
34: Fleetside pickup

The eighth digit determines the year, the ninth the assembly plant, and the last six numbers are the sequential number.

1968–1971
No changes until 1972.

1972

In 1972, GM started including an engine code in the VIN to identify the powerplant.

1C80J2B100001

The first digit represents the division within GM. In this case 1 stands for Chevrolet Division.

The second digit determines the model series, in this case an El Camino. The third and fourth digits identify the body style, a two-door pickup delivery. The fifth digit is the one most important for our purpose. For the first time, GM has included one letter to specifically pinpoint the powerplant. This theme has carried on, with minor changes, through today.

The sixth digit determines the model year, the seventh the assembly plant, and the last six the serial part of the VIN.

The engine codes, the fifth digit, for this year are:
F: 307 2 bbl, 130hp
H: 350 2 bbl, 165hp
J: 350 4 bbl, 175hp

K: 350 4 bbl, 200hp
L: 350 4 bbl, 255hp
R: 400 2 bbl, 170hp

In 1972, the truck VIN breakdown also changed to indicate the powerplant used in the vehicle. It does not, however, pinpoint the exact type of engine as well as the automobile codes.

TGE1362P100001

1: Division
2: Truck type
3: Engine type. E: V-8 gasoline, G: V-6 Toro-Flow diesel, M: V-6 Gasoline, S: six-cylinder in-line gasoline

4: Series
5 and 6: Body or chassis type
7: Year
8: Assembly plant
9: Sequential number

From 1972 through 1980, the serial number configuration for both cars and trucks remained the same, with the exception of the engine code changes over the years. The position of this code is the third digit. Please refer to the VIN code chart listing all the codes.

1981
In 1981, GM expanded its VIN to include yet more information.

1G4AZ27AXE5100001

1: Country. 1: United States, 2: Canada
2: Manufacturer. G: General Motors
3: Division
4: Restraint system
5: Car line or series
6 and 7: Body style
8: Engine code
9: Check digit
10: Year
11: Assembly plant
12: Sequential number

VIN Code Chart

first year	last year	VIN code	RPO code	cid	hp	carb	application	comment
1987	90	E		305		TBI	cars	
1972		F		307	130	2	cars	
1973		F		307	115	2	cars	
1981	86	F		305		4	truck	
1985	87	F	LB9	305		EFI	truck	
1985	86	F		305			cars, truck	
1987	88	F		305		TPI	cars	
1989	90	F8		305		TPI	cars	
1975	76	G		262	110	2	Monza	
1979	81	G		305		2	cars, truck	
1984	86	G	L69	305		4	cars	high output
1987	88	G		305		4	cars	
1972		H		350	165	2	cars	
1973	75	H		350	145	2	cars	
1978		H	L82	350	220	4	Corvette	
1978	86	H	LG4	305		4	cars, truck	
1987	90	H		305		EFI	cars, truck	
1972		J		350	175	2	cars	
1973		J		350	190	4	cars	
1974	75	J		350	165	4	cars	
1979	82	J		267		2	cars	
1972		K		350	200	4	cars	
1973		K		350	175	4	cars	
1974		K		350	185	4	cars	
1985	86	K		350		4	truck	
1987	90	K		350		TBI	truck	
1972		L		350	255	4	Z-28, Corvette	
1974		L		350	160	4	cars	
1975		L		350	155	4	cars	
1976	86	L		350	165	4	car, truck 180hp	Corvette
1979	90	M		350		4	truck	

first year	last year	VIN code	RPO code	cid	hp	carb	application	comment
1980	85	P		350		2	truck	
1976		Q		305	140	2	cars	
1972		R		400	170	2	cars	
1973		R		400	150	2	cars	
1974	80	R		400	150	2	cars, trucks	
1983		S		305		TBI	cars	
1973	74	T		350	245	4	Z-28 250hp	Corvette
1975		T	L82	350	205	4	Corvette	
1974	75	U		350		4	truck	export
1974		U		400	180	4	cars	
1977	78	U		305	145	2	cars, trucks	
1974	76	V		350	145	2	truck	
1974		W		350		4	truck	LPG
1973		X		307	130	2	truck	
1976	77	X	L82	350	210	4	cars	Corvette
1980		X		400		4	truck	
1973		Y		350	155	4	truck	
1974	75	Y		350	160	4	truck	
1987	88	Y		305		4	cars	
1989	90	Y		305		TBI	cars	
1979		4		350		4	cars	
1980	81	6		350		4	cars	
1983	86	6		350		4	cars	police
1982	83	7		305		TBI	cars	
1979	80	8		350		4	cars	
1982		8		350		TBI	Corvette	
1982	84	8		350		TBI	cars	
1985	90	8		350		TPI	cars	

Chapter 3

Body Codes

This chapter is going to be short and sweet. The reason I would like to mention something about body codes is that I will be using an extension of GM's coding system.

Up until 1972, bodies were designated by a model number. After that, GM started using letters to specify chassis or lineup of cars.

To help condense all the information in this book, you will notice that I use these letters from time to time. Although they may not abide strictly to the rules set out by the manufacturer, you will be able to easily decipher them.

For example, the Nova or Chevy II did not get the X body code until 1972, but I will refer to this series of cars as the X body in this manual, irrelevant of the year of the car.

The list of letters is as follows:

A: Chevelle, Monte Carlo, El Camino (except 1959-60)
B: Full-size cars, El Camino (1959-60)
C: Conventional pickup and truck
G: Chevelle, Monte Carlo, El Camino (1978-86)
F: Camaro, Firebird
K: Four-wheel-drive pickup
M: Vans
X: Nova
Y: Corvette

Chapter 4

Date Codes

The letter "L" was not used too often within date codes, because it could be mistaken for an "I" or a "1." Here, the letter "M" (the thirteenth letter in the alphabet) is used instead of the letter "L" (the twelfth letter). Thus, the date of this casting is December 12, 1966.

Since the inception of the small-block Chevy, General Motors has used date coding to keep track of production runs or production changes to castings. This has turned out to be invaluable for anybody wanting to identify engine components. The coding is cast directly onto the parts in question. This casting code is included on engine blocks, cylinder heads, intake manifolds, crankshafts, water pumps, and exhaust manifolds. The same coding is stamped on certain assemblies, such as distributors, alternators, and carburetors. The coding, in the latter cases, does not determine the casting date of the core but the final production date of the assembly.

For our purpose, this coding has some limitations, as you will see in the breakdown explanation.

The code has three, four, or five digits to it. The first digit is a letter. It represents the month of production—A being January, B February, and so on. There is an exception to this rule. In some cases, the letter I is not used or jumped over because of its similarity to the number 1. This means that J, K, and L can be moved up by one month, and when M appears, even though it is the thirteenth letter in the alphabet, it means December.

Before I go any further, I should explain how this coding could be contrived of three, four, or five digits. Most codings are made up of three or four digits. The first, as we already know, determines the month of production, the last digit always represents the last digit of the production year.

Example A: A82
Example B: B123
Example C: C2774

Example A. This code is interpreted as the first month on the 8th day of 1962, 1972, 1982, or 1992. I think you may realize where the possibility for confusion comes from.

Example B. This one means, second month, twelfth day of 1963, 1973, 1983, or 1993.

Example C. In the mid-70s, the Tonawanda plant began marking the year by using the two last digits. This would explain the situation where five digits are used for the date coding.

Let's get back to that little bit of confusion produced by this coding. The date coding, in most cases, will not specifically determine the year of the part all by itself. It really is a complement to the casting number. When identifying a core, the casting number will set the range of years in which it was available, and the date coding will pinpoint the origin more precisely.

The location of these codes has changed somewhat over the years. The parts we are most concerned with are blocks and heads. The location of the coding on the blocks is generally on the bell housing flange at the rear of the block on the top side. Some are on the same side of the casting number or driver's side, and some are on the passenger side. In the 70's, the date coding has been used on the side of the block in much larger size, and it can also be found on the inside of the block (sump area) at the rear at the bottom of number eight cylinder.

On many castings, a clock can be seen. This determines the time and shift within the date code. The casting plants generally operated in two ten-hour shifts. The clock is comprised of ten dots with the first hour of every shift having double dots. The dots are read in the clockwise fashion. The shift involved is determined by the type of fastener showing in the middle of the clock. A flat-head screw means the first shift, and a rounded-head screw means the second.

The location of the date codes on the cylinder heads is under the rocker cover between the valves or rocker studs. There is no absolute rule for location on the other castings, or none that I can see, as they seem to have been put on at random. They usually are placed in a prominent area so as to give easy access. However, aluminum intake manifolds may have the date coding cast in the area under the oil deflector shield. Removal of this component may be required to find the marks.

Chapter 5

Identification at a Glance

In this chapter, I will describe what I look for initially when trying to determine the type of small-block engine. In many cases, there are typical characteristics that give away the origin of the engine. To make this chapter most useful, I will classify this information by state of assembly—the level of assembly or disassembly of the parts.

Complete in the vehicle. Look for the stamping pad at the front on the passenger side of the block at the block deck. When the engine is installed, the alternator will often be right on top of the pad, so actually reading the numbers on it is not what one is attempting to do, but determining the size of the pad will tell you if it's pre-1978 or post-1978. The size of the pad also can tell you, within the pre-1978 engines, if the engine is a 350, 400, 283, or 307ci engine. Refer to the block identification chapter for specific sizes. Along with this, you should look at the cylinder head casting marks to determine if the heads are lightweight. At the same time, look to see if there are bolt holes in the end of the cylinder head. Once these things have been established, look at the balancer. Unless it has been replaced, it is a very good indication of the engine's displacement, as there are several different types of balancers. The type of carburetion can sometimes go a long way in identifying the engine, but unfortunately, it is usually the first thing to be changed when an engine is modified; therefore, this check is not always foolproof. The dipstick location also is a way of identifying pre-1978 and post-1978 models. The early style is located on the

driver side coming out of the block at the deck. Newer types after 1978 have the dipstick located at the oil pan on the passenger side. The ignition, like carburetion, can sometimes help if it has not been swapped with HEI (introduced in 1974). As far as the spark plug type, it too can be a good indicator. In 1971, GM changed the type of plugs from a nonresistor 13/16in hex with washer to a resistor 5/8in taper seat plug. The accessory mounting changed in 1969. The usual location of the alternator up to 1968 was on the driver side. From 1969 on, the alternator was relocated to the passenger side.

One of the most sought-after engines is the 350ci four-bolt. In 1968, when the 350ci was introduced, the four-bolt was born. This block is most desirable for any high-performance application. This block has been used in trucks, Corvettes, Z-28s, and marine applications. There are a few identifying marks on the block that are apparent from the outside, even when the engine is completely installed. The only block to have the oil pressure takeoff drilled and tapped at the front of the block is the four-bolt 350ci. The exact location of this pressure feed is just above the timing cover slightly to the passenger side. The pressure feed has been used on trucks to supply oil pressure to accessories, such as power takeoff. On the Corvettes, it has been used for the oil pressure sensor (GM felt there was not sufficient room at the back for the sending unit). In most cases, the 1/8in pipe thread hole is plugged with a square-head pipe plug. Although having a block with this plug in the front

almost guarantees it of being a four-bolt, many four-bolts were not drilled. Another good indication of the engine being used in a heavy-duty application is the large 8in balancer. Only trucks and high-performance applications got this size balancer. On trucks, the bell housing flange may have an extra (seventh) bolt hole drilled. Most all small-blocks have six bolt holes for mounting the transmissions. Certain heavy-duty and marine applications required an extra bolt hole to be drilled into the block. This hole is located dead center at the top on the block's bell housing flange. This may not be easy to see in some cases, but if you see the top bolt in, it sure is a good indication.

Within the pre-1978 models, other obvious features can be useful. The oil filler pipe in front of the intake manifold was used until 1968. At the same time, the rear ventilation port or road draft tube also disappeared. To recognize the really old blocks, you can look for a missing oil filter on the early 265ci and a really small balancer (really a hub for a balancer) on the 265ci and early 283ci engines. Most of these early models will not have any bolt holes in the ends of the cylinder heads. The next thing you will notice is the cartridge-type oil filter. This is not an absolute clue, since many have been converted to the spin-on type oil filter with the help of an adapter kit. Another way to recognize an early block is by the missing boss for the ball-to-clutch linkage hole; it would be on the driver side at the back. The engine mount boss on the side of the block is not included in the first year of production. The only way to mount these engines is by using the front-mount bosses. Talking about those, many of the blocks from the 1970s and up have the bosses cast onto the front of the block, but they are not drilled and tapped.

The 400ci, my personal favorite, is most easily recognizable by the large balancer with the notch out of it. This only applies when the engine is still original and using the 400ci crankshaft. If it is a rebuilt, it could be a 383ci or a 350ci with a 400ci crank. The presence of this balancer is a sure indication of a 3.75in stroke crank. The other external indication of a 400ci block is often difficult to see if it is installed in the vehicle. The 400ci block is cast for three frost plugs on the side of the block. Most often, the side of the block will be coated with a generous layer of oil and dirt. On top of that, the plugs are shielded by manifolds and the starter. If it is one of the early 511 four-bolts, it will have three frost plugs on the side. It would have to be a really dirty block for you not to see them.

A common way of shopping for a core is to visit your friendly neighborhood scrapyard. Some yards organize or catalog their engines properly, and they can usually tell you what they are. Other yards don't care, and the engine department is a pile in the back. It may be more work to get a good core out of there, but the price is sure to be better. There may be some jewels hiding in there, and no one is the wiser. The unfortunate thing is that the engine pile is likely to have just about anything in it from all different manufacturers. Once you have sorted through these, there are certain things you should be looking for.

If the engine is mostly together and upright, then the preceding paragraphs apply. If the engine has the oil pan on, but is upside down, the crank flange and the oil pan itself can be a good indication of a usable engine. The crank flywheel flange is a very good indicator of the engine's displacement and vintage. I will not get into this at this point, since I describe the sizes and shapes in detail in the crankshaft chapter. However, look for a counterweight type flange or a plain round rear flange. A steel crank signifies a performance and heavy-duty application, and the dowel pin on a counterweighted flange signifies a 400ci engine. The oil pan can be read several ways. Car pans have a very short deep end of the sump. Many truck pans have a longer deep end than the car pans. Corvettes get a larger capacity pan. This one can be easily recognized, since the drain plug is located in the center to the back of the deep part of the sump. Most other drain plugs are located on the driver-side edge. The one-piece rear main seal is a dead giveaway for engines built after 1985. The starter's bolt pattern is also an indication.

There are other things to look for. The rocker covers have changed several times over the years for cosmetic, pollution control, and functional reasons. Carburetors and intake manifolds, along with fuel injection systems, are always key in engine identification. They very often include a date marking, which could help date the piece. As soon as I see an original-type installation using a Holley carburetor, it means either a performance engine or a heavy-duty truck engine. Exhaust manifold configurations help in dating the piece, but somehow they seem to be very much chassis-oriented. The air cleaner can be a small indicator. The ones with a cold air duct are no older than 1970, and the twin snorkels are no newer than 1974. The ones on Corvettes aim very much forward at an approximately 30deg angle from the straight ahead, and the others are on a 45deg angle. Most of these criteria only apply to engines in their original state. This is something you will have to keep in mind.

Engine Regular Production Order Codes (RPO)

years	rpo #	cid	h/p	intake	comp ratio	special body application	manif
1989-92	1LE	350	230	TPI	10	tuned port	F
1987	B2L	350	225	TPI	10	tuned port	F
1988-89	B2L	350	230	TPI	10	tuned port	F
1990-92	B2L	350	245	TPI	10	tuned port	F
1991-92	B4C	350	245	TPI	10	tuned port	F
1984	L03	305	-	TBI	-	-	-
1968	L14	-	-	-	-	-	-
1963-67	L30	327	-	4	-	-	-
1963-64	L30	327	250	-	-	turbo-fire	-
1966-68	L30	327	275	-	-	turbo-fire	-
1963-64	L32	283	-	-	-	-	-
1976	L32	350	-	2	-	-	-
1974-77	L34	350	-	4	-	-	-
1980-81	L39	267	-	2	-	-	-
1967-72	L48	350	295	4	-	-	-
1973	L48	350	-	4	-	-	-
1986	L49	350	-	EFI	-	-	-
1969-73	L65	350	-	2	-	-	-
1970-72	L65	350	-	2	-	-	-
1981-86	L69	305	-	4	-	-	-
1968	L73	327	250	-	-	turbo-fire	-
1965	L74	327	300	-	-	turbo-thrift	-
1975	L76	350	-	4	-	-	-
1963-66	L77	283	220	-	-	turbo-fire	-
1975	L77	350	-	4	-	-	-
1975	L78	350	-	4	-	-	-
1965-68	L79	327	350	-	-	turbo-fire	-
1973-82	L82	350	-	4	-	-	-
1973	L82	350	-	4	-	-	-
1973	L83	350	-	-	-	-	-
1973	L98	350	-	TPI	-	al cyl heads	-
1973	LB9	305	-	TPI	-	-	-
1973	LF6	400	-	2	-	-	B
1973	LG3	305	-	2	-	-	-
1987	LG4	-	-	-	-	-	-
1987	LG4	305	-	4	-	-	-
1987	LG9	305	-	2	-	-	-
1969-80	LM1	350	-	-	low	-	El Camino
1974	LM1	350	-	4	-	catalytic	-
1974	LS9	350	-	4	-	-	-
1970-72	LT1	350	-	-	-	-	-
1974	LT4	400	-	4	-	-	-
1974	LT5	350	-	MPI	-	ohc	-
1974	LT9	350	-	4	-	-	truck
1975	LTF	400	-	4	-	-	-
1982-83	LU5	305	-	TTBI	-	cross-fire	-
1975	LV1	262	-	2	-	-	Monza
1967-69	Z28	302	-	4	-	-	F

Chapter 6

Cylinder Heads

You will find the cylinder head casting number between two intake valves on top of the intake ports.

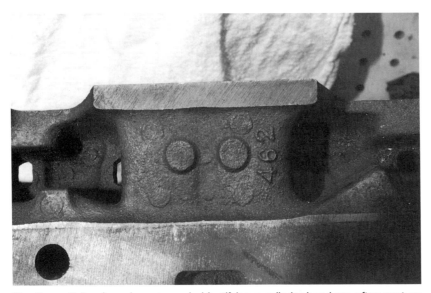

The three digits of any importance in identifying a cylinder head are often cast on the back side of the intake port.

In this chapter I will describe cylinder heads by family groups. The reason for this is that most cylinder heads have much in common, and most of the modifications done over the years have little impact on the casting. There are, however, some changes that are significant, and I will classify the cylinder heads by those changes. I refer to cylinder heads by the last three digits in the casting number. They are the only parts of the number that matter. Some castings with the same last three digits may have different preceding numbers with no significant change to the casting. The location of this number is, in full, under the rocker cover face in between two springs or rocker studs on top of an intake port. In many cases, the three-digit number will be cast on the lifter valley side on the back side intake port. The date code is under the rocker cover face as well.

Combustion Chamber Volumes

Instead of describing each casting individually, it seems more practical to group them by certain critical features. The most important feature is the combustion chamber. As I describe these combustion chambers, I will refer to them by their volume. This by no means indicates the absolute size of the chamber. I have measured several supposedly 64cc chambers to be as much as 68cc. The same holds true with 74cc open chamber castings which have measured almost 80cc. So this sizing is nominal and not necessarily accurate. The other thing about the chamber's volume is that I

28

will refer to them in the charts by these sizes.

The first configuration is the 64cc 265ci head. These heads were also used in some early 283ci engines. To achieve an adequate compression ratio on a relatively small displacement engine, the combustion chamber had to be made as small as possible. To do that, the engineers felt that shrouding around the spark plug was a good way of increasing the compression ratio. Of course, they soon realized the drawbacks of this design—the flame propagation was seriously compromised. With this in mind, the combustion chamber was redesigned to eliminate this flaw.

The 64cc head was used extensively until 1968, when it was modified. The 1968 version had the spark plug moved toward the center of the chamber. This did not change the volume but did improve flame travel. A peculiar characteristic of this type of chamber is the double squish design. Squish is the flat part of the combustion chamber as it meets the flat part of the piston. If clearances are at a minimum, every time the piston comes up, it almost touches the flat of the head. This is most beneficial in

This is the casting that has been so popular: the double bumps or camel humps. Castings 461, 462, and 291 carry these marks. They are the 300hp type heads.

Right
The 186 casting also carries the double bumps, but it also has the bolt holes. This is an LT1 head.

Below
Lightweight castings began to appear in 1978. With the exception of Mexican 882 and 993 castings, they still survive today. The straight versus contoured patterns are what one should look for. The extra bolt hole for the exhaust manifolds is a later feature.

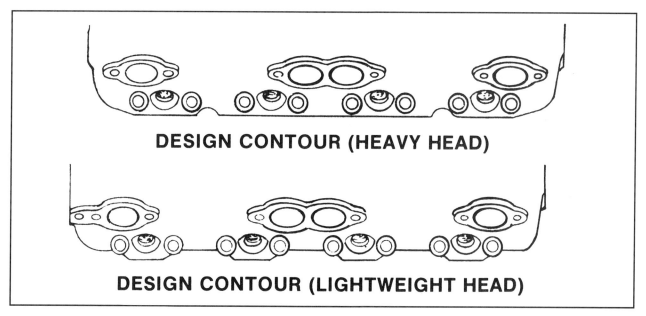

DESIGN CONTOUR (HEAVY HEAD)

DESIGN CONTOUR (LIGHTWEIGHT HEAD)

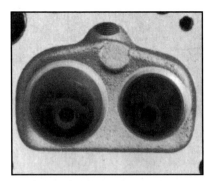

The 265ci head is unique in the sense that it is the only head to have the spark plug shrouded in material. This type of head was also used on early 283ci engines.

helping turbulence in the chamber, just before the spark. This helps overall combustion efficiency. The underneath of the spark plug, since it is so far into the chamber, has a small squish area. Hence, it is a double squish chamber. This type of combustion chamber has also been used on the later 262ci, 267ci, and 305ci engines.

The second configuration is the nominal 66cc head. It is nearly identical to the 64cc design but does not have the squish under the spark plug. In this case, the squish is laid down toward the spark plug side of the chamber. This reduces the tendency to detonate, and it enhances flame propagation. This style eventually became the standard combustion chamber design of choice for high-performance applications.

The first open-chamber type head, the 74cc head, made its appearance in the mid-1960s. This configuration was produced to accommodate the lower compression ratios required for heavy-duty truck applications. This type of head eventually spread to other applications that required stringent exhaust quality standards. The 74cc head became the norm, with some exceptions, in 1971. In 1972, the chamber volume increased in size to 76cc. The 400ci heads were 78cc.

In the mid-1970s, the small displacement engines required a smaller 60cc head to achieve a decent compression ratio.

The next major change occurred in 1986 with the advent of the electronic fuel-injection systems. The spark plug was relocated closer to the exhaust valve. This is an extension of the philosophy that brought about the angle plug. Over-the-counter performance castings are often referred to as turbo heads. The

This is a 462 chamber fit with small 1.94in/1.50in valves.

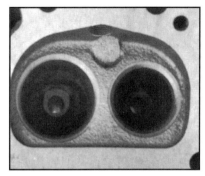

Here is an example of a fully closed combustion chamber. Notice the flat, or squish, area under the spark plug.

This is the second type of combustion chamber design. This one was unshrouded for the large valves at the factory. Notice the machined area behind the intake valve seat.

Corvette heads got combustion chambers as small as 58cc. To achieve that small volume, the relief to the valves was specially contoured to reduce the chamber size to a minimum, without hurting airflow too much.

Casting Numbers

It would be nice to absolutely classify cylinder heads by combustion chamber volume, but unfortunately, within certain groups of configurations, there are exceptions. These I will discuss in the next paragraphs as they arise. I will focus on the most common and popular head designs. If I leave out some castings, it is because they are likely to be low-performance or odd models not used for long periods of time.

The early 265ci cylinder heads are only good for a 265ci engine. They do not spread or enhance the burn very well. They do not have any bolt holes in the ends. They are easily recognized by the recessed spark plug.

The 520 and 896 castings, for the 283ci engine, have a 58cc chamber. Most all other 283ci heads are 64cc. The intake port has an approximate 140cc volume size. The Power Pack heads carry a marginally larger intake port over other 283ci heads. This feature made this casting the most desirable in the early years. Several other castings have been used on the 283ci engine, includ-

ing some larger combustion chamber styles used on heavy-duty truck applications.

The next cylinder head is the 461. Although the combustion chamber has been imitated on many other castings, the port configuration of this casting best lends itself to high-horsepower development. First cast in 1962, it was originally used on the fuel-injection engines; this explains the "fuelly" nickname it has. It features a 160cc intake runner. The 461X was produced for special high-performance applications and got a 175cc intake runner. The 461 heads are recognizable by the double bumps on the ends of the casting. The 461X castings have been most valuable in class racing, be it superstock drag racing or stock car circle track racing where no porting is allowed. If porting is done, the advantage is negated, since most of the enlargement of the port is in the bowl. A good head porter can duplicate and improve on that. The 461 casting has been equipped with both the 1.94in/1.50in and 2.02in/1.60in sizes of valves. The castings orig-

inally equipped from the factory with the larger valves were unshrouded in the combustion chamber to accommodate the larger valves and provide better flow. I have seen some examples of these heads, which were originally fit with 1.94in/1.50in valves, modified to accept the 2.02in/1.6in valves. They were not unshrouded, and they actually managed to reduce the airflow capacity of the castings. The GM engineers were certainly aware of this and properly machined around the valves to push the edge of the combustion chamber away from the valve to allow flow in between. This can be recognized by a circular machined shape and smooth finish on both sides of the spark plug as opposed to the cast texture of the ones using the small valves.

The next family of heads includes the numbers 462, 186, 291, 041, 292, and 492. They all use the 66cc combustion chamber with the relief under the spark plug and a slightly higher plug location. The port configuration is akin to the 461. The 462 and 291 have the double bumps but no

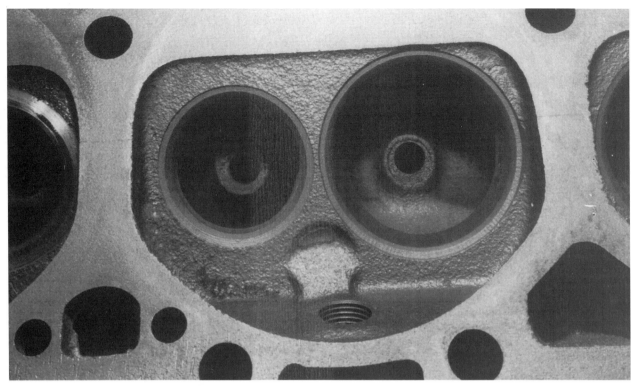

In the late 1960s, the move to lower compression ratios required this type of open chamber. These could range in size from 74cc to 78cc.

This 882 chamber is nearly identical to the low-compression 74cc open chamber except that the underside of the 45deg seat has an undercut from the factory. The roof of the exhaust port is flush with the guide boss, as opposed to being contoured.

bolt holes. The 186 has bolt holes and the short double bumps. The 041 has bolt holes and a different casting mark. It is intended for mid-performance engines and is equipped with 1.94in/1.5in valves, but the chamber and port configuration remains the same. Some of the others in this family have had the large valves installed at the factory (for the 302ci Z-28 and the LT1). The same enshrouding machining was performed on these as on the 461. As far as the stud arrangement goes, the large valve models were usually fitted with screw-in studs and guide plates.

The engineers were finally allowed to put some nice things in the LT4 heads. The intake valve grew .060in, and the exhaust valve grew .050in; both have hollow stems. With the convoluted shape of the chamber, angle plugs, and minimum size, it is obvious that enormous attention was paid to every detail.

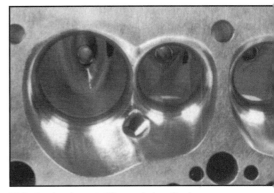

This is the latest Chevrolet cylinder head design. Although you may not come across this combustion chamber very often, it is becoming available.

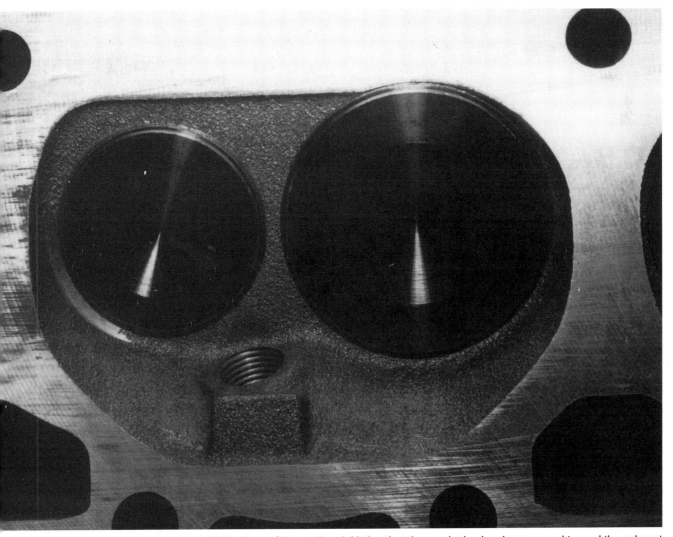

The 58cc chamber of the late-model aluminum Corvette head. Notice that the spark plug has been moved toward the exhaust valve and is angled.

The 441 and 126 castings were made between 1967 and 1970. They are open-chamber, large-valve cylinder heads. The port configuration is similar to the previous family but has slight bowl changes and a large combustion chamber of 74cc. The heads have the bolt holes in the end and use the large 13/16in washer-type spark plugs.

The 336, 993, 920, 991, and 487 castings are essentially the same as the 441 and 126 castings but use a 5/8in resistor-type spark plug. They are found on mid-performance engines built between 1970 and 1973. As I have mentioned earlier, some castings will have an X cast after the casting number. This is indicative of an over-sized intake port. Unlike the 461X, however, the volume increase is not as generous and is in the order of 5-7cc. These castings were produced for heavy-duty truck applications requiring more power.

In 1974, when GM was forced to produce engines that would run on unleaded fuel, many changes were made to the cylinder heads. The addition of an extra heat crossover port on the center exhaust port and the re-designed exhaust port did reduce emissions and raised the operating temperature. GM also began flame-hardening the exhaust seats to keep them from eroding under the new unleaded fuel conditions. On top of that, GM went on a lightening binge. All these changes contributed to a rash of cracking cylinder heads. Cracks usually formed around the exhaust seats of the center cylinder. The new exhaust port configuration did not improve flow. The most common casting you will find is the 882 for the 350ci engine and the 454 for the 305ci engine. These castings have a strangely cast area under the intake ports which make them very easy to spot. These castings have a 76cc chamber.

By 1978, another new series of castings, which were even lighter, was introduced. The 624 was created for the 350ci engine, and the 450, 416, and 601 were made for the 305ci engine. These can be recognized by the chiseled side at the short head bolts and the extra exhaust manifold bolt hole at the left end when viewing them from the same angle. Although the 624 casting has a 76cc chamber, the 450, 416, and 601 castings don't. The early 305ci engine used a large chamber volume head, but as the 1980s rolled around, the need for more power from this engine mandated a smaller chamber to yield higher compression ratios. The 450 cast-

The factory exhaust port has changed very little over the years. This late-model Corvette head shows one of the few changes. Here, the port was raised about 1/2in and is "D" shaped.

ing has a 1.72in/1.5in combination with a 62cc chamber. The 416 has 1.85in/1.5in valves with the same chamber. In 1984 and 1985, the Z-28 and Monte Carlo SS received a High Output 5.0ltr engine. The 601 casting was used for this engine; it had 1.85in/1.50in valves and a smaller 60cc chamber.

In 1986, a lot of changes were made to the cylinder heads. The rocker cover no longer was fastened on the outside edge. Instead, it was held by four bolts in the center of the cover. The gasket surface was also raised and machine finished. Something that may not be so obvious is the realignment of

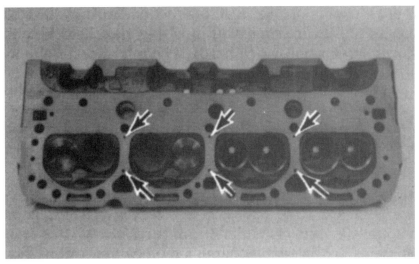

The 400ci head contains open-chamber 76–78cc combustion chambers. The head has six steam holes drilled.

Here you can see the difference between a smog 882 casting and a 441 casting typical of most all other heads. The 882, the front head, has ribs machined flush with the deck. This feature makes these heads very easy to spot. Only the 434 casting of early 305ci heads has the same feature.

the four center mounting bolts of the intake-to-head location. I have modified heads and manifolds to interchange, but the new alignment, which is more straight up, is far more easily accessible than the old style.

The 350ci engine casting has a 76cc head, and the 305ci engine has a 64cc head. The exception is the Corvette and its aluminum cylinder heads. Some of these are as small as 58cc. There are two different types of intake ports for the iron heads: the swirl port and standard port. On the swirl port, the bowl has a swirl ramp cast into it. These heads were produced for high fuel efficiency in trucks and heavy car applications. The standard port is found on F body cars, some 350ci engine trucks, and heavy-duty applications.

The newest head available is the reverse cooling LT1 aluminum cylinder heads. With a chamber volume of 58cc and less, they are unique and will not interchange with other earlier standard cooling engines. The water passages have been seriously modified.

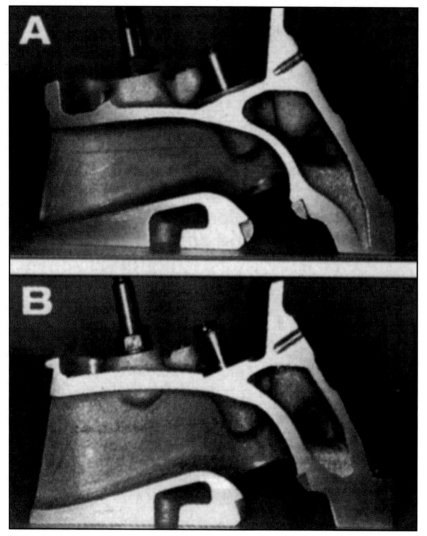

The raised roof of the LT4 intake port (photo B) is where the head gained most of its 15cc displacement over the LT1 (photo A). This required modified machining at the rocker rail. The short radius is also improved.

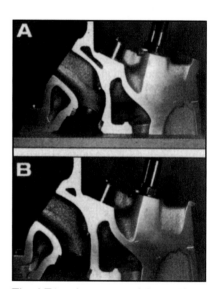

The LT1 exhaust port (photo A) already has the raised "D" port design, which is most effective, but the LT4 (photo B) gets a revised short radius.

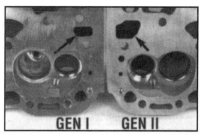

Reverse cooling in a Generation II head requires a larger opening to allow water to migrate into the head first instead of running into the block first.

In a Generation II head, the bolt angle and cooling passages are altered. The water return passages at the end of the cylinder heads where they meet the intake manifold are eliminated since coolant returns to the radiator via the block.

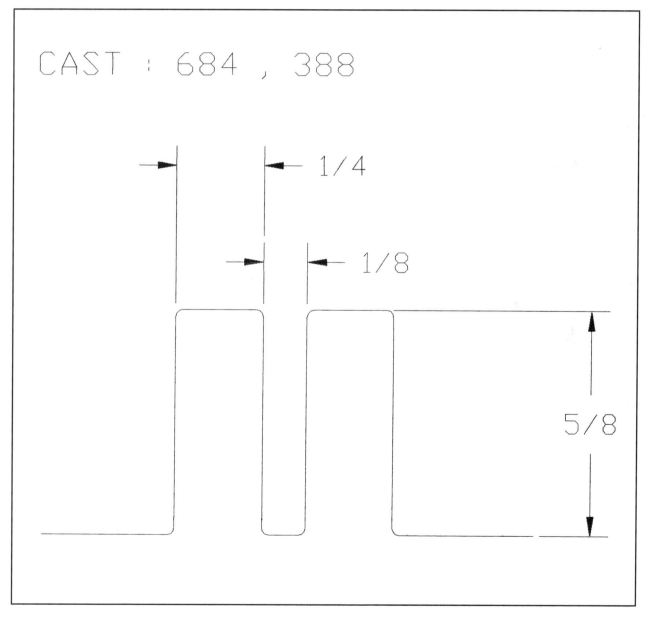

CAST : 684 , 388

1/4

1/8

5/8

Cylinder Heads Sorted by Casting Number

years	cast #	cid	intake vlv	exh vlv	cc	bolt holes	carburetion
1971-75	330545	307, 350	1.72	1.5001	74	yes	-
1971-73	330862	400	1.94	1.5001	-	-	-
1971-76	333881	350	1.72	1.5001	-	-	-
1970-80	333882	350, 400	1.94	1.5	76	yes	may have 1.72 & 1.6
1973-80	340292	350	2.02	1.6	66	yes	serv casting, turb head
1975-76	354434	262, 305	1.72	1.3	62	yes	exh 1.5 on 305
1976-79	358741	305	1.72	1.5	66	yes	-
1975-76	367450	262, 305	1.72	1.3	-	yes	exh 1.5 on 305
1980-84	376445	350	1.72	1.5001	-	-	3/8 exh guide
1969-79	376495	350	-	-	-	-	-
1970-73	399380	400	-	-	-	-	-
1978-80	460703	350	-	-	-	-	-
1979-85	462624	350	1.94	1.5	-	yes	-
1979-83	468642	350	1.72	1.5001	-	yes	Vette
1979-82	517513	267	1.72	1.3	-	yes	-
1968-69	3238882	350	-	-	-	-	-
1963-67	3297185	327	1.72	1.5001	-	-	-
1955	3636839	265	1.72	1.5	-	no	-
1955	3703523	265	1.72	1.5001	-	no	car, Vette, truck
1955-56	3713358	265	1.72	1.5	-	no	truck
1955-56	3713569	265	1.72	1.5	-	no	-
1962-67	3714482	327	1.72	1.5	-	no	-
1956-57	3725306	265	1.72	1.5	-	no	-
1969-73	3727185	307	1.72	1.5001	-	-	-
1956	3731262	265	1.72	1.5	-	no	2 four bbl, Vette
1957	3731539	283	1.72	1.5	-	no	FI, 2 four bbl, Vette
1955-56	3731544	265	1.72	1.5	-	no	two bbl
1957-66	3731554	283	1.72	1.5	-	no	car, truck
1957	3731556	283	1.72	1.5	-	no	truck
1956	3731762	265	1.72	1.5001	-	-	2 four bbl, Vette
1960-61	3737465	283	1.72	1.5	-	no	-
1962-67	3737775	283	1.72	1.5	-	no	also on 327
1957	3740997	283	1.72	1.5	-	no	2 four bbl, FI
1958	3743056	283	1.72	1.5	-	no	truck
1962-67	3743096	327	1.72	1.5	-	no	GMC, truck
1957	3747363	265	1.72	1.5	-	no	-
1958-61	3747363	265	1.72	1.5	-	no	-
1962-67	3748056	327	1.72	1.5001	-	-	truck
1957-58	3748720	283	-	1.5	-	no	4 bbl, 2 fours, FI Vette
1957-62	3748770	283	1.72	1.5	-	no	-
1958-59	3748772	283	1.72	1.5	-	no	-
1957-59	3755537	283	1.72	1.5	2	no	-
1959	3755538	283	1.72	1.5001	-	-	FI, Vette
1958-59	3755539	283	1.72	1.5	-	no	staggered cover
1957-59	3755549	283	1.72	1.5	-	no	car, truck
1957-62	3755550	283	1.72	1.5	-	no	staggered cover
1962-67	3755585	327	1.72	1.5	-	no	truck
1959	3760116	283	1.72	1.5	-	no	Vette, FI & 4bbl
1962-64	3767460	327	1.72	1.5	-	no	-
1962-67	3767462	327	1.94	1.5	68	no	dbl bump, hi perf
1959	3767465	283	1.72	1.5001	-	-	FI, 2 four bbl, Vette
1960-61	3767754	283	1.72	1.5	-	no	-
1960-67	3767792	283	1.72	1.5	-	no	truck

years	cast #	cid	intake vlv	exh vlv	cc	bolt holes	carburetion
1967-70	3770126	327	1.94	1.5	74	yes	-
1955	3773012	265	1.72	1.5001	-	-	Vette
1964-67	3774634	327	-	-	-	-	-
1960-67	3774682	283, 327	1.72	1.5	-	no	truck
1962-64	3774684	283, 327	1.72	1.5	-	no	GMC, truck
1958	3774690	283	-	-	-	-	FI, Vette
1960-67	3774692	283	1.72	1.5	-	no	-
1962-67	3782461	327	1.94	1.5	-	no	dbl bump, hi perf
1962-67	3782879	327	1.94	1.5	-	no	Vette
1964-67	3790721	283	1.72	1.5	-	no	-
1965-67	3792563	327	1.72	1.5	-	no	-
1963-67	3795896	283, 327	1.72	1.5	-	no	-
1963-67	3798996	327	1.72	1.5	-	no	-

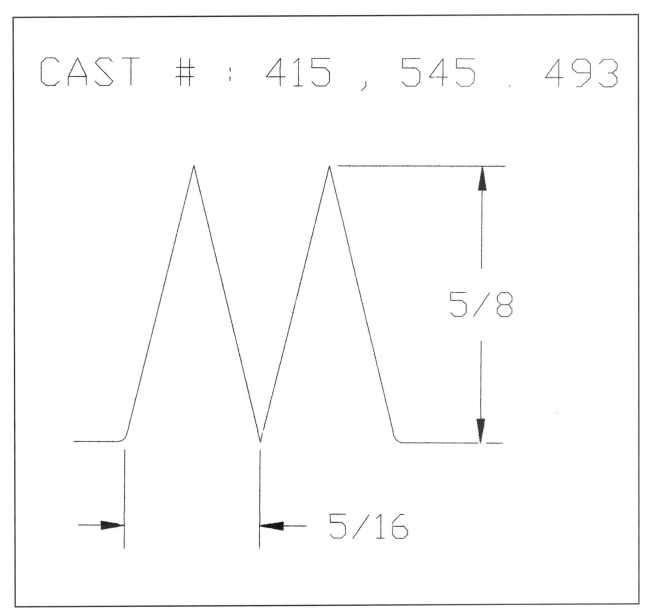

years	cast #	cid	intake vlv	exh vlv	cc	bolt holes	carburetion
1967	3814462	350	1.94	1.5001	-	-	-
1962-67	3814480	283, 327	1.72	1.5	-	no	-
1962-67	3814482	283, 327	1.72	1.5001	-	-	350 in 1967
1959	3817680	283	1.72	1.5	-	no	FI & 4 bbl
1966-67	3817681	327	1.72	1.5	-	no	-
1967	3817681	350	1.72	1.5	-	no	-
1961-62	3817682	283	1.72	1.5	-	no	2 bbl
1955-56	3836839	265	1.72	1.5	-	no	-
1962-67	3836842	283, 327	1.72	1.5	-	no	-
1963-64	3836924	283	1.72	1.5001	-	-	-
1958-62	3836942	283	1.72	1.5001	-	-	-
1958-62	3837063	283	1.72	1.5001	-	-	-
1956	3837064	265	1.72	1.5	-	no	-

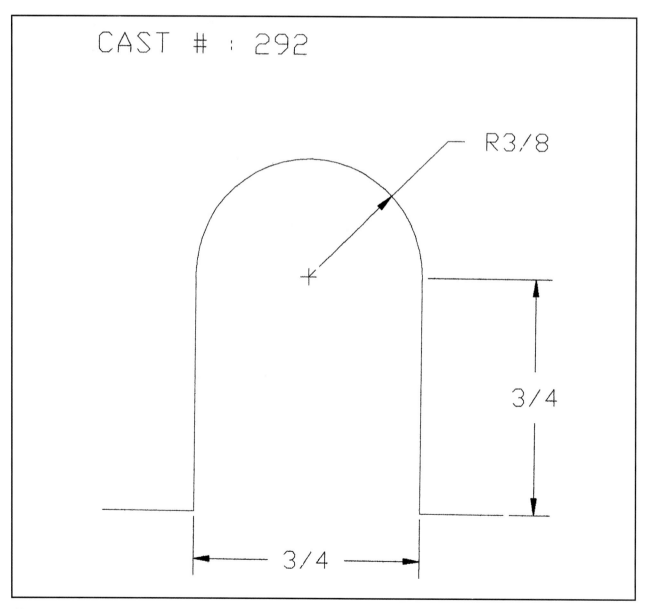

CAST # : 292

R3/8

3/4

3/4

years	cast #	cid	intake vlv	exh vlv	cc	bolt holes	carburetion
1955-56	3837065	265	1.72	1.5	-	no	-
1957	3837739	283	1.72	1.5	-	no	truck
1962-67	3837775	283	1.72	1.5001	-	-	also on 327
1957-58	3848720	283	1.72	1.5	-	no	-
1965	3849820	327	1.72	1.5001	-	-	-
1965-67	3849935	283	1.72	1.5	-	no	-
1962-64	3852174	327	1.72	1.5	-	no	-
1962-67	3854520	283	1.72	1.5	-	no	-
1962-67	3854520	327	1.72	1.5	-	no	-
1968-76	3855961	350	1.72	1.5	-	yes	-
1957-60	3867802	283	1.72	1.5	-	yes	FI, Vette
1956-57	3873064	265	1.72	1.5001	-	-	-
1962-67	3876132	327	1.94	1.5	-	no	Vette
1971-73	3876487	350	1.94	1.5001	-	-	-
1960-67	3876775	283, 327	1.72	1.5	-	no	-
1960-67	3876775	327	1.72	1.5	-	no	-
1962-67	3884520	283, 327	1.72	1.5	-	no	-
1967	3890462	302, 327	2.02	1.6	66	-	-

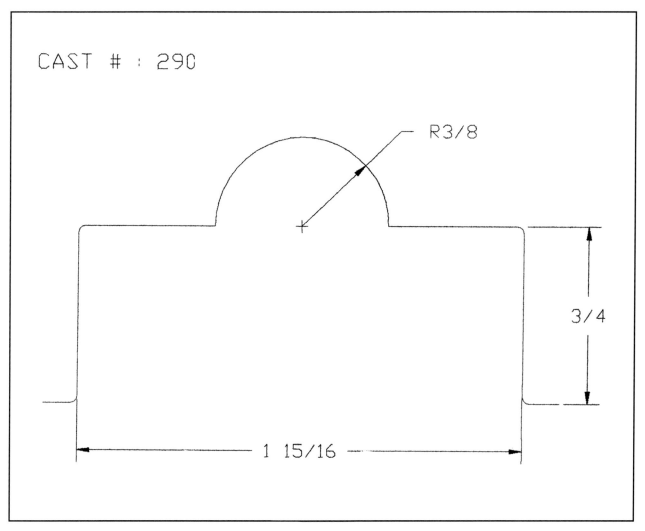

CAST # : 290

R3/8

3/4

1 15/16

years	cast #	cid	intake vlv	exh vlv	cc	bolt holes	carburetion
1962-67	3891462	327	1.94	1.5001	-	-	lrg valvs
1968	3911011	327	1.72	1.5001	-	-	-
1968-69	3911032	307, 327	1.72	1.5	-	-	-
1958-62	3912264	283	1.72	1.5	-	no	car, truck
1963-64	3912265	283	1.72	1.5	-	no	-
1968-70	3912291	327	1.94	1.5001	-	-	also on 350, lrg valvs
1967	3912311	350	1.94	1.5	-	yes	-
1965-67	3912313	327	1.72	1.5	-	yes	-
1968-73	3914636	307	1.72	1.5	-	yes	-
1967	3917264	302	2.02	1.6	-	no	-
1968-69	3917290	307, 327	1.72	1.5	-	yes	-
1967-69	3917291	302, 327	2.02	1.6	-	no	dbl bump
1968-69	3917291	350	1.94	1.5	-	no	dbl bump
1968	3917292	327	1.94	1.5	-	no	dbl bump
1968-69	3917293	307, 327	1.72	1.5	-	no	-
1966	3921175	327	2.02	1.6	-	no	w 350hp
1968-72	3923441	350	1.94	1.5001	76	-	-
1968-73	3927185	307, 350	1.72	1.5	-	yes	-

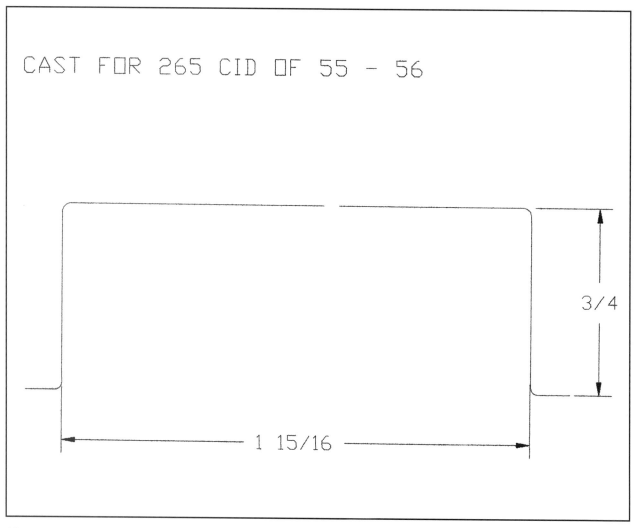

CAST FOR 265 CID OF 55 - 56

3/4

1 15/16

years	cast #	cid	intake vlv	exh vlv	cc	bolt holes	carburetion
1969	3927185	327	1.72	1.5	-	yes	-
1968-69	3927186	302	2.02	1.6	-	yes	Z-28
1968-69	3927186	327	2.02	1.6	-	yes	-
1970-72	3927186	350	2.02	1.6	-	yes	LT1
1969-70	3927187	302, 350	2.02	1.6	-	yes	-
1969	3927188	307	1.72	1.5	-	yes	light truck
1969	3927188	327	1.72	1.5	-	yes	light truck
1969	3927188	350	1.72	1.5	-	yes	light truck
1968	3928454	307	1.72	1.5	-	yes	-
1968	3928455	302	2.02	1.6	-	yes	w 325hp & 350hp
1968	3928455	327	2.02	1.6	-	yes	w 325hp & 350hp
1968	3928494	327	2.02	1.6	-	yes	hi perf, 4 bbl

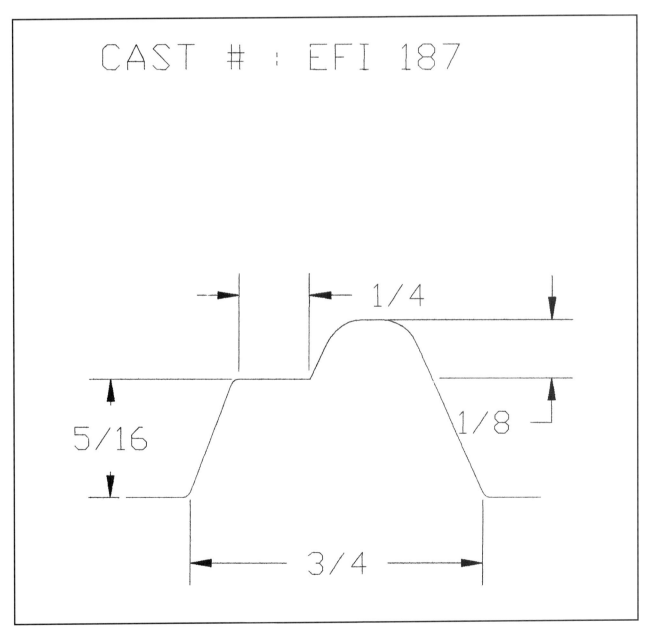

CAST # : 185 , 339

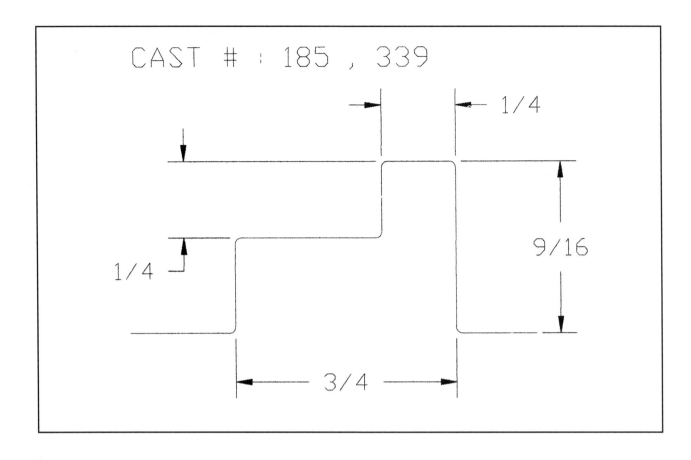

CAST # : 487 , 997 , 993
601 cast same but 1/16 smaller all around

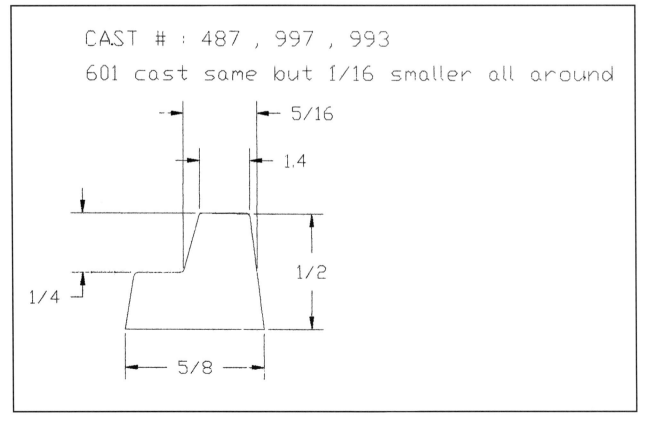

44

years	cast #	cid	intake vlv	exh vlv	cc	bolt holes	carburetion
1968	3928494	350	2.02	1.6	-	yes	hi perf, 4 bbl
1968	3928495	327	1.94	1.5	-	yes	w 250hp
1968-73	3931633	307	1.72	1.5	-	yes	-
1968-76	3931635	350	1.72	1.5	-	yes	-
1968-69	3931637	327	1.94	1.5	-	-	car, Vette
1968	3931638	327	1.72	1.5	-	-	truck
1968	3931639	302	2.02	1.6	-	-	-
1968-73	3932373	307	1.72	1.5	-	yes	-
1969-72	3932441	327, 350	1.94	1.5	-	yes	-
1968-69	3932454	307	1.72	1.5	-	yes	-
1976	3932882	400	1.94	1.5	-	yes	-
1968-73	3933148	350	-	-	-	-	-
1968	3941174	327	-	-	-	-	-
1969	3946812	350	1.72	1.5	-	yes	truck

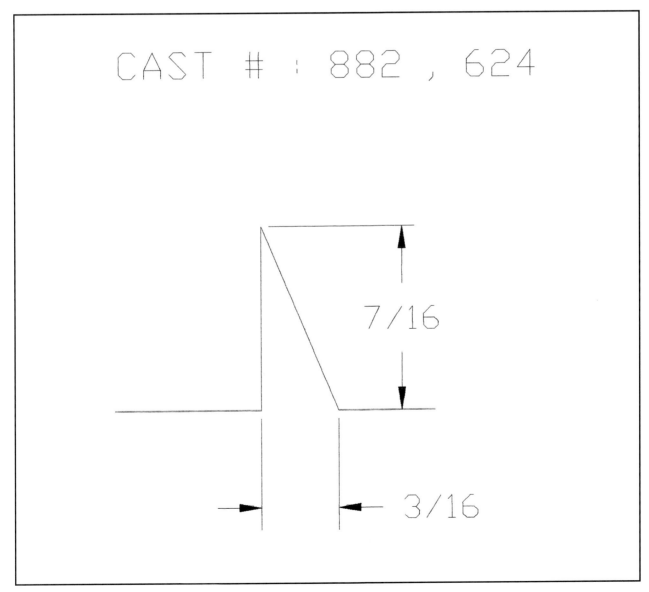

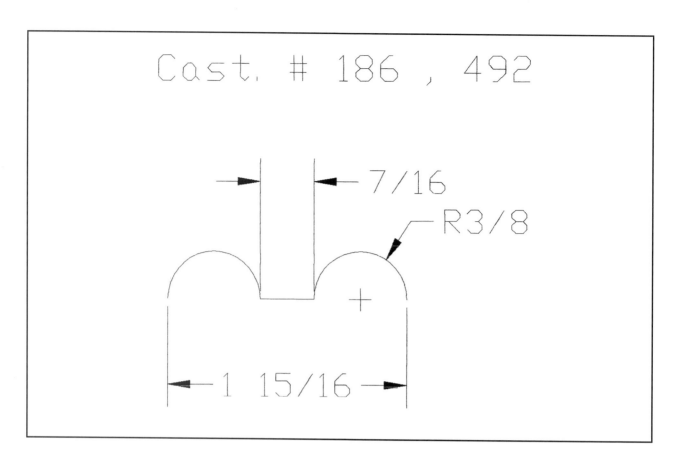

Cast. # 186 , 492

7/16

R3/8

1 15/16

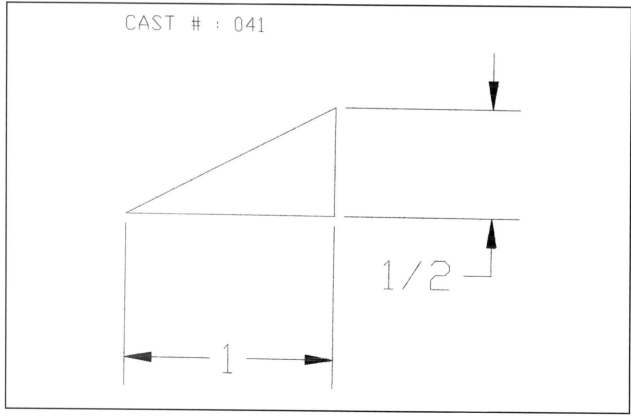

CAST # : 041

1/2

1

years	cast #	cid	intake vlv	exh vlv	cc	bolt holes	carburetion
1969-70	3946813	350	1.72	1.5	-	yes	-
1969-70	3947014	350	-	-	-	-	-
1968-70	3947041	350	1.94	1.5	-	yes	w 300hp & 64cc
1970-71	3951598	400	1.94	1.5	-	yes	-
1968-77	3964286	350	1.72	1.5	-	yes	-
1967-70	3970126	327	1.94	1.5	-	yes	w 13/16in sprk plg
1971-73	3973195	400	-	-	-	-	truck
1964-70	3973414	327	2.02	1.6	-	-	also on 350, Vette
1968-72	3973487	350	1.94	1.5	-	yes	-
1968-73	3973487	350	2.02	1.6	-	yes	LT1
1972-76	3973493	400	1.94	1.5	-	yes	-
1967	3981462	302	1.94	1.5	-	no	dbl bump
1962-67	3981462	327	1.94	1.5	-	no	dbl bump
1967	3981462	350	1.94	1.5	-	no	dbl bump
1971-72	3986316	350	-	-	-	-	-
1969-79	3986330	350	-	-	-	-	-
1968-69	3986339	307	1.72	1.5	-	yes	-
1970-76	3986339	350	1.72	1.5	-	yes	-

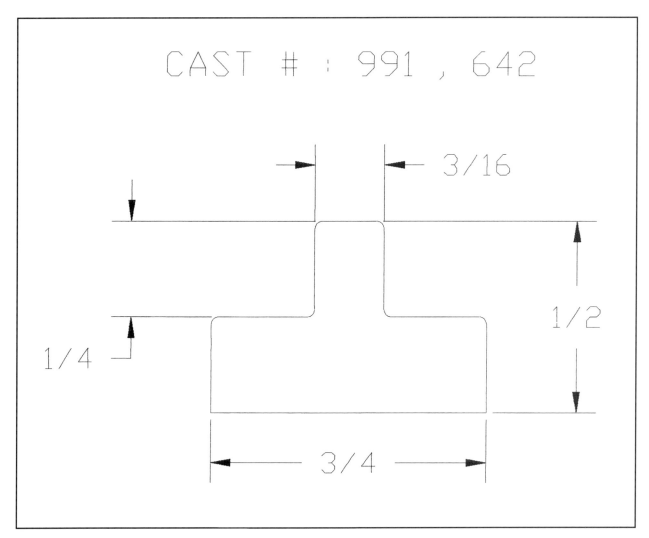

CAST # : 991 , 642

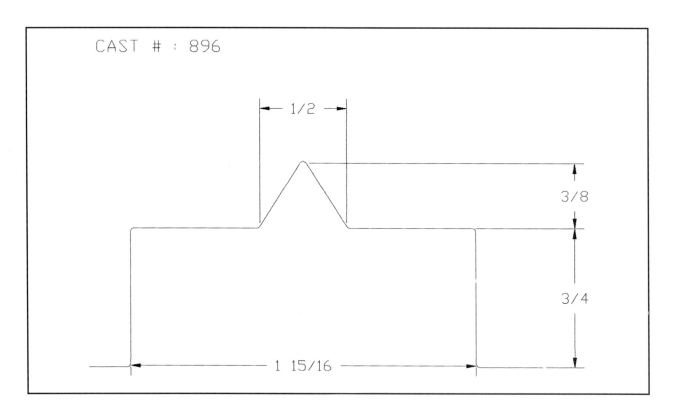

CAST # : 896

1/2

3/8

3/4

1 15/16

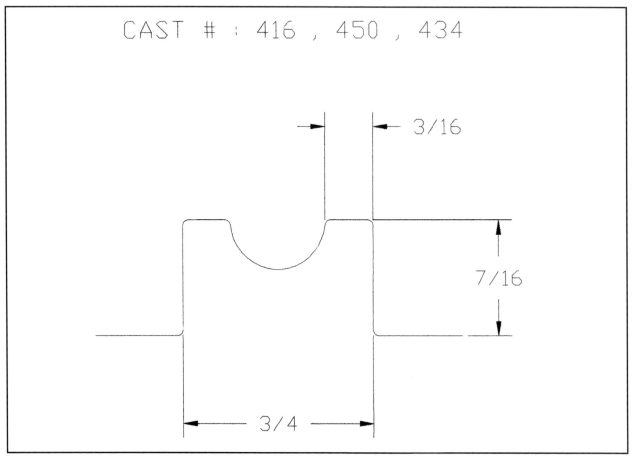

CAST # : 416 , 450 , 434

3/16

7/16

3/4

years	cast #	cid	intake vlv	exh vlv	cc	bolt holes	carburetion
1968-71	3986388	307	1.72	1.5	-	yes	-
1972-76	3986388	350	1.72	1.5	-	yes	-
1962-68	3990462	327	1.94	1.5	-	no	dbl bump
1962-68	3990462	327	2.02	1.6	-	no	dbl bump
1969-72	3991492	350	2.02	1.6	-	yes	service only
1971	3997417	307	1.72	1.5001	72	-	cars
1972	3998916	400	1.94	1.5	-	yes	-
1972-74	3998920	350	1.94	1.5	-	yes	-
1968-69	3998991	307	1.72	1.5	-	yes	-
1970-76	3998991	350	1.72	1.5	-	yes	-
1968-76	3998993	350	1.72	1.5	-	yes	truck
1972	3998997	400	1.94	1.5	-	yes	-

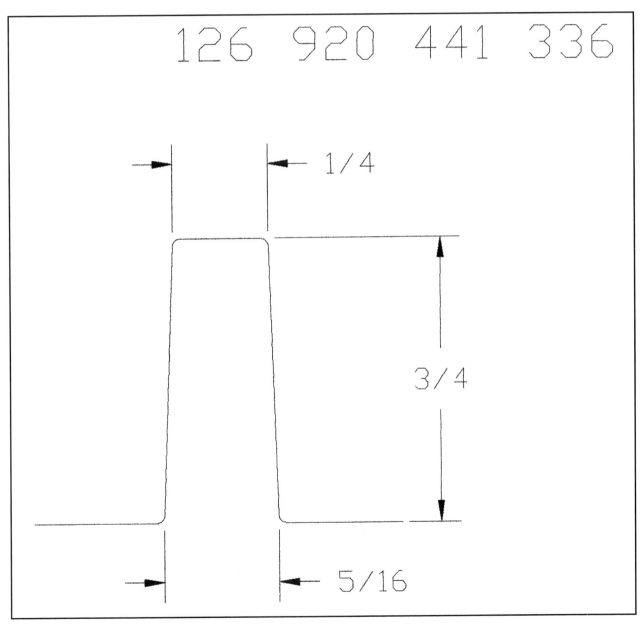

years	cast #	cid	intake vlv	exh vlv	cc	bolt holes	carburetion
1968-76	6259425	350	1.72	1.5	-	yes	-
1973	6259515	350	1.94	1.5001	76	-	cars
1968-76	6260856	350	1.72	1.5	-	yes	-
1972-73	6272070	350	1.72	1.5001	76	-	-
1987	10065206	350	1.94	1.5001	-	-	EFI
1980-82	14014415	267	1.72	1.3	-	yes	-
1980-84	14014416	305	1.85	1.5	-	yes	4 bbl
1984-88	14019261	350	1.94	1.5001	-	yes	-
1980	14020517	350	-	-	-	-	-
1981	14020555	305	-	-	-	-	-
1981	14020556	350	-	-	-	-	-
1985	14022056	350	1.94	1.5001	-	-	-
1980-84	14022301	305	1.85	1.5	-	yes	-
1980-82	14022601	267	1.72	1.3	-	yes	-
1980-86	14022601	305	1.84	1.5001	-	yes	-
1986	14085963	350	1.94	1.5001	-	-	-
1986-88	14089119	350	1.94	1.5001	-	-	EFI
1987	14101083	350	1.94	1.5001	-	-	EFI
1987	14101128	350	1.94	1.5001	-	-	EFI
1986-88	14102191	350	1.94	1.5001	-	-	EFI, swirl port
1986-88	14102193	350	1.94	1.5001	-	-	EFI
1986-91	10110810	305	1.84	1.5001	-	-	EFI, swrl prt, stat wgn
1986-91	14101081	305	1.84	1.5001	-	-	EFI, std port
1988-93	14102188	350	1.94	1.5001	-	-	EFI, swirl port
1986-91	14102187	305	1.84	1.5001	-	-	EFI, swirl port

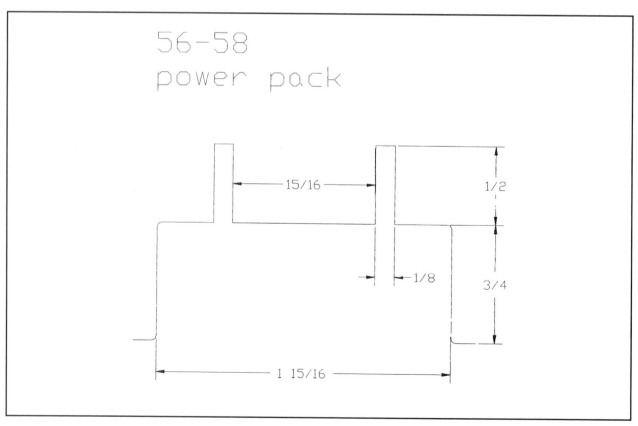

56-58 power pack

Cylinder Heads Sorted by Short Numbers

years	cast #	short #	cid	intake vlv	exh vlv	cc	bolt holes	carburetion
1968	3911011	011	327	1.72	1.5001	-	-	-
1955	3773012	012	265	1.72	1.5001	-	-	Vette
1969-70	3947014	014	350	-	-	-	-	-
1968-69	3911032	032	307	1.72	1.5	-	-	-
1968-70	3947041	041	350	1.94	1.5	-	yes	w 300hp & 64cc
1958	3743056	056	283	1.72	1.5	-	no	truck
1962-67	3748056	056	327	1.72	1.5001	-	-	truck
1985	14022056	056	350	1.94	1.5001	-	-	-
1958-62	3837063	063	283	1.72	1.5001	-	-	-
1956	3837064	064	265	1.72	1.5	-	no	-
1956-57	3873064	064	265	1.72	1.5001	-	-	-
1955-56	3837065	065	265	1.72	1.5	-	no	-
1972-73	6272070	070	350	1.72	1.5001	76	-	-
1987	14101083	083	350	1.94	1.5001	-	-	EFI
1962-67	3743096	096	327	1.72	1.5	-	no	GMC, truck
1959	3760116	116	283	1.72	1.5	-	no	Vette, FI & 4bbl
1986-88	14089119	119	350	1.94	1.5001	-	-	EFI
1967-70	3970126	126	327	1.94	1.5	-	yes	w 13/16in sprk plg
1987	14101128	128	350	1.94	1.5001	-	-	EFI
1962-67	3876132	132	327	1.94	1.5	-	no	Vette
1968-73	3933148	148	350	-	-	-	-	-
1962-64	3852174	174	327	1.72	1.5	-	no	-
1968	3941174	174	327	-	-	-	-	-
1966	3921175	175	327	2.02	1.6	-	no	w 350hp
1963-67	3297185	185	327	1.72	1.5001	-	-	-
1969-73	3727185	185	307	1.72	1.5001	-	-	-
1968-73	3927185	185	307	1.72	1.5	-	yes	-
1968-69	3927185	185	327	1.72	1.5	-	yes	-
1970-76	3927185	185	350	1.72	1.5	-	yes	-
1968-69	3927186	186	302	2.02	1.6	-	yes	Z-28
1968-70	3927186	186	327	2.02	1.6	-	yes	-
1970-72	3927186	186	350	2.02	1.6	-	yes	LT1
1969	3927188	188	307	1.72	1.5	-	yes	light truck
1969	3927188	188	327	1.72	1.5	-	yes	light truck
1969	3927188	188	350	1.72	1.5	-	yes	light truck
1986-88	14102191	191	350	1.94	1.5001	-	-	EFI
1986-88	14102193	193	350	1.94	1.5001	-	-	EFI
1971-73	3973195	195	400	-	-	-	-	truck
1987	10065206	206	350	1.94	1.5001	-	-	EFI
1984-88	14019261	261	350	1.94	1.5001	-	yes	-
1956	3731262	262	265	1.72	1.5	-	no	two 4 bbl, Vette
1958-62	3912264	264	283	1.72	1.5	-	no	car, truck
1967	3917264	264	302	2.02	1.6	-	no	-
1963-64	3912265	265	283	1.72	1.5	-	no	-
1968-77	3964286	286	350	1.72	1.5	-	yes	-
1968-69	3917290	290	307	1.72	1.5	-	yes	-
1968-69	3917290	290	327	1.72	1.5	-	yes	-
1968-70	3912291	291	327	1.94	1.5001	-	-	302 & 350 lrg valvs
1967-69	3917291	291	302	2.02	1.6	-	no	dbl bump
1967-69	3917291	291	327	2.02	1.6	-	no	dbl bump
1968-69	3917291	291	350	1.94	1.5	-	no	dbl bump
1973-80	340292	292	350	2.02	1.6	66	yes	turbo casting
1968	3917292	292	327	1.94	1.5	-	no	dbl bump

years	cast #	short #	cid	intake vlv	exh vlv	cc	bolt holes	carburation
1968-69	3917293	293	307	1.72	1.5	-	no	-
1968	3917293	293	327	1.72	1.5001	72	-	cars
1980-84	14022301	301	305	-	-	-	-	-
1980-84	14022301	301	305	1.72	1.5	-	yes	-
1956-57	3725306	306	265	1.72	1.5	-	no	-
1967	3912311	311	350	1.94	1.5	-	yes	-
1965-67	3912313	313	327	1.72	1.5	-	yes	-
1971-72	3986316	316	350	-	-	-	-	-
1969-79	3986330	330	350	-	-	-	-	-
1968-69	3986339	339	307	1.72	1.5	-	yes	-
1970-76	3986339	339	350	1.72	1.5	-	yes	-
1955-56	3713358	358	265	1.72	1.5	-	no	truck
1957	3747363	363	265	1.72	1.5	-	no	-
1968-73	3932373	373	307	1.72	1.5	-	yes	-
1970-73	399380	380	400	1.94	1.5001	-	yes	-
1968-71	3986388	388	307	1.72	1.5	-	yes	-
1972-76	3986388	388	350	1.72	1.5	-	yes	-
1964-70	3973414	414	327	2.02	1.6	-	-	also on 350, Vette
1980-82	14014415	415	267	1.72	1.3	-	yes	-
1980-84	14014416	416	305	1.85	1.5	-	yes	4 bbl
1971	3997417	417	307	1.72	1.5001	72	-	cars
1968-76	6259425	425	350	1.72	1.5	-	yes	-
1975-76	354434	434	262	1.72	1.3	62	yes	-
1968-72	3923441	441	350	1.94	1.5001	76	-	-
1967-72	3932441	441	327	1.94	1.5	-	yes	-
1980-84	376445	445	350	1.72	1.5001	-	-	truck
1975-76	367450	450	262	1.72	1.3	-	yes	-
1976-79	367450	450	305	1.72	1.5	-	yes	2 bbl
1968	3928454	454	307	1.72	1.5	-	yes	-
1968-69	3932454	454	307	1.72	1.5	-	yes	-
1968	3928455	455	302	2.02	1.6	-	yes	w 325hp & 350hp
1968	3928455	455	327	2.02	1.6	-	yes	w 325hp & 350hp
1962-64	3767460	460	327	1.72	1.5	-	no	-
1962-69	3782461	461	327	1.94	1.5	-	no	dbl bump, hi perf
1962-67	3767462	462	327	1.94	1.5	-	no	dbl bump, hi perf
1967	3782462	462	327	1.94	1.5001	-	-	lrge valvs
1967	3814462	462	350	1.94	1.5001	-	-	-
1967	3890462	462	302	2.02	1.6	66	-	Z-28
1967	3890462	462	327	2.02	1.6	66	-	cars
1962-67	3891462	462	327	1.94	1.5001	-	-	302 & 350, lrg valvs
1962-67	3981462	462	327	1.94	1.5	-	no	dbl bump
1967	3981462	462	302	1.94	1.5	-	no	dbl bump
1967	3981462	462	350	1.94	1.5	-	no	dbl bump
1962-68	3990462	462	327	2.02	1.6	-	no	dbl bump
1962-68	3990462	462	327	1.94	1.5	-	no	dbl bump
1960-61	3737465	465	283	1.72	1.5	-	no	-
1960-61	3767465	465	327	1.72	1.5001	-	-	FI 4, two 4 bbl, Vette
1960-67	3814480	480	283	1.72	1.5	-	no	-
1962-67	3714482	482	327	1.72	1.5	-	no	-
1967	3814482	482	327	1.72	1.5001	-	-	-
1971-73	3876487	487	350	1.94	1.5001	-	-	-
1968-72	3973487	487	350	1.94	1.5	-	yes	-
1968-73	3973487	487	350	2.02	1.6	-	yes	LT1
1969-72	3991492	492	350	2.02	1.6	-	yes	service
1972-76	3973493	493	400	1.94	1.5	-	yes	-

years	cast #	short #	cid	intake vlv	exh vlv	cc	bolt holes	carburation
1968	3928494	494	327	2.02	1.6	-	yes	hi-perf, 4 bbl
1968	3928494	494	350	2.02	1.6	-	yes	hi-perf, 4 bbl
1969-79	376495	495	350	-	-	-	-	-
1968	3928495	495	327	1.94	1.5	-	yes	w 250hp
1979	517513	513	267	1.72	1.3	-	yes	-
1973	6259515	515	350	1.94	1.5001	76	-	cars
1980	14020517	517	350	-	-	-	-	-
1962-67	3854520	520	283	1.72	1.5	-	no	-
1962-67	3854520	520	327	1.72	1.5	-	no	-
1960-67	3884520	520	283	1.72	1.5	-	no	Power pack
1960-67	3884520	520	327	1.72	1.5	-	no	Power pack
1955	3703523	523	265	1.72	1.5001	-	-	car, Vette, truck
1957-62	3755537	537	283	1.72	1.5	2	no	-
1959	3755538	538	283	1.72	1.5001	-	-	FI, Vette
1957-66	3731539	539	283	1.72	1.5	-	no	truck, Vette
1958-62	3755539	539	283	1.72	1.5	-	no	truck
1955-56	3731544	544	265	1.72	1.5	-	no	-
1971-75	330545	545	350	1.94	1.5001	-	-	-
1957-62	3755549	549	283	1.72	1.5	-	no	car, truck

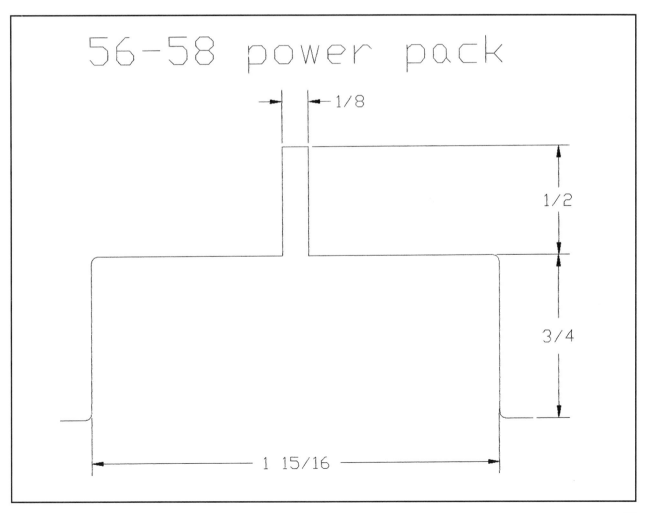

56-58 power pack

years	cast #	short #	cid	intake vlv	exh vlv	cc	bolt holes	carburation
1957-62	3755550	550	283	1.72	1.5	-	no	-
1957-66	3731554	554	283	1.72	1.5	-	no	car, truck
1981	14020555	555	305	-	-	-	-	
1957	3731556	556	283	1.72	1.5	-	no	truck
1981	14020556	556	350	-	-	-	-	-
1965-67	3792563	563	327	1.72	1.5	-	no	-
1955-56	3713569	569	265	1.72	1.5	-	no	-
1962-67	3755585	585	327	1.72	1.5	-	no	GMC truck
1970-71	3951598	598	400	1.94	1.5	-	yes	-
1980-82	14022601	601	305	1.72	1.3	-	yes	-
1980-86	14022801	601	305	1.84	1.5001	-	-	also on 267
1979-85	468624	624	350	1.94	1.5	-	yes	-
1979-83	468624	624	350	2.02	1.6	-	yes	L-82 for Vette
1968-73	3931633	633	307	1.72	1.5	-	yes	-
1964-67	3774634	634	327	-	-	-	-	-
1968-76	3931635	635	350	1.72	1.5	-	yes	-
1968-73	3914636	636	307	1.72	1.5	-	yes	-
1968-69	3931637	637	327	1.94	1.5	-	-	car & Vette
1968	3931638	638	327	1.72	1.5	-	-	truck
1968	3931639	639	302	2.02	1.6	-	-	-
1959	3817680	680	283	1.72	1.5	-	no	FI & 4 bbl
1962-67	3817681	681	327	1.72	1.5	-	no	-
1967	3817681	681	350	1.72	1.5	-	no	-
1960-64	3774682	682	283	1.72	1.5	-	no	car, truck
1961-62	3817682	682	283	1.72	1.5	-	no	2 bbl

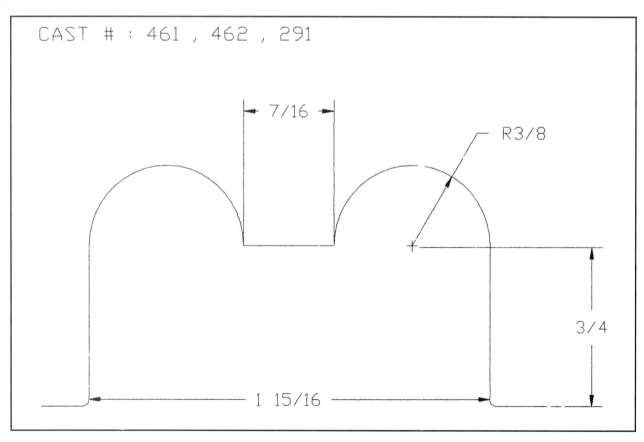

CAST # : 461 , 462 , 291

7/16

R3/8

3/4

1 15/16

years	cast #	short #	cid	intake vlv	exh vlv	cc	bolt holes	carburation
1962	3774684	684	283	1.72	1.5	-	no	Chevy & GMC truck
1963-64	3774684	684	283	1.72	1.5	-	no	Chevy & GMC truck
1958	3774690	690	283	-	-	-	-	FI, Vette
1958-64	3774692	692	283	1.72	1.5	-	no	-
1978-80	460703	703	350	-	-	-	-	-
1957-58	3748720	720	283	-	1.5	-	no	4 bbl, two 4 bbl, FI, Vette
1957-58	3848720	720	283	1.72	1.5	-	no	-
1964-67	3790721	721	283	1.72	1.5	-	no	-
1957	3837739	739	283	1.72	1.5	-	no	truck
1976-79	358741	741	305	1.72	1.5	-	yes	-
1960-61	3767754	754	283	1.72	1.5	-	no	-
1956	3731762	762	265	1.72	1.5001	-	-	two 4 bbl, Vette
1955-56	3748770	770	265	1.72	1.5	-	no	-
1957-62	3748770	770	283	1.72	1.5	-	no	-
1957-61	3748772	772	283	1.72	1.5	-	no	-
1962-67	3737775	775	283	1.72	1.5	-	no	-
1962-67	3737775	775	327	1.72	1.5	-	no	-
1962-67	3837775	775	283	1.72	1.5001	-	-	also on 327
1960-67	3876775	775	283	1.72	1.5	-	no	-
1960-67	3876775	775	327	1.72	1.5	-	no	-
1960-67	3767792	792	283	1.72	1.5	-	no	car, truck
1957-60	3867802	802	283	1.72	1.5	-	yes	FI, Vette
1969	3946812	812	350	1.72	1.5	-	yes	truck
1969-70	3946813	813	350	1.72	1.5	-	yes	-
1965	3849820	820	327	1.72	1.5001	-	-	-
1955	3636839	839	265	1.72	1.5	-	no	-
1955-56	3836839	839	265	1.72	1.5	-	no	-
1958-67	3836842	842	283	1.72	1.5	-	no	-
1962-67	3836842	842	327	1.72	1.5	-	no	-
1968-76	6260856	856	350	1.72	1.5	-	yes	-
1971-73	330862	862	400	1.94	1.5001	-	-	-
1962-67	3782879	879	327	1.94	1.5	-	no	Vette
1971-76	333881	881	350	1.72	1.5001	-	-	-
1970-76	333882	882	350	1.94	1.5	76	yes	-
1970-76	333882	882	400	1.94	1.5	80	yes	some w 1.6in exh
1968-69	3238882	882	350	-	-	-	-	-
1976	3932882	882	400	1.94	1.5	-	yes	-
1963-67	3795896	896	283	1.72	1.5	-	no	-
1968-72	3795896	896	307	1.72	1.5	-	no	-
1972	3998916	916	400	1.94	1.5	-	yes	-
1972-74	3998920	920	350	1.94	1.5	-	yes	-
1963-64	3836924	924	283	1.72	1.5001	-	-	-
1965-67	3849935	935	283	1.72	1.5	-	no	-
1958-62	3836942	942	283	1.72	1.5001	-	-	-
1968-76	3855961	961	350	1.72	1.5	-	yes	-
1986	14085963	963	350	1.94	1.5001	-	-	-
1968-69	3998991	991	307	1.72	1.5	-	yes	-
1970-76	3998991	991	350	1.72	1.5	-	yes	-
1968-76	3998993	993	350	1.72	1.5	-	yes	truck
1963-67	3798996	996	327	1.72	1.5	-	no	-
1957	3740997	997	283	1.72	1.5	-	no	-
1972	3998997	997	400	1.94	1.5	-	yes	-

Chapter 7

Engine Blocks

Identifying blocks involves using several casting numbers from various block locations. The primary number is at the rear of the block on top of the bell housing

The block casting number can be found at the back of the block on the driver side. The date code is sometimes located in that area.

flange on the driver side. Once this has been determined, you may be given a range in which this casting number was available. To more specifically determine the original configuration and chassis installation, look at the stamping number located on the deck at the front on the passenger side. The final set of numbers to check is the casting date. These numbers can be located in several places (please refer to the chapter on date coding).

265ci Engine

This is the original configuration of this little engine. It is most easily recognized by its missing oil filter boss. Obviously, it was felt that oil filtration was not required. This was soon corrected. These blocks also used the road draft tube for

crankcase ventilation. The draft tube worked through a baffle bolted under the intake manifold in the lifter valley at the rear of the block. There is a special passage cast right in the block, and the outlet is directly behind the rear of the intake beside the distributor. This system was used until 1968 on 283ci and 327ci engines. Another less obvious feature involves the cam bearing housing bores. They were not annular grooved as most later blocks were. These engines need a camshaft with a grooved main journal to feed oil to the lifter galleries. The rear cam plug is 2-1/64in. This block can also be recognized by the missing motor mount bosses on the side of the block. In those years the block was mounted into the chassis using the front mounting holes. The rear main seal used in the early blocks was a rope style. This was upgraded, with the addition of the oil filter boss, to a neoprene-type seal. The seal housing is machined differently.

283ci Engine

The original one was simply the second-design 265ci engine bored to 283ci. This block was used until 1962. At this point, the advent of the 327ci engine required a casting change to accommodate the longer stroke. These blocks have their insides at the base of the cylinders cast in an arc fashion, as opposed to the straight design of the previous models. These 283ci blocks

Right
The lightweight blocks have a stamping pad that is smaller than that of the heavy blocks.

When looking for a block with a high-nickel, high-tin mix, the numbers to look for are "010" and "020." They are cast under the timing cover area.

can, in most cases, be bored 0.125in without a problem. A quick way to tell them apart is by the crank. If your 283ci block has a cast crank, it is definitely relieved for the larger counterweights. In 1958, the rear cam plug size was increased from 2-1/64in to 2-7/32in.

In the mid-1960s, the block received clutch linkage bolt hole bosses to the side of the block at the rear on the driver side. The Nova got a special block modified at the filter housing.

327ci Engine

Up until 1967, this block used a small-journal crank. The Nova got a special block with the oil filter boss recessed into the block 2-1/2in. The lack of clearance between the oil filter and the steering linkage is most certainly what prevented Chevrolet from

installing this hot little engine in their most lightweight chassis until the block was modified in 1964. The dipstick was also in the pan at the front, and the dipstick hole in the block was plugged. For the small-journal 327ci block, most rules pertaining to the 283ci block are still in effect, with the obvious bore size difference (3-7/8in for the 283ci and 4in for the 327ci). In 1968, all small blocks carried the large-journal configuration. In many cases, the 327ci engine and the 350ci engine shared the same block.

302ci Engine

This engine used a small-journal 283ci block in 1967 and a large-journal 327ci block in 1969. The only way to determine these is by the stamping number, since the block is 283ci. These engines can be readily recognized by the

rear crank flange, as it is unique to the large-journal 302ci block.

307ci Engine

In 1968, this engine was introduced to fill the void left by the

The 509 block is the only 400ci engine block to have the standard frost plug configuration.

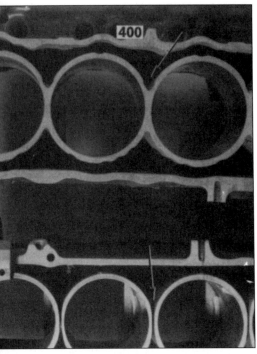

The bores on the 400ci block are siamesed; they touch each other. The blocks with smaller bores (350ci and less) allow coolant to flow between the bores.

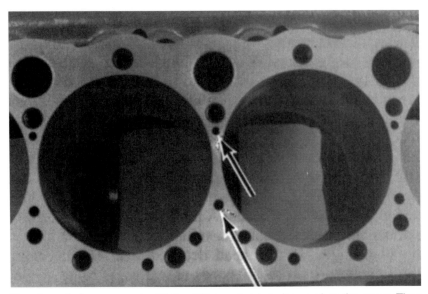

The steam holes are required if the 400ci engine is to be used on the street. They allow coolant flow in these critical areas.

283ci engine. Using the then new large-journal crank, it retains the bore of the 283ci block, but uses the 3.25in stroke of the 327ci engine. It is not a particularly desirable block, as most of them were cast with very little nickel and no tin to improve the cast mix. This was an attempt to lower the production costs of the bottom-line engine. It seems to have an increased bore wear rate because of that. In any case, it is still a small-bore block, and that alone makes it second best.

262ci Engine

Produced between 1975 and 1976, it was installed in the Monza and Nova. The casting number is the only external feature available to recognize this block. It does, however, have a unique bore size of 3.671in.

267ci Engine

Introduced in 1979 and produced until 1982, this engine has the smallest bore size of all at 3.5in. Expect to find the dipstick on the passenger side of the block.

305ci Engine

The 305ci engine was introduced in 1976 and is still in production. It carries a 3.736in bore and the 350ci engine crank. The early blocks have the dipstick on the driver side at the deck face. The newer models, from 1978 on, have the dipstick on the passenger side at the bottom by the oil pan. The models from 1986 on have the one-piece rear main seal and provisions for the roller camshaft. Some late 1980s 305ci blocks may have the fuel pump boss cast into them, but it may not be machined. Most blocks cast this way use an electric fuel pump for the fuel injection, as opposed to a mechanical fuel pump for the carbureted versions. There are some exceptions for the 305ci block. Some blocks have "305" cast right onto the block at the front directly opposite of the fuel pump boss on the other side. With EFI blocks, not all are cast with the provisions for the roller camshaft. All the early ones did, but in the late 1980s, as GM was not putting roller cams in truck applications, and the truck segment being the greatest V-8 user, GM discontinued making all the blocks the same. Only the F body car received a roller 305ci engine.

350ci Engine

Introduced in 1967 to go into the newly developed Camaro, this engine has to be the most popular block available for hot rodding purposes. It has always had the large-journal crank and has been offered under several different casting numbers. It can be found in two- and four-bolt main configurations. In 1978, the 350ci block got the dipstick change (like other small blocks) and in 1985, due to the EFI redesign, received more changes. The early blocks up to 1970 have four ribs cast into the lifter valley going up along the cylinders. The most popular block of the early 1970s has to be the K series. These can be recognized by the "K" prefix on the serial number and a "K" cast by the casting number and on the main caps. This block was made at the McKinnon casting foundry. The lightweight blocks from 1978 on often have "350" cast onto the rear bell housing flange opposite side of the casting number. The EFI blocks from 1986 on have the displacement cast beside the casting number. These sizes are metric: 5.0ltr is 305ci, and 5.7ltr is 350ci. The Mexican blocks are identified by the "hecho en Mexico" usually cast in the same area.

400ci Engine

Introduced in 1970 and produced until 1980, this block has several identifying features. The early blocks, 1970 to 1972, have three frost plugs on the side of the block and have four-bolt main bearing caps. The newer design has provisions for the three frost plugs cast into its side, but only the two outside ones are machined. These blocks have two-bolt mains. This is not an end-all, be-all rule, as I presently have a two-bolt 400ci block in my shop, and it has the three frost plugs on the side. I suspect this one is a crossover oddball. Another distinguishing feature of the 400ci block is the two-bolt main caps design. It is very much like a big-block engine on the three center caps. What I mean by this is that the caps go on in a 45deg angle from the head of the bolt to the block register, as opposed to straight down

Many engines sold over the parts counter were made in Mexico. This is clear by the "hecho en Mexico" markings on the block.

The stamping pad can be a good indication of the type and vintage of small block you are dealing with. This is an example of a large pad found on a 350ci block.

on all other two-bolt mains. Another identifying feature is the steam holes between the cylinders. There are six per side. These steam holes vent the air pockets from the top of the cooling jacket from between the cylinders. The reason they are required in the 400ci block is simple. Because the bores are so big, GM had to cast them touching each other. In other words, there is no space between them to circulate coolant, so some air pockets could develop and create unmanageable localized hot spots. These are called siamesed bores. The cylinder heads and head gaskets must have matching holes to allow flow. Another identifying attribute of the 400ci block is the relief at the oil pan rail of the block. These are cast into the block to clear the connecting rods. It is required to allow the longer stroke.

The original design for the rear main seal has been very reliable over the years.

In 1985, GM improved on the few leak-prone components and integrated a one-piece, 360deg rear main seal. The newer block has obvious machined surfaces and the drilled holes to fasten down the seal housing.

Stamping Pad

Over the years, the stamping pad part of the cast has been changed several times. Whether it was for identification purposes or not, the fact remains that most distinct series of block have a different size pad. The early small-journal 265ci, 283ci, and 327ci engines have a pad that is approximately 3in wide. I have noticed that the pad size will vary as much as 1/4in, plus or minus from the size quoted. It can still be a good indicator, since all the pad's nominal sizes are further apart than that. The early large-journal blocks—262ci, 302ci, 305ci, 307ci, and 350ci—have the largest pad of all at 4-1/4in wide. These are considered the old style large-journal or heavy castings. In 1975, GM began a diet which was full in by 1978. The second series of large-journal blocks—267ci, 305ci, and 350ci—got a considerably smaller pad at 1-3/4in wide. Finally, the EFI engines—305ci and 350ci of 1985 vintage and newer—have a pad 1-5/8in wide. The 400ci has a pad size all its own at 3-1/2in. Please keep in mind that all these sizes are nominal and are not to be considered as exact. When using this information, please go to the nearest size for identification.

This block is equipped with four-bolt main bearing caps. It also has a two-piece rear main seal and a driver side dipstick. The end caps only have two bolts on any block.

It is very easy to date a block by determining the type and location of the dipstick. Up to 1978, it was on the driver side at the deck. After 1978, the dipstick has the tube coming out at the bottom of the block on the passenger side. This is not an absolute rule; both are common.

In 1963, in order for the engine to fit in the tight confines of the Chevy II, GM had to recess the oil filter pad into the block.

The year 1986 saw the arrival of roller lifters. This required that retaining bosses be cast and tapped in the valley of the block. A spring cover holds down eight alignment bars. This is required since roller lifters do not spin like flat tappets.

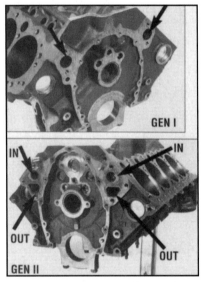

The flow of coolant in a Generation II block is directed to the head from the top holes and is returned out the bottom. The difference is obvious when it is set against a first-generation small-block.

Engine Block Data

years	cast #	cid	power low	power high	main caps	body application/comment
1980-85	140029	350	-	-	2	car
1973-80	330817	400	-	-	2	car, truck
1975	355909	262	-	-	2	car, truck
1976-85	355909	305	-	-	2	A
1975	360851	262	-	-	2	Monza
1976-79	361979	305	-	-	2	car, truck
1978-86	366245	350	-	-	-	car
1982-86	366286	350	-	-	4	Chevrolet, siamese
1982	366299	350	-	-	4	Chevrolet, aluminium
1956-67	383810	283	-	-	2	-
1967-68	389257	302	-	-	2	Z-28
1968-73	391436	307	-	-	2	-
1965-67	393288	283	-	-	2	car, truck
1976-79	460776	305	-	-	2	car, truck
1976-79	460777	305	-	-	2	car
1978-79	460778	305	-	-	2	car, truck
1979-82	471511	267	-	-	2	car, truck
1976-85	581671	305	-	-	2	A
1985-94	1489363	350	-	-	2	-
1979-82	2135412	267	-	-	2	-
1979-82	2404929	267	-	-	2	-
1973-76	3030817	400	-	-	2	car, truck
1958-61	3556519	283	-	-	2	car, truck
1955	3703524	265	195	-	2	car, no filter
1955-56	3720991	265	195	225	2	car, truck
1957	3731548	283	220	283	2	-
1956-67	3736935	283	-	-	2	-
1957-59	3737739	283	220	290	2	car, truck
1958-62	3756519	283	230	315	2	car, truck
1956-67	3756935	283	-	-	2	-
1962-65	3782870	327	250	375	2	car, truck
1956-67	3789187	283	-	-	2	-
1962-67	3789817	327	210	275	2	car, truck
1961-64	3789935	283	230	315	2	car, truck, Vette
1966-67	3790721	283	-	-	2	Chevy II
1964-67	3791362	327	300	300	2	Chevy II
1958-62	3794226	283	220	220	2	truck
1968-69	3794460	327	250	250	2	truck
1968-69	3814660	327	-	-	2	F A
1968-69	3814660	302	-	-	4	Camaro, Z-28, Vette
1956-67	3832338	283	-	-	2	-
1956-67	3834812	283	-	-	2	-
1958-62	3837739	283	-	-	2	-
1957-66	3849852	283	220	-	2	car, truck
1956-67	3849859	283	-	-	2	-
1956-67	3849935	283	-	-	2	-
1964-67	3852174	327	-	-	2	car, truck
1968-76	3855961	350	-	-	2	car
1964-67	3858174	327	300	350	2	A
1964-67	3858180	327	250	375	2	-
1962-67	3858190	327	-	-	2	-
1966-67	3862194	283	-	-	2	Chevy II
1962-66	3864812	283	230	-	2	car, truck

years	cast #	cid	power low	power high	main caps	body application/ comment
1964-67	3868657	327	300	-	2	-
1962-67	3876132	327	-	-	2	-
1963	3889935	283	-	-	2	truck
1962-67	3892657	327	-	-	2	car, truck
1967	3892657	302	290	-	2	Z-28, small journal
1968-69	3892659	327	210	-	2	-
1962-66	3896944	283	230	-	2	-
1965-67	3896948	283	-	-	2	-
1964-67	3903352	327	250	-	2	-
1969-80	3911460	350	-	-	2	A
1968-73	3914635	307	-	-	2	car
1968-73	3914636	307	-	-	2	car, truck
1968-69	3914638	327	-	-	2	-
1968-73	3914653	307	-	-	2	A
1968-69	3914660	327	250	-	2	truck
1968-69	3914678	302	290	-	4	Camaro, Z-28
1968-69	3914678	327	210	295	4	car, truck
1968	3914678	350	210	295	4	cars
1965-67	3932288	283	-	-	2	A
1956-67	3932338	283	-	-	2	-
1974-75	3932368	350	-	-	2	-
1969-73	3932371	307	-	-	2	car, truck
1969-73	3932373	307	-	-	2	car, truck
1968-69	3932386	350	300	350	4	LT1, 4
1968	3932386	327	-	-	2	A
1969	3932386	302	290	-	4	Camaro, Z-28
1969-76	3932388	350	165	300	2	car, truck
1968-69	3933100	327	-	-	2	-
1968-69	3933180	327	-	-	2	-
1968	3941174	307	-	-	2	truck
1956-67	3949852	283	-	-	2	-
1973-80	3951509	400	-	-	2	car, truck
1970-73	3951511	400	-	-	4	truck
1962-67	3953512	327	-	-	2	-
1968-69	3955618	327	-	-	4	A F, Vette
1969	3956618	302	290	-	4	Z-28
1969-79	3956618	350	165	350	4	car, truck, Vette
1969-76	3958618	350	-	-	2	A
1962-63	3959512	327	250	-	2	-
1956-67	3959532	283	-	-	2	-
1968	3970010	327	-	-	2	A
1969-79	3970010	350	185	370	2	car, truck, Vette
1968-76	3970014	350	-	-	2	car, truck
1969-73	3970020	307	-	-	2	car, truck
1968-76	6259425	350	-	-	-	car, truck
1980-84	14010201	305	-	-	2	car, truck
1980-84	14010202	305	-	-	2	car, truck

The water pump on a Generation II engine is gear-driven. Its two-way thermostat mixes hot and cold liquid to reduce thermal shock to the engine.

This number reveals that this is a 1970 LT1 block. It is one of the most sought-after engines. Unfortunately, many LT1 blocks have been rebuilt, modified, or cannibalized of good parts.

years	cast #	cid	power low	power high	main caps	body application/ comment
1980-84	14010203	305	-	-	2	car, truck
1980-82	14010205	267	-	-	2	-
1980-85	14010207	350	-	-	4	truck
1980-85	14010209	350	-	-	4	truck
1978-86	14010231	305	-	-	2	-
1979-82	14010280	267	-	-	2	car
1982	14011064	350	-	-	4	Chevrolet, high tin
1979-82	14016375	267	-	-	2	-
1979-82	14016376	267	-	-	2	car
1978-85	14016379	350	-	-	-	car, truck
1980-84	14016381	305	-	-	2	car, truck
1978-88	14016383	305	-	-	2	-
1979-82	14040205	267	-	-	2	-
1978-86	14049047	305	-	-	2	-
1986-94	14079287	350	-	-	-	-
1987	14088526	350	-	-	2	Camaro
1986-94	14088548	350	-	-	-	-
1986-92	14088551	305	-	-	2	-
1988-94	14093627	305	-	-	2	-
1986-94	14093638	350	-	-	-	-
1988-94	14094766	305	-	-	2	-
1986-94	14101148	350	-	-	-	-
1987-88	14102058	305	-	-	2	-
1969-85	14316379	350	-	-	2	-

A close look at the water pump drive system on a Generation II block shows you how the side load of the old belt drive has been eliminated. This certainly improves the durability of the seal and bearing in the pump.

Chapter 8

Crankshafts

Over the years, several crankshafts have been offered. They were made from two basic manufacturing processes: forging and casting. All early cranks were forged. The reason for this is that there where no casting techniques thought adequate in those days. In the mid-1960s, the foundry processes improved to the point were it was felt safe to cast a crank strong enough to withstand the rigors of service. The only small-journal crankshaft ever cast was for the 283ci. All small-journal 3.25in cranks made for the 327ci engine are forged.

Three different sizes of journals have been produced over the years. There is the small-journal crank with 2.300in mains and 2.000in rods, the large-journal crank with 2.450in mains and 2.100in rods, and the 400ci crank with 2.650in mains and 2.100in rods.

The way of distinguishing the forged crank from the cast crank

The crankshaft casting number is located on one of the sides as shown.

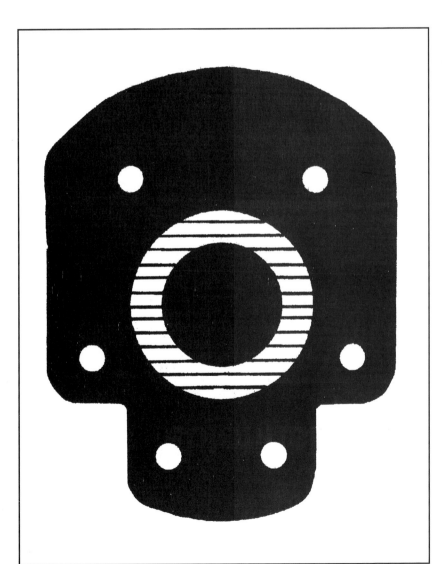

The flange of a 400ci crankshaft.

The difference between a forged crank and a cast crank. The cast crank to the left has a narrow parting line; the forged crank has a larger parting line.

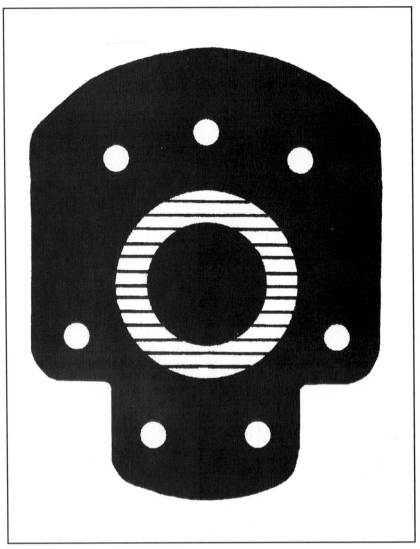

The flange of a 350ci crankshaft.

ture of the material. Most forged steel cranks have the counterweights machined to size. It gives them a brighter smoother finish than the cast ones. Two cranks were never forged: the 3.100in crank of the 262ci and the 3.75in crank of the 400ci.

A feature applied only to the forged cranks is the Tuftriding process. It is a chemical heat-treating technique that hardens the journal and makes them more resistant to scratching and scuffing. This process leaves the forged crank with a dull gray finish. These cranks can be identified by the cross-drilling process used on high-load applications. Be aware that not all cross-drilled forged cranks got Tuftrided.

The casting (or forging) number located on the side of one of the counterweights will help identify the type of crank. Refer to the list of numbers. Another way of telling cranks apart is by the rear flange. Many different flanges have been used, and they are indicative of the age and stroke of the crank.

The 3in-stroke crank was used in the 265ci and 283ci engines. It has been forged and cast. The 302ci engine used that stroke in a small-journal forged design in 1967 and in a unique forged large-journal type in 1968 and 1969.

The 3.1in-stroke crank is unique to the 262ci engine and was only cast for the 1975and 1976 model years. The 262ci engine was available in the Monza and Nova only.

The 3.25in-stroke crank was originally used in the small-journal 327ci engine. The same stroke was used in the large-journal 307ci and 327ci engines. Only the high-performance and truck applications got forged cranks.

The 3.48in-stroke crank has to be the most common stroke ever used. Introduced in 1968 for the 350ci engine, it has only been made in the large-journal configuration. Both cast and forged processes have been used for this

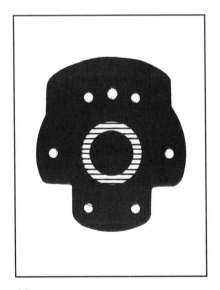

is by the parting line left by the manufacturing process. The forged crank has a wide parting line running from front to back of the crank and is approximately 1/2in wide. It is the forging flash left by the dies. This flash is then ground off. Distinct grinding marks are left after this process. The cast crank has a very narrow parting line, which is where the mold halves separate and leave a thin line. Another way of telling them apart is by the overall tex-

The flange of a 327ci large-journal crankshaft.

crank. The 267ci, 305ci, and 350ci engines all used the same stroke. The only difference among the three cast cranks is the counterweight sizes for balancing purposes. In many cases, a 305ci crank can be used in a 350ci engine. When lighter than stock pistons are used, proper balancing can be achieved. I don't suggest using a 267ci crank in a 350ci engine, because the balancing differences are too great.

The 3.750in-stroke crank of the 400ci engine has two distinguishing features. It is the only crank to have the first throw drilled all the way through. You may notice that some other cranks may be partially drilled in the same location. These have been done that way for balancing requirements. The other feature is the fact that these cranks usually have the dowel pin in the flywheel flange. This is so the flywheel can be installed only one way. The flywheel as well as the balancer are part of the reciprocating assembly. The 400ci crank is externally balanced.

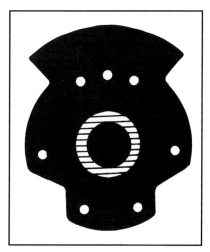

The flange of a 307ci crankshaft.

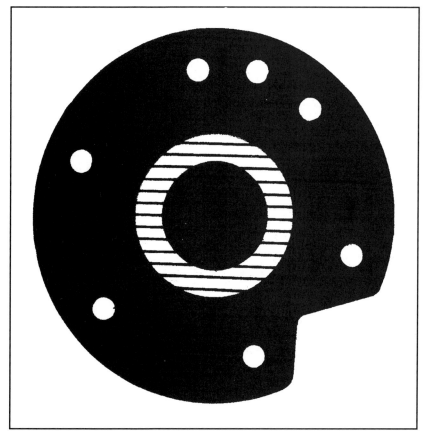

The flange of a 302ci crankshaft.

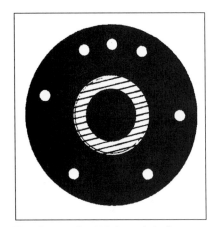

The flange of a 283ci crankshaft.

The left crankshaft is a 1986 and newer style. It has a one-piece rear main seal. The right crank is a two-piece pre-1986 style.

Crankshaft Data

years	cast #	cid	material	journal	rear main	application
1968-73	1130	307, 327	cast	large	two	all
1968-76	1181	350	cast	large	two	all
1968-69	3279	302	forged	large	two	Z-28
1962-67	4577	327	forged	small	two	-
1968-73	4672	307, 327	cast	large	two	-
1975-85	310514	350	-	large	two	-
1975-76	354431	262	cast	large	two	Monza, Nova
1955-67	3727449	265, 283	forged	small	two	-
1962-67	3734627	327	forged	small	two	-
1955-67	3735236	265, 283	forged	small	two	-
1957-63	3735263	283	forged	small	two	-
1962-67	3782680	327	forged	small	two	-
1955-67	3815822	265, 283	forged	small	two	-
1957-65	3835236	283	forged	small	two	-
1956-63	3836266	265, 283	forged	small	two	-
1963-67	3849847	283	cast	small	two	-
1964-67	3876764	283	cast	small	two	-
1964-67	3876768	283	cast	small	two	-
1967-76	3892690	350	cast	large	two	-
1968-73	3911001	307, 327	cast	large	two	-
1969-85	3932442	305, 350	cast	large	two	in 1979-82 267
1968-73	3941174	307, 327	cast	large	two	-
1968-69	3941178	302	forged	large	two	Z-28
1964-67	3949847	283	-	small	two	-
1970-80	3951529	400	cast	XL mns	two	-
1986-on	14088526	305, 350	cast	large	one	-
1986-on	14088532	350	forged	-	one	truck
1986-on	14088535	305, 350	cast	large	one	all
1969-85	39411182	350	forged	large	two	Z-28, Vette, truck

Chapter 9

Connecting Rods

Connecting rods are relatively difficult to nail down to their date and origin. There are two different forgings: the small-journal rod and the large-journal rod. The second has been machined in several different fashions, but it's still the same basic forging. It has also been made lighter over the years, but it's still the same in most respects. Some will argue that the 400ci engine got a special rod when in fact it's a large-journal rod that just got forged shorter. The only other exception is that some early 305ci engine rods were cast as opposed to forged. These were a problem and were soon discontinued.

The original rod design remained mostly unchanged until the small-journal/big-journal changeover in 1968. The bearing housing bore became smaller, the rod bolt stud size became 11/32in, and the rods had an oil pressure passage cut into the rod at the cap parting line. This squirt hole was used to lubricate the piston and its pin. It was thought unnecessary and was discontinued in 1965.

The large-journal rod has a 2.225in housing bore and uses a 3/8in rod bolt. All small-block Chevy connecting rods have a center-to-center length of 5.703in, with the exception of the 400ci engine which is 5.565in.

Over the years, the engineers felt that high-performance applications required rods with a little special attention paid to them. The manufacturing processes involved heat treating, magnafluxing, and shot peening. Some even got full-floating pins as opposed to interference fit pins. Some early maximum-effort Corvette 327ci small-journal rods got heat treated, magged, and peened. The Z-28 and LT1 rods got all that and a full-floating pin.

These processes led up to the famed LT1 pink rod. When this engine was being designed, the engineers felt they had to put the best rods in it. The forgings were first magnafluxed to eliminate any marginal parts. They were then heat treated to relieve any residual stresses left by the forging process. They were magnafluxed again and finally shot peened to return some surface tension to the material and, therefore, increase the strength and durability of the rod. When the rod had passed all the tests, it was colored with a pink die, hence the "pink rod" nickname. Many also received full-floating pins. These are most definitely the best connecting rods ever installed in a stock-production small-block engine.

Since the connecting rods lack any clear identification markings,

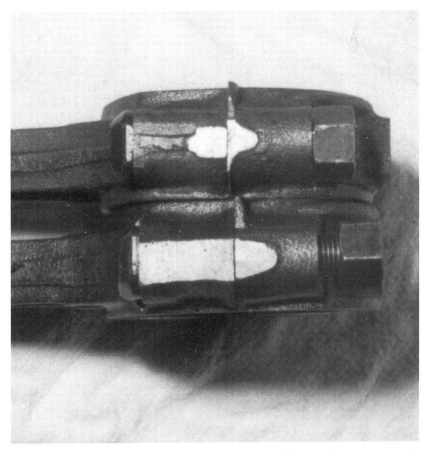

The way of identifying a standard-duty connecting rod from a heavy-duty one is by the forging pad on the side of the rod. The rod with the larger pad has more metal in the crucial area under the head of the bolt. This type of rod appeared in the mid-1970s.

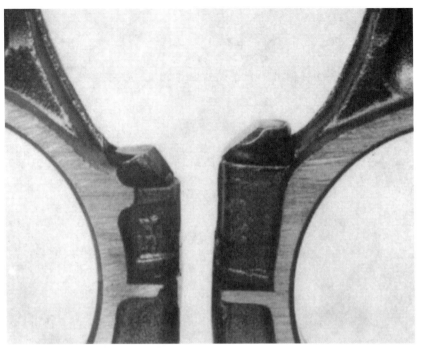

The difference between the 400ci rod on the left and the 5.7in rod on the right is clearly illustrated.

I will describe the differences between the standard-duty pieces and the heavy-duty ones. The beam is usually one of the weakest points of the rod. If you were to measure the width of the beam, looking at it from the bolt side, the two sizes found are .500in and .575in. This will determine the type of rod you have. Obviously the second one, the heavy-duty type, is the best choice.

There is one letter per rod that seems to have some significance in some cases. Just inside the rod nut on the bearing cap, there is a letter forged into the piece. From my experience, "O" rods were the ones used for the LT-1 engines. "K" rods go with the K series blocks, and "X" rods were used throughout the 1970s as the heavy-duty truck and high-performance rod. Later, many other letters were used with no correlation to the actual type of rod. The 305ci rods got a dimple near the parting line.

Chapter 10

Intake Manifolds

Since its inception, the small-block engine has used many different types of intake systems. Until 1986, the entry-level applications have had two-barrel carburetors, mid-level vehicles had four-barrel carbs, and special engines have been equipped with one four-barrel carb, two four-barrel carbs, and mechanical fuel injection.

The carburetors used have been made by several different companies. These are Carter, Holley, and Rochester, a GM division. The mechanical fuel-injection system of the late 1950s and early 1960s was a Rochester design.

A noteworthy feature of the intake manifolds is that they are completely interchangeable from 1955 to 1985. The bolt pattern changed somewhat after 1985.

One can identify these components by the casting number. If I have not included the number that you are looking for in the following list, the manifolds usually carry a date code that can be very helpful. There are some distinct features that help in determining the origin of these pieces. The oil filler tube located at the front next to the thermostat housing is a feature that was discontinued after 1968. In 1969, the two-barrel throttle bores were enlarged to accommodate the greater power requirements. In 1973, the EGR passage was cast into the side of the intake. By 1974, the choke heating system was changed from the manifold-residing, spring-in-box, divorced-style choke to a hot air pipe powered by vacuum. The four-barrel intakes have seen more changes over the years. These include a small bolt pattern square bore spread bore and large bolt pattern Holley type bolt pattern. The changes that were made to the 1968–1975 two-barrel manifolds were also made to the four-barrel manifolds.

In 1967, GM designed and installed on the Z-28 and Corvette a new aluminum intake manifold. This was around for production cars until 1971. This manifold featured a high-rise plenum and a Holley square-bore flange. This manifold is still available, in a slightly modified manner, from GM. It has been altered to accept the HEI ignition, so keep in mind that some early manifolds will not clear the larger ignition housing. These manifolds were produced at the Winters foundry in Ohio and carry the snowflake insignia on them.

Special-equipment intake systems have been used over the years. From 1956 (on the 265ci engine) to 1961 (on the 283ci engine), GM used a dual four-barrel intake on its high-end equipment. These are aluminum low-rise models that fit under the hood. The Carter WCFB carbs completed the set. Another interesting intake system is the mechanical fuel injection. In two different appearance packages, it was offered from 1957 through 1965. The two distinct styles can be differentiated by their looks. The early version, from 1957 through 1961, is the plain top. The version from 1962 through 1965 has a removable finned cover and is somewhat wider at the top. These fuel injection systems were never very popular because of their cost and the added inconvenience of service difficulties. In 1965, the FI system cost $300 more than the Holley four-barrel system and made 10hp less. After the era of fuel injection, the only special intake manifold offered was the high-rise aluminum single Holley four-barrel configuration for the 302ci, 327ci, and 350ci engines. The Z-28 302ci engine got a cross-ram twin four-barrel intake system as an option for 1967, 1968, and 1969. It used two 600cfm Holley carbs.

As the fuel shortage crisis arrived in the early 1970s, the variety of intake manifolds got drastically smaller. By 1973, Rochester carburetors were the only passenger car carburetors available. This meant cast-iron two-barrel or iron-spread-bore four-barrel intakes only. All remained the same until 1982 when electronic fuel injection appeared. There is one exception to the Quadrajet spread-bore intake. Corvettes got an aluminum

Here is a common Quadrajet intake manifold found on 350ci engines built from 1975 on. It was machined to accept an EGR valve and the tube to heat the crossover-type choke. This particular manifold, being aluminum, is from an L-82 engine. The same lightweight unit found its way onto high-output 305ci engines built between 1983 and 1985.

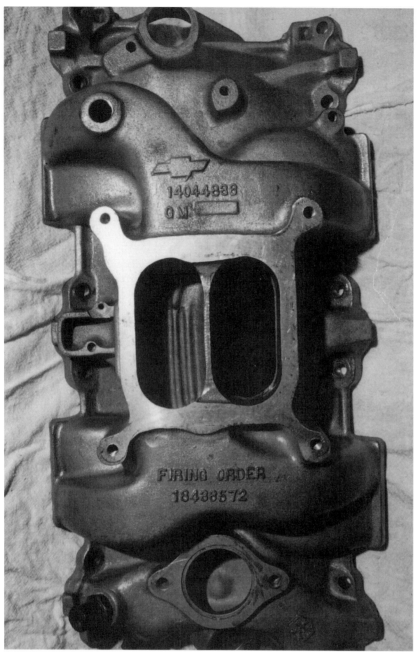

This is a reproduction LT1 intake manifold available from GM.

version of the same design in the late 1970s. The early attempts at throttle body fuel injection involved a strangely similar type of manifold used on the Z-28 cross ram of the 1960s. These twin throttle body systems were met with lukewarm success, as they did not deliver the extra punch for the extra money. The throttle body electronic fuel injection became the standard intake system almost all across the board in 1986. It used a unique two-barrel type intake manifold. The Z-28, Corvette, and Trans Am got the tuned port injection in 1984. This system offered excellent throttle response and generous horsepower. The system is very distinctive by its individual curved runners and its central air intake. This intake system remained mostly unchanged until 1993 when a new F body required yet a lower intake line to accommodate the lower hood line of the latest Camaro and Firebird. The Corvette also got a redesigned intake plenum. The shortcomings of the tuned port injection were eliminated in these last designs.

Intake Manifold Data

years	cast #	cid	bbls	material	carb	body application
1974-76	340261	350	4	iron	Q-jet	A B F X
1973-81	340266	305, 350	2	iron	-	A B F G
1982-85	340281	305, 350	4	iron	Q-jet	B F
1976-82	346249	305, 350	4	iron	Q-jet	all
1976-82	346250	305, 350	4	iron	Q-jet	all
1973-77	346260	305, 350	2	iron	-	A B F
1978-80	373598	305	2	al	-	G
1976-82	458520	305, 350	4	al	Q-jet	all
1980-82	1403372	305, 350	TTBI	al	cross-fire	F Y
1955	3704790	265	2	iron	-	B
1955	3711348	265	4	iron	-	B Y
1956	3728725	265	8	al	WCFB	Y
1986-57	3731394	283	8	al	WCFB	Y
1957	3731398	283	4	iron	WCFB, 4jet	B Y
1957	3732880	265, 283	2	iron	-	B
1956	3735444	265	2	iron	-	B
1956	3735448	265	4	iron	-	Y
1956	3737109	265	4	iron	-	B
1957	3739653	283	8	al	-	Y
1957	3741193	283	FI	al	-	B
1957	3746826	265, 283	2	iron	-	B
1958-61	3746829	283	4	iron	WCFB, 4jet	B Y
1962-63	3783244	327	4	iron	WCFB, 4jet	B Y
1963	3794129	327	4	al	-	Y
1962	3795397	327	4	iron	-	Y
1972	3797771	350	4	iron	-	A B F
1962-64	3799349	327	4	iron	AFB	B Y
1963-65	3826810	327	FI	-	-	Y
1956-57	3837109	265, 283	4	iron	WCFB, 4jet	B Y
1964-65	3840905	283	2	iron	-	A B X C K
1964-65	3844457	327	4	iron	-	A B X Y
1963-65	3844459	327	4	iron	-	A B X Y
1964-65	3844461	327	4	al	-	Y
1962-65	3866922	283, 327	4	iron	-	A B X
1966-67	3872783	327	4	iron	-	A B X
1965	3877652	283, 327	2	iron	-	truck, A B C K
1966-67	3890490	327	4	al	-	X Y
1966-68	3905393	327	4	iron	Q-jet	A B F X
1967-68	3910601	327	2	-	-	A F X
1969-70	3916313	307, 350	2	-	-	all
1967-68	3917610	302	4	al	-	Z-28, F
1968	3919801	307, 327	2	iron	-	A B C K
1967-68	3919803	327, 350	4	iron	-	A B F X Y
1969	3927183	307, 327	2	iron	-	A B F X
1969	3927184	350	4	iron	-	A B F X Y
1969	3932472	302	4	al	-	Z-28, F
1967-68	3941126	302	8	al	X ram (bot)	-
1968-69	3941130	302	8	al	X ram (top)	-
1969-70	3958622	307, 327	2	iron	-	-
1969-70	3958626	350	2	iron	-	-
1971-72	3959594	350	4	al	LT1	Y F
1970	3965577	350	4	iron	-	B F X
1970	3972110	350	4	al	LT1	F Y

years	cast #	cid	bbls	material	carb	body application
1970	3972114	350	4	al	-	Z-28, F
1971	3972361	350	4	al	-	Z-28, F
1969-71	3973465	307, 327	2	-	-	A B F X
1971	3973469	350	4	iron	-	B F Y
1969-70	3987361	350	-	iron	-	-
1971	3990948	350	-	iron	-	-
1973	3991004	350	-	iron	-	-
1971	3991005	307	-	iron	-	-
1973	3997770	350	-	iron	-	-
1973	3997771	350	4	iron	-	A B F X
1973	3997772	350	-	iron	-	-
1972	6262928	307	-	iron	-	-
1972	6262930	350	-	iron	-	-
1971-72	6262932	350	-	iron	-	-
1972	6263751	350	4	iron	-	Y
1973	6271060	350	-	iron	-	-
1957	7014360	283	FI	al	-	-
1957	7014520	283	FI	al	-	-
1957-58	7014800	283	FI	al	-	-
1958-59	7014900	283	FI	al	-	-
1958	7014960	283	FI	al	-	-
1959-61	7017200	283	FI	al	-	-
1959-60	7017250	283	FI	al	-	-
1959-60	7017300	283	FI	al	-	-
1960-61	7017310	283	FI	al	-	-
1960	7017320	283	FI	al	-	-
1962	7017355	327	FI	al	-	-
1962	7017360	327	FI	al	-	-
1962-63	7017375	327	FI	al	-	-
1964-65	7017380	327	FI	al	-	-
1979-80	14007374	305	2	al	-	-
1981	14014432	350	4	al	-	-
1978-85	14057053	305, 350	4	al	-	-

Chapter 11

Carburetors

As original equipment, several different brands of carburetors have been used on the small-block Chevy. The brands are Holley, Carter, and Rochester.

The Carter WCFB model was used in single and twin four-barrel configuration until 1964.

Holley carburetors were used in the maximum effort engines starting in 1964 and were used until 1971 in car bodies. Large trucks, C-40 and bigger, have used the Holley carbs through the 1970s and into the 1980s.

The Rochester carbs have been, by far, the most common type used. Starting in 1956, they have been used until 1986, and even further in the case of trucks.

The Z-28 302ci engine was offered with a cross-ram dual four-barrel-carburetor setup but only as an option.

Chapter 12

Exhaust Manifolds

The ram's horns-type exhaust manifold has been used on several different body styles, but only the Corvette used the ones with a 3in outlet.

Although the exhaust manifolds are more indicative of the chassis installation than anything, they can help in dating the core you are looking at.

The earliest manifolds ran on top of the spark plugs and dumped down in between the first and second spark plugs on the driver side and directly on top of the starter on the passenger side. These manifolds are only good for a restoration project requiring absolute originality. They are rather poor flowing and somewhat rare today.

Soon after, the "ram's horns" came to be. They are called this because they look like the horns on a ram. The ram's horns manifold has been cast in several different sizes with or without accessory mounting bosses. With the exception of the Corvette, these went out of production by the 1970s. The outlet size varies from 2in on trucks and low-performance cars to 2-1/2in and 3in on some Corvette applications. Many driver-side manifolds were cast with a bend to clear steering linkages of passenger cars. The Chevy II got a bent manifold on the passenger side as well.

By the late 1960s, a new type of exhaust manifold was designed. This one ran under the spark plugs. I call this type the log manifold. It became the most common type available on trucks, A, B, and X bodies, and some mid-1970s Corvettes. These have been cast in two different configurations, with or without the reinforcing bars in between the exhaust ports. Be aware that when overheated, the manifolds without the bars will warp and tend to curl themselves together, not allowing the outside bolt holes to line up anymore. GM was certainly aware of this problem. You will notice that these manifolds have larger bolt holes in the end ports compared to the center port's bolt holes.

In the mid-1970s, the designers had to come up with a compact design to fit into the Monza. They created a manifold that resembled the early over-the-sparkplug design. The outlet was relocated to the rear between the second last and last spark plug on the driver side and exits at the rear on the passenger side. This required modification of the cylinder head (an extra bolt hole was added). These manifolds have been used on most of the 305ci engines, until the mid-1980s, in G and B bodies and, until 1993, in the F bodies. These manifolds were also used in some 350ci applications, but the engineers realized the poor flow characteristics of these and returned to the log-type manifolds wherever possible. The F bodies got an enlarged version of these in the mid-1980s to try and help performance.

The last exhaust manifold is used on the trucks made from 1988 on. This is a redesigned version of the log which has the outlet pointing at 45deg rearward on both sides. The earlier version of this one had the driver side outlet pointing down from in between number five and number seven spark plugs. The new manifolds angle away from the cylinder head as they go back, as opposed to being parallel to the engine.

The 1993 Z-28 and Trans Am exhaust manifolds are an absolute work of art. They are still cast iron but model a short header design. The redesign of these manifolds has freed up some untapped horsepower.

Exhaust Manifold Data

first year	last year	cast #	cid	side	application
1973	76	336709	350	R	F
1973	75	336710	307, 350, 400	L	A B F G
1973	80	346222	307, 350, 400	R	A B F G
1975	77	346247	350	L	A B F G
1975	77	346248	350	R	A B F G
1976	80	364753	305, 350, 400	L	all
1970	82	372243	350	R	Y
1978	82	462697	267, 305	L	G
1978	82	462698	267, 305	R	G
1955	-	3704791	265	L	B Y
1955	-	3704792	265	R	B Y
1956	-	3725563	265	both	B Y
1956	-	3731557	265	L	B Y
1956	-	3731558	265	R	B Y
1957	-	3733975	283	L	B Y
1957	-	3733976	283	R	B Y
1965	-	3746563	327	L	Y
1962	68	3747038	283, 327	R	B Y
1958	67	3747042	283	R	B Y
1964	-	3747938	327	L	-
1964	-	3747942	327	L	-
1958	63	3749965	283, 327	L	B Y
1958	65	3750556	283, 327	R	B Y
1964	67	3790729	283, 327	L	Chevy II
1965	-	3790730	283, 327	R	Chevy II
1965	-	3791162	283, 327	R	Chevy II
1966	67	3791182	283, 327	R	B
1962	63	3797901	327	L	Vette
1962	65	3797902	327	R	Vette
1963	-	3797942	327	both	Vette
1967	68	3834947	283, 327	L	B
1955	-	3836968	265	R	B
1955	-	3837069	265	-	Y
1964	-	3840715	283, 327	L	A
1964	68	3840912	all	R	A F X
1964	71	3846559	327, 350	L	Vette
1964	65	3846563	327	L	Vette
1964	67	3849288	283, 327	R	Chevy II
1964	67	3849290	283, 327	R	Chevy II
1964	68	3855163	283, 327	L	B C K
1966	67	3872723	283, 327	L	Chevy II
1966	-	3872729	283, 327	L	A
1967	68	3872730	all	R	A F
1966	67	3872738	283, 327	R	Chevy II
1966	68	3872741	283, 327	L	B
1967	71	3872765	327, 350	L	Vette
1966	68	3872778	283, 307, 327	R	B C K Y
1964	67	3890424	283, 327	R	Chevy II
1967	-	3892679	all	L	A F X
1967	68	3892683	all	L	A F
1966	68	3893604	283, 327	R	B
1967	-	3893608	all	R	A F
1967	68	3896956	283, 307, 327	R	C K

first year	last year	cast #	cid	side	application
1967	68	3905364	307, 350, 400	R	C K
1969	70	3932376	307, 350	R	A F
1970	72	3932461	350	both	Vette
1969	70	3932465	327, 350	R	B
1969	70	3932469	350, 400	L	B
1969	70	3932473	307, 350	L	B
1969	-	3932481	350	R	Y
1967	-	3940972	350	R	F
1969	71	3942527	302, 307, 350	L	A F X
1969	70	3942529	307, 350	L	A F X
1969	-	3946826	302, 307, 350	R	A F X
1969	-	3946826	302	R	-
1972	73	3959562	307, 350	R	A F
1971	72	3973432	307, 350	R	A B F X
1972	74	3986330	307, 350	R	F
1970	72	3989036	350, 400	R	B Y
1969	73	3989041	302, 307, 350	L	A F X
1970	73	3989043	307, 350	L	A B F X

Chapter 13

Balancers

The vibration damper, which is commonly referred to as the balancer, has been changed several times. The engine's displacement and intended service determine the size of the component. The specific material of the crankshaft also has a bearing on the balancer's configuration.

The physical properties of forged steel and nodular cast iron are important if we are to understand why certain balancers have been used. Without getting too far into it, let me say that the fundamental differences between the two materials will have the cast crank absorbing some of the vibrations and the steel crank transferring a greater amount. Putting the crank failure possibilities aside, when using a steel crank, other components surrounding it may be affected by all the transferred vibrations, at least more so than with a cast crank. Enough said, this is another book all on its own.

In the early days, there were no damping devices attached to the hubs of the 265ci and early 283ci engines, both of which used a steel crank. Some valvetrain failures, along with other problems, have been attributed to this lack of crankshaft damping on the early engines. In 1963, GM, recognizing this, started using a balancer made of two distinct metal parts: the center hub and the outer ring, which were separated by a rubber layer. The larger stroke of the 327ci mandated it, and the technique was applied to the 283ci as well. With the ever-increasing rpm and power expectations, the balancers got larger, up to 8in in diameter. With the exception of the 305ci balancer, and the zero degrees timing mark location, no changes have been made since the early 1970s.

As far as interchangeability is concerned, all balancers will physically press onto any crank. Before you get lulled into a false sense of security, even though they will all clear the water pump and line up with your original pulleys, they are not created equal. First of all, the 400ci balancer must only go on a 400ci crank. It is not balanced to itself, as all others, but out of balance for the externally balanced 400ci. The next problem you will run into is the different timing locations between pre-smog and smog-era balancers.

The 265ci and early 283ci engines contain just a hub. It is a hub because it is not made of two different parts. It is only a hub to bolt the pulley onto.

I group the balancers into two basic hub sizes: The smaller diameter is 4-3/8in, and the second is 6-1/4in. A list of all factory-delivered balancers appears at the top of page 80.

The most common ones today have to be the 305ci and the small 350ci types.

Of course, with all these different sizes of balancers, there are matching timing covers to go with them. Many have the timing mark spot-welded directly onto it. Some have a separate timing marker that bolts on with two of the timing cover bolts. The

The 400ci balancer is the one to the far left. It is distinguished by its notching. The second one from the left is the special high-performance piece. Next is the last 8in balancer; it was used on trucks. The fourth balancer is the 7in model that was used on passenger cars with 305ci and 350ci engines. The fifth balancer, the smallest of the group, was used on 283ci and 307ci engines. The last balancer was used on 267ci and 305ci engines.

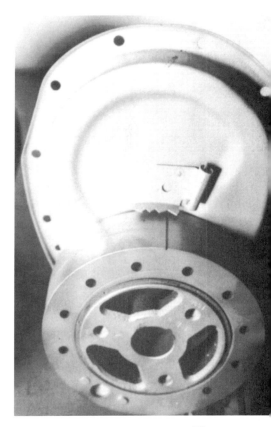

Right
Until the mid-1970s, 0deg top dead center was at about the two o'clock position. The increasing number of accessories required a relocation of top dead center closer to twelve o'clock.

Factory Delivered Balancers

Hub size	outside dia.	thickness	ci
4-3/8in	hub only		265, 283
4-3/8in	6-1/8in	3/4in	262, 307
4-3/8in	6-3/4in	1-3/16in	305, 327, 350
4-3/8in	6-3/4in hollow	1-11/16in	267, 305
6-1/4in	8in	1-1/2in	350 heavy-duty
6-1/4in	8in w/cut-out	1-1/2in	400 only
6-1/4in	8in	1-3/4in	302, 327, 350 high performance

The damper on the left is for internally balanced engines, like the 350ci. The one on the right is for the externally balanced 400ci. The cutout on the inside of the outer ring is a dead giveaway.

latter is my preferred way of timing an engine, and there is a simple way of telling them apart. The markers for the small 6-3/4in ones only go to 12deg BTDC; the 8in timing markers go to 16deg BTDC.

Earlier I mentioned that there are different timing mark locations on the various balancers. In the early 1970s, electronic engine diagnostic equipment became standard in dealerships and quite popular in many repair shops. These pieces of equipment required a locating bracket for the timing light pick-up. At first, these were installed on covers with the zero timing mark at the two o'clock position (when facing the engine). This was later altered to the twelve o'clock position. The two reasons for the change involve better accessibility and better visibility in all chassis. To reflect this change, the balancer itself was marked for top dead center in a different spot, so be careful not to interchange these, as the timing mark will be out by about 30deg.

This early style 8in timing cover has timing graduations up to 16deg. The 7in setup looks similar but has a timing marker that only goes up to 12deg.

Chapter 14

Flywheels and Starters

I will include both flywheels (manual transmission) and flexplates (automatic transmissions) in this chapter. I will also include the starters, as they are matched to the flywheel size.

As far as interchangeability is concerned, there are only two different bolt patterns for all. The second bolt pattern began in 1986 on engines with one-piece rear main seals. In order to fit the new type seal, GM had to reduce the bolt pattern diameter on the rear of the crankshaft. The only other swapping problem you may encounter is when you are working on a 400ci engine. You may remember that this one is externally balanced, and the flywheel, although it will bolt on, will be out of balance for any other engine.

There are two basic sizes of flywheel as delivered by the factory: The first is 12-3/4in and has 153 teeth; the larger second is 14in and has 198 teeth. These sizes apply to the flexplates as well. The starters used are specific to the size of the flywheel, so be careful if exchanging components. The starters are mostly identical except for the nose. They may also have different size driving motors. For the flywheel, the large one may be drilled to accept both the 10-1/2in and 11in clutches. The large flexplate may also be drilled to accept both the large and small bolt pattern torque converters. The small fly-wheels and flexplates can only accept small components.

I suspect that you are familiar with the bolt location and alignment of the Chevy starters; they go straight up. It wasn't always this way. Many trucks with cast-iron bell housings have a completely different bolt pattern. These bolts go in horizontally very much like the Fords. These are not too popular anymore, and I will explain the differences you may encounter with the first type. There are two different bolt patterns for these starters. The small light-duty gets a straight-across bolt pattern, and the heavy-duty gets a staggered, or angled, bolt pattern.

Chapter 15

Oil Pans

There have been enough different types of oil pans used on the small-block to warrant some discussion.

As far as interchangeability, pans made before 1978 have a driver side dipstick; pans made between 1978 and 1985 have a passenger side dipstick. In 1985, the rear main seal was upgraded to a one-piece unit. The seal housing requires a larger semicircle at the rear of the pan. The two adjacent bolt holes have been moved farther apart. The new pan also comes with a one-piece neoprene gasket from the factory. The aftermarket, however, has designed a three-piece rubber-and-cork gasket set to replace these. I suspect that price is at the root of this aftermarket design.

In the pre-1985 design, there are two different sizes of front semicircle type. The change occurred around 1969. For that reason, when you purchase a full gasket set, it usually comes with both the thick- and thin-style end piece.

As far as any other differences, the Corvette has often been equipped with a special high-capacity oil pan. It can be identified by its longer sump and the drain hole located in the center of the sump to the back. The reason for this is that the engine sits farther back in a Corvette and allows for a longer sump.

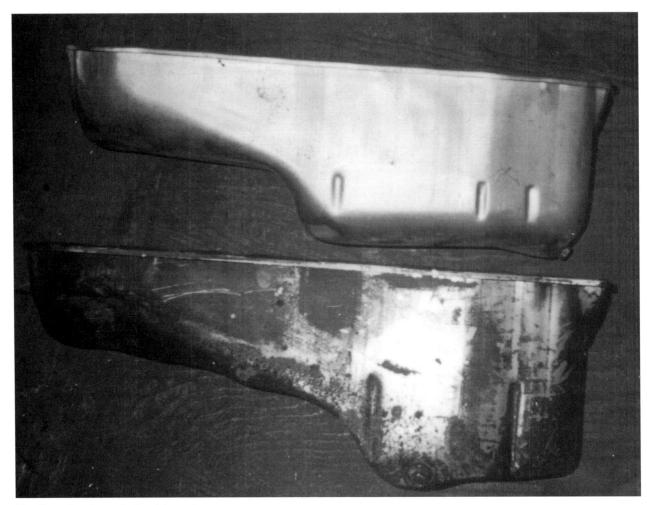

The Corvette oil pan (bottom) has a longer sump.

The standard car oil pan was designed to clear a crossover exhaust pipe routed just ahead of the sump. This required the sump to be shorter. Trucks also get larger-capacity oil pans, because they are subjected to more severe service and have more room in the chassis.

The Z-28 in the late 1960s and early 1970s also used a slightly larger-capacity oil pan. Unfortunately, it does not have any distinct features other than having a larger sump.

Each different pan uses a specific oil pump pickup. If you are switching pans around, make sure that the proper pickup is used.

I have seen engines ruined because a deep sump pan was used with a stock, short pickup. This will surely starve the pump and burn out the bearings.

Several high-performance applications got a windage tray.

Right
In 1993, the LT1 required a new timing cover (right) that would provide access for a distributor drive. A new die-cast aluminum cover with water pump and distributor drive seals was the first real change in this area since the inception of this engine.

The Corvette got a full-length tray fastened by studs at the main bearing caps. The Camaros, Novas, and Chevelles got a shorter version of the same. This is because the pan's deep sump of the Corvette's will clear the extra studs at the front.

Right
From 1955 to the early 1970s, a small cover/oil pan seal was used. The thicker style seal (bottom) was used between 1970 and 1985. The thicker seal made it easier to remove and replace the front cover without disturbing the oil pan gasket.

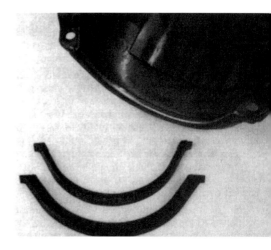

GEN I   GEN II

Chapter 16

Rocker Covers

The hydraulic roller lifter has been around for ten years. Now, the LT4 receives cast aluminum roller rockers, specially designed for GM and embossed with a Bow Tie. This complete roller valvetrain with egg-shaped springs permits a more aggressive camshaft.

The rocker covers can be indicative of the vintage and application of the small-block. The Corvette has always been blessed with the prettiest models available and in many cases it got special pieces to top the engine.

The first rocker covers do not have any vent holes in them and have Chevrolet stamped on top. By 1962, when GM started putting stickers on the rocker cover to advertise the size and rating of the engine, a pad was included in the stamping. Still, these covers did not have any vent or filler holes. Only in 1968, when the road draft and manifold front filler tube was done away with, did the covers get a filler hole and provision for PCV. Until 1978, the covers didn't change. In 1978, a minor cosmetic design change involved the deletion of the two ribs running longitudinally. This gives the cover a smoother look. In 1985, the cylinder head change, designed to eliminate leaks, required a completely different cover. This one has the fastener holes in the center of the cover, as opposed to being on the periphery. The new covers also have a ribbed look.

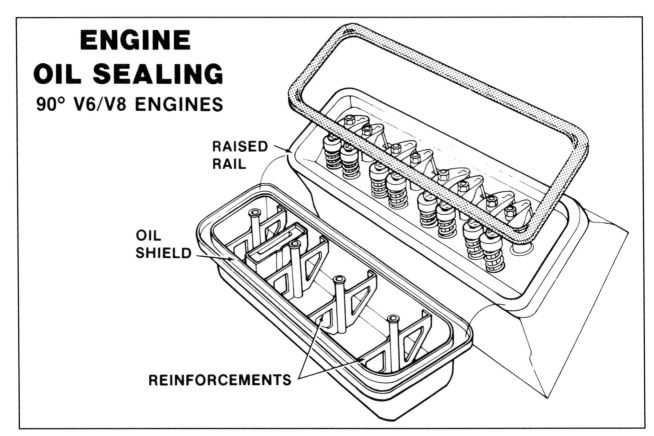

ENGINE
OIL SEALING
90° V6/V8 ENGINES

RAISED RAIL

OIL SHIELD

REINFORCEMENTS

The rocker covers were redesigned in 1986. They bolt down through the center of the cover and have sleeves that prevent overtightening. The machined rail, along with a superior seat for the gasket, have eliminated oil leaks.

As noted earlier, the Corvette almost always got special covers. From the beginning, the base engines got stamped steel covers with Corvette written on them. The optional engines got finned aluminum covers with Corvette cast in them. In 1968, the style of the finned cover changed as the Corvette word was dropped in favor of the crossed checkered flags insignia. This design remained unchanged until 1986, when the Corvette received another special aluminum cover. Gone are the fins, but the flags remain.

The 1970–74 Z-28s also got the finned aluminum covers with the flags.

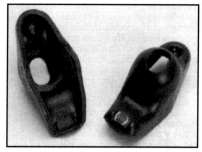

In 1988, a new type of rocker with a valve tip guide rail eliminated the need for pushrod guide plates.

In 1985, GM started using hydraulic roller lifters in the Corvette and F body cars. This lifter is longer than the flat tappet lifter and requires shorter pushrods to work properly.

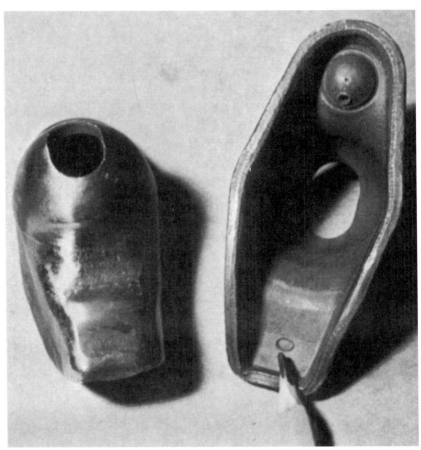

The 1970 LT1 received rocker arms that had the valve contact face hardened. These are identified by an "O" on the reverse side.

The early-style LT1/L-82 rocker covers had a natural aluminum color. The covers made after 1978 were painted black.

Chapter 17

Studebaker

You may wonder why this chapter exists at all. Well, in 1965, when Studebaker was on its decline, the company had to find another powerplant to replace the Ford 289ci engine that had been used until then.

When the South Bend plant shut down in December of 1963, all the production was moved to Hamilton, Ontario. The 283ci engine was used in the Studebaker Daytona models. Rated at 195hp, the engine was only available in this base configuration. This was a step backwards for this company, since they had had several performance engine packages in the past. It seems that performance wasn't a major concern, since survival was foremost on the company's mind. The 283ci got the name of Thunderbolt. About 25,000 of these were produced in 1965 and 1966.

In 1965, the Avanti started using small-blocks. This model, still in production today, has used many different versions of the small-block. The lineup of these is as follows:

1965-70:	327ci, 300hp
1969-70:	350ci, 300hp
1971-72:	350ci, 270hp
1973:	400ci, 245hp
1974-75:	400ci, 180hp
1976:	350ci, 210hp
1977-79:	350ci, 180hp
1980-81:	350ci, 190hp
1982-83:	350ci, 200hp
1984:	305ci, 180hp
1985-87:	305ci, 205hp
1988-90:	305ci, 220hp

The production of the Avanti has been limited to approximately 200 units per year.

Chapter 18

Marine Engines

Many small-block engines have been installed by numerous pleasure craft manufacturers. These have been used in both freshwater and saltwater applications.

Chris-Craft has used small-block engines as early as the original 283ci engine and has also used the 327ci and 350ci.

Mercury Marine has also used the small-block extensively and today offers the 305ci and the 350ci in its lineup.

From what I have seen, the engines can be of significantly different configuration. The lower horsepower-rated models usually are stock two-bolt, cast-crank, small-valve motors. The optional high-output models have the steel crank, heavy-duty rods, four-bolt main bearings, and better heads. These are certainly worth investigating as a core if ever they become available to you. Be aware, however, that by the nature of their cooling system, some freshwater engines may have the cooling passages of the block and heads either plugged or severely corroded. The saltwater closed systems usually use antifreeze and are not prone to this as much. Problems occur if antifreeze or a corrosion preventing product was not used in the cooling system. Unfortunately, some mechanics in the southern states do not know the meaning of this product and never use it, in which case, problems in the cooling passages may exist.

As far as identifying these engines, they did not get special parts cast for them. In other words, whatever castings were available to GM at the time are what got put in the boats. I have noticed that the Mercury Marine engines that I have worked on had a stamping number suffix that starts with an M. This certainly can be a good indication. Another indicative clue is the brass tag that the marine manufacturer rivets to the side of the block. For warranty purposes, these tags often get removed when the engine is replaced so that the tag can be put onto the replacement unit. This will, on the original engine, leave the two holes along with a stain where the tag used to be. Another clue to an engine's marine origin is the frost plugs. Marine engines only come with brass plugs, as opposed to steel ones on automotive applications. This is by no means a sure thing; many engine rebuilders like to use brass plugs on all their engines.

To my knowledge the 400ci engine has never been installed as original equipment in a marine application.

Chapter 19

Stamping Prefix Codes and Suffix Codes

The prefix, when referring to the engine stamping codes, generally refers to the production facility.

F: Flint, Michigan
K: St. Catherines, Ontario, Canada
M: Mexico
T: Tonawanda, New York

After the casting number, the suffix stamping codes are proba-bly the best identifying marks left on the engine. The word suffix, by definition, means to be affixed to the end of something. In this case, the stamped number on the deck of the block at the front on the passenger side.

As you may notice, several codes have been used on different occasions. For example, "CHA" can be a 307ci in 1971 and a 350ci in 1978. To accurately de-termine the proper identification via the stamping code, having the block casting number may be necesssary. The casting number will identify the block type and general years of use. The suffix then pinpoints the original facto-ry installation. In some cases, the stamping code has only been used once, and it can instantly determine the engine type with-out looking any further.

Suffix Stamping Codes

first year	last year	stamp RPO	cid	application	VIN	h/p	bbls	body styles
1978	-	3N	305	U LG3	-	145	2	Firebird/school bus
1978	-	3T	350	L LM1	-	170	4	Firebird/school bus
1978	-	3X	305	U LG3	-	145	2	Phoenix/school bus
1980	-	9A	305	H LG4	-	155	5	full size/school bus
1976	79	AAA	350	m/t	LF5	160	2	C-50 & 60/school bus
1976	79	AAB	350	m/t	LF5	160	2	C-60
1976	79	AAC	350	a/t	LF5	160	2	C-60
1975	79	AAD	350	m/t	LF5	160	2	C-50 & 60
1976	79	AAF	350	a/t	LF5	160	2	C-60
1975	79	AAH	350	m/t	LF5	160	2	C-60
1976	79	AAJ	350	a/t	LF5	160	2	C-60/school bus
1976	-	AAK	350	LF5	-	160	2	C-60/school bus
1976	-	AAL	350	LF5	-	160	2	C-60/school bus
1976	77	AAM	350	LF5	-	160	2	C-50/school bus
1978	-	ABA	350	LF5	-	160	2	C-50/school bus
-	-	-	-	-	-	-	-	Omega/Monte/
-	-	-	-	-	-	-	-	Malibu
1978	-	ABB	350	LF5	-	160	2	C-50/school bus
1978	-	ABC	350	LF5	-	160	2	C-60/school bus
1978	-	ABD	350	LF5	-	160	2	C-60/school bus
1978	-	ABF	350	LF5	-	160	2	C-60
1978	-	ABH	350	LF5	-	160	2	C-60/Impala
1978	-	ABJ	350	LF5	-	160	2	C-60
1978	-	ABK	350	LF5	-	160	2	C-60
1978	-	ABL	350	LF5	-	160	2	C-60
1978	-	ABM	350	LF5	-	160	2	C-60/school bus
1973	-	ACA	350		-	155	2	C-50/school bus
1973	-	ADA	350		-	155	2	C-50/school bus
1973	-	ADR	350	LPG fuel	-	155	2	C-60/school bus
-	-	-	-	-	-	-	-	Impala
1973	-	AJA	350		-	155	2	C-50/Impala

first year	last year	stamp RPO	cid	application	VIN	h/p	bbls	body styles
1973	-	AJD	350		-	155	2	C-50/school bus
-	-	-	-	-	-	-	-	Monte
1973	-	AJF	350	-	-	155	2	C-60/Omega
1973	-	AJH	350	-	-	155	2	C-50 & 60/school bus
-	-	-	-	-	-	-	-	Impala
1973	-	AJJ	350	-	-	155	2	C-60/Impala
1973	-	AJK	350	-	-	155	2	C-60/Monte
1973	-	AJM	350	-	-	155	2	C-60/Omega
1973	-	AJN	350	-	-	155	2	C-60/Monte
1973	-	AJR	350	-	-	155	2	C-60/Omega
1973	-	AJS	350	-	-	155	2	C-60/Monte
1973	-	AJT	350	-	-	155	2	C-30 & 35
1989	-	AKH	305	L03	E	170	TBI	Firebird
-	-	-	-	-	-	-	-	Monte
1989	-	AKJ	305	L03	E	170	TBI	Firebird
1989	-	ATA	305	LB9	F	190	TPI	Firebird
1989	-	ATB	305	LB9	F	190	TPI	Firebird
1989	-	ATF	305	LB9	F	190	TPI	Firebird
1989	-	ATM	305	LB9	F	190	TPI	Firebird
-	-	-	-	-	-	-	-	Omega
1989	-	AWA	350	L98, a/t	8	225	TPI	Firebird
1989	-	AWK	350	L98, a/t	8	225	TPI	Firebird/Omega
1981	-	BD	305	LG4	H	150	4	Firebird
1981	-	BJ	305	LG4	H	150	4	Firebird/Omega
1990	-	BLC	305	L03	E	170	TBI	Firebird
1990	-	BLD	305	L03	E	170	TBI	Firebird/trucks
-	-	-	-	-	-	-	-	Omega
1990	-	BLF	305	LB9	F	190	TPI	Firebird/trucks
1990	-	BLH	305	LB9	F	190	TPI	Firebird
1990	-	BLJ	305	LB9	F	190	TPI	Firebird
1990	-	BMK	350	L98, a/t	8	235	TPI	Firebird
1957	-	C	265	m/t, 3 spd	-	-	-	cars/Vette/Omega
1958	60	C	283	m/t, 3 spd	-	185	2	cars
1960	64	C	283	m/t	-	170	2	cars/Omega
1977	-	C2K	305	LG3	U	145	2	F X
1977	-	C2L	305	LG3	U	145	2	F X/Omega
1977	-	C2M	305	LG3	U	145	2	F X
1982	-	C2R	305	Roch E4ME carb.	H LG4	155	4	B F G/Monte
1982	-	C2S	305	Roch E4ME carb.	H LG4	155	4	B F G
1982	-	C2T	305	Roch E4ME carb.	H LG4	155	4	B F G
1982	-	C2U	305	Roch E4ME carb.	H LG4	155	4	B F G/Impala
1982	-	C2W	305	Roch E4ME carb.	H LG4	155	4	B F G/Monte
1982	-	C2X	305	Roch E4ME carb.	H LG4	155	4	B F G/Omega
1978	-	C3N	305	LG3	U	145	2	Camaro/Monte
1978	-	C3P	305	LG3	U	145	2	G/Omega
1978	-	C3T	350	L	-	-	-	Camaro
1984	-	C4A	305	Roch E4ME carb.	H LG4	150	4	B F G/Impala
1984	-	C4B	305	Roch E4ME carb.	H LG4	150	4	B F G
1984	-	C4C	305	Roch E4ME carb.	H LG4	150	4	B F G/Omega
1984	-	C4D	305	Roch E4ME carb.	H LG4	150	4	B F G/Omega
1982	-	C4N	267	Roch E2ME carb.	J L39	-	2	A B/Monte
1985	-	C4P	305	Roch E4ME carb.	H LG4	150	4	B F/Monte
1982	-	C4R	267	Roch E2ME carb.	J L39	-	2	B G
1985	-	C4R	305	Roch E4ME carb.	H LG4	150	4	B
1982	-	C4S	267	Roch E2ME carb.	J L39	-	2	B

first year	last year	stamp RPO	cid	application	VIN	h/p	bbls	body styles
1982	-	C4T	267	Roch E2ME carb.	J L39	-	2	B G/Omega
1982	-	C4U	267	Roch E2ME carb.	J L39	-	2	B G
1982	-	C4W	267	Roch E2ME carb.	J L39	-	2	B G/Impala
1984	-	C4W	305	Roch E4ME carb.	H LG4	150	4	F B/Omega
1982	-	C5A	350	LM1	L	-	4	police/Impala
1982	-	C5B	350	LM1	L	-	4	police
1985	-	C5P	350	Tuned port inj.	6	-	-	Parisien/Monte
1985	-	C7A	305	Roch E4ME carb.	H LG4	150	4	B F G/Omega
1985	-	C7B	305	Roch E4ME carb.	H LG4	150	4	B F G
1986	-	C7D	305	Roch E4ME carb.	H LG4	150	4	F
1986	-	C7H	305	Roch E4ME carb.	H LG4	150	4	F
1987	-	C7L	305	Roch E4ME carb.	H LG4	150	4	F/police/taxi/Monte
1987	-	C7M	305	Roch E4ME carb.	H LG4	150	4	F/Kingswd
1979	-	C8B	305	LG3	G	130	2	F X/Impala
1979	-	C8C	350	LM1	L	-	4	F/Monte
1980	-	C8X	267	Roch E2ME carb.	J L39	-	2	F/Monte
1972	-	CAR	350	tur 350, Calif emis	-	165	2	A B
1985	-	CAR	305	Roch E4ME carb.	H LG4	150	4	F/Monte
1972	-	CAT	400	t/h trans, Calif	LF6	-	2	B
1972	-	CAZ	307	Powerglide NB2	-	130	2	A F X/Monte
1958	-	CB	283	m/t	-	185	2	truck/1271/Monte
1963	64	CB	283	m/t, police, h/p	-	-	-	cars/Monte/Impala
1971	-	CBG	350	Powerglide	-	-	-	full size/Impala
1971	-	CCA	307	manual trans.	-	200	2	A F X
1971	-	CCC	307	Powerglide	-	200	2	A F X/Monte
1957	-	CD	265	m/t, O.D.	-	-	2	car/truck
1958	62	CD	283	m/t, O.D.	-	185	2	truck/1271/Impala
1972	-	CDA	350	m/t, Calif	L65	165	2	A X
1981	-	CDA	350	m/t, fed., L81	6	-	-	Vette/Monte
1972	-	CDB	350	Powerglide, Calif	L65	-	2	A B/Monte
1982	-	CDB	267	Roch E2ME carb.	J L39	-	2	B G
1982	-	CDC	267	Roch E2ME carb.	J	-	2	B G/Monte
1972	-	CDD	350	t/h NB2	L48	200	-	Camaro/Impala
1972	-	CDD	350	tur hydro, Calif	-	175	4	Chevelle
1972	-	CDD	350	t/h NB2	-	165	2	Monte
1982	-	CDD	267	Roch E2ME carb.	J	-	2	B G/Omega
1985	-	CDD	305	Roch E4ME carb.	H LG4	150	4	B G F
1985	-	CDF	305	Roch E4ME carb.	H LG4	150	4	B F G/Omega
1972	-	CDG	350	m/t NB2	-	175	4	Chevelle/SS/Omega
1972	-	CDH	350	4 spd, NB2	K	200	4	Vette/Omega
1985	-	CDH	305	Roch E4ME carb.	H LG4	150	4	B F G/Bel Air
-	-	-	-	-	-	-	-	Kingswd/Omega
1972	-	CDJ	350	base, tur 400, NB2	K	200	-	Vette/SS
1982	-	CDJ	267	Roch E2ME carb.	J	-	2	B G/Bel Air
-	-	-	-	-	-	-	-	Kingswd/Monte
1985	-	CDJ	305	Roch E4ME carb.	H LG4	150	4	B F G/Impala
1985	-	CDK	305	HO E4ME carb.	G L69	175	4	Z-28/T/A/SS
1972	-	CDL	400	t/h trns, pol/taxi	LF6	170	2	Caprice
1985	-	CDL	305	Roch E4ME carb.	H LG4	150	4	B F G/Impala
1972	-	CDM	400	t/h, pol/taxi, Calif	LF6	170	2	Caprice
1985	-	CDM	305	HO E4ME carb.	G L69	175	4	Z-28/T/A/SS
-	-	-	-	-	-	-	-	Impala
1985	-	CDN	305	LB9	F	190	TPI	Z-28/T/A/B
1985	-	CDR	305	LB9	F	190	TPI	Z-28/T/A/B
-	-	-	-	-	-	-	-	Impala

first year	last year	stamp RPO	cid	application	VIN	h/p	bbls	body styles
1957	-	CE	265	H.D. clutch	-	-	-	cars/Impala
1980	-	CEA	305	auto trans.	H LG4	155	4	G
1980	-	CEC	305	auto trans.	H LG4	155	4	G
1980	-	CED	305	auto trans.	H LG4	155	4	B/Fbird −5hp
1980	-	CEH	305	auto trans.	H LG4	155	4	full size/Fbird −5hp
1978	-	CEJ	305	auto trans.	U LG3	145	2	full size
1980	-	CEJ	305	-	H LG4	155	4	Camaro/Impala
1982	-	CEJ	305	LU5, Cross-Fir inj.	7	165	TTBI	F B
1978	-	CEK	305	auto trans.	U LG3	145	2	full size/Impala
1980	-	CEL	305	-	H LG4	155	4	Camaro
1980	-	CEM	305	-	H LG4	155	4	Camaro/1200/
-	-	-	-	-	-	-	-	Omega
1978	-	CER	305	-	U LG3	145	2	G/Impala
1980	-	CER	305	-	H LG4	155	4	G/Omega
1980	-	CET	305	-	H LG4	155	4	Camaro
1980	-	CEU	350	-	L LM1	190	-	Camaro
1958	59	CF	283	m/t	-	230	4	truck/1271/Omega
1960	-	CF	283	m/t	-	170	2	truck/1100/Impala
1961	-	CF	283	-	-	-	4	full size/Impala
1962	-	CF	283	m/t, 4 spd	-	-	-	Chevy II/Impala
1982	-	CFA	305	Roch E4ME carb.	H LG4	155	4	B F G
1985	-	CFA	305	LB9	F	190	TPI	Z-28/T/A/B/Monte
1982	-	CFB	305	Roch E4ME carb.	H LG4	145	4	B F G/Monte
1985	-	CFB	305	LB9	F	190	TPI	Z-28 T/A/B/Monte
1982	-	CFC	305	Roch E4ME carb.	H LG4	145	4	B F G/Impala
1982	-	CFD	305	Roch E4ME carb.	H LG4	145	4	B F G/Monte
1982	-	CFF	305	Roch E4ME carb.	H LG4	145	4	B F G/Impala
1985	-	CFF	305	HO	G L69	175	4	Z-28/T/A/SS
1982	-	CFH	305	Roch E4ME carb.	H LG4	145	4	B F G/Impala
1985	-	CFH	305	HO	G L69	175	4	Z-28/T/A/SS
1982	-	CFJ	305	Cross-Fir Fuel inj.	LU5 7	165	TTBI	Z-28/T/A/Impala
1982	-	CFK	305	Cross-Fir Fuel inj.	LU5 7	165	TTBI	Z-28/T/A/B
1982	-	CFL	305	Cross-Fir Fuel inj.	LU5 7	165	TTBI	Z-28/Monte
1982	-	CFM	305	Cross-Fir Fuel inj.	LU5 7	165	TTBI	Z-28/T/A/B
1982	-	CFN	305	Cross-Fir Fuel inj.	LU5 7	165	TTBI	Z-28/T/A/B
1982	-	CFR	305	Roch E4ME carb.	H LG4	145	4	F B G/Omega
1982	-	CFT	305	Roch E4ME carb.	H LG4	145	4	F B G
1982	-	CFW	305	Roch E4ME carb.	H LG4	145	4	F B G
1982	-	CFY	305	Roch E4ME carb.	H LG4	145	4	F B G/Kingswd
1982	-	CFZ	305	Roch E4ME carb.	H LG4	145	4	F B G
1958	59	CG	283	m/t, O.D.	-	230	4	truck & cars
1960	-	CG	283	m/t, O.D.	-	170	2	truck & cars
1962	64	CG	283	m/t, 4 spd, a/c	-	-	-	Chevy II/Kingswd
1971	-	CGA	350	manual trans.	-	245	2	A B
1975	76	CGA	262	LV1	G	110	2	Monza/Kingswd
1971	-	CGB	350	Powerglide	-	245	2	A B F X
1975	76	CGB	262	LV1	G	110	2	Monza
1971	-	CGC	350	tur hydro	-	245	2	El Camino
1971	-	CGC	350	std trns, pol/taxi	-	245	2	full size
1971	-	CGJ	350	t/h trns, pol/taxi	-	-	2	B
1975	-	CGJ	262	LV1	G	110	2	Monza
1971	-	CGK	350	manual trans.	-	270	4	A F X
1975	-	CGK	262	LV1	G	110	2	Monza
1971	-	CGL	350	t350	-	270	4	A F X
1971	-	CGP	350	m/t, 4 spd	LT1	330	4	Z-28

first year	last year	stamp RPO	cid	application	VIN	h/p	bbls	body styles
1970	-	CGR	400	manual trans.	-	265	2	full size/truck
1971	-	CGR	350	t400	LT1	330	4	Z-28
1971	-	CGS	350	4 spd trans.	-	270	4	Vette
1971	-	CGT	350	tur 400	-	270	4	Vette
1971	-	CGY	350	H.D. 4 spd	LT1	330	4	Vette/Monte
1971	-	CGZ	350	m/t, 4 spd	LT1	330	4	Vette
1958	59	CH	283	m/t, 3 spd	-	250	FI	full size
1962	64	CH	283	manual 3 spd	-	-	-	Chevy II
1973	-	CHA	307	tur hydramatic	-	115	2	F B X
1975	-	CHA	350	m/t	J L48	165	4	Vette
1980	-	CHA	305	LG4	H	155	4	Camaro/Monte
1980	-	CHA	350	LM1	L	190	4	Camaro
1988	-	CHA	305	LB9	F	190	TPI	Firebird
1973	-	CHB	307	manual trans.	-	115	2	F B X
1975	-	CHB	350	a/t, fed	J L48	165	4	Vette
1988	-	CHB	305	LB9	F	190	TPI	Firebird
1973	-	CHC	307	tur hydro, Calif	NB2	115	2	F B X
1975	-	CHC	350	m/t, h/p	T L82	205	4	Vette
1976	-	CHC	350	m/t, h/p	X L82	210	4	Vette
1980	-	CHC	350	auto trans.	L	-	-	full size
1973	-	CHD	307	-	-	115	2	X
1977	-	CHD	350	a/t, Calif	L L48	180	4	Vette/Chevelle
-	-	-	-	-	-	-	-	Monte
1978	-	CHF	350	auto trans. LM1	L	170	-	F B
1973	-	CHH	307	tur hydro trans.		115	2	F X
1978	-	CHH	350	auto trans. LM1	L	170	4	full size
1973	-	CHJ	307	m/t, NB2	-	115	2	Camaro
1978	-	CHJ	350	auto trans. LM1	L	170	4	B F
1973	-	CHK	307	tur hydro, Calif	NB2	115	2	B F X
1978	-	CHK	350	auto trans. LM1	L	170	4	full size
1978	-	CHL	350	auto trans. LM1	L	170	4	F B X
1978	-	CHM	350	auto trans. LM1	L	170	4	full size
1988	-	CHP	305	LB9	F	190	TPI	Firebird
1975	-	CHR	350	a/t, s h/p, Calif	T L82	205	4	Vette/Camaro
1978	-	CHR	350	auto trans. LM1	L	170	4	Camaro
1975	-	CHS	400	-	-	-	-	Chevelle
1978	-	CHS	350	auto trans. LM1	L	170	4	Camaro
1978	-	CHT	350	auto trans. LM1	L	170	4	Camaro
1978	-	CHU	350	auto trans. LM1	L	170	4	Camaro
1975	-	CHW	350	-	-	155	4	Chevelle/1200
1978	-	CHW	350	m/t	L L48	185	4	Vette/Chevy II
1977	-	CHX	350	auto trans. LM1	L	170	4	A X
1977	78	CHY	350	auto trans. LM1	L	170	4	B/Kingswd
1975	-	CHZ	350	a/t, Calif/em	J L48	165	4	Vette
1958	59	CJ	283	hi lift cam, m/t 3 sp		290	FI	full size
1959	-	CJ	283	m/t	-	290	FI	truck/1100
1964	-	CJ	283	man 3 spd, A/C	-	-	-	Kingswd
1971	-	CJB	350	4 spd, pol/taxi	-	270	4	B
1988	-	CJB	305	L03	E	150	TBI	Firebird
1988	-	CJC	305	L03	E	150	TBI	Firebird
1971	-	CJD	350	t350	-	270	4	A F X
1971	-	CJG	350	m/t	-	270	4	A F X/Monte
1971	-	CJH	350	four spd,pol/taxi	-	270	4	B/Monte
1971	-	CJJ	350	m/t	-	270	4	A
1971	-	CJK	350	tur 400	LT1	330	4	Vette/Chevelle

first year	last year	stamp RPO	cid	application	VIN	h/p	bbls	body styles
-	-	-	-	-	-	-	-	Monte
1971		CJL	350	m/t, 4 spd	-	270	4	Vette
1972	-	CKA	350	manual trans.	L65	165	2	F A X
1973	-	CKA	350	manual trans.	-	145	2	F A X
1977	-	CKA	350	LM1	L	170	4	B
1985	-	CKA	305	Roch E4ME carb.	H LG4	150	4	G B F
1972	-	CKB	350	tur 400 trans.	L65	165	2	A B
1973	-	CKB	350	m/t, 4 spd	L48	175	4	F A X/Monte
1974	-	CKB	350	m/t, 3 & 4 spd	-	185	4	F X
1973	-	CKC	350	m/t	NB2	145	2	A X
1975	-	CKC	350	a/t, s h/p, w/fed	T L82	205	4	Vette
1976	-	CKC	350	a/t, s h/p, w/fed	X L82	210	4	Vette
1972	-	CKD	350	tur hydro trans	-	175	4	F A B X
1973	-	CKD	350	tur hydro, Calif	L48	200	4	A B F X
1974	-	CKD	350	T350 NB2	-	-	4	A B F X
1977	-	CKD	350	a/t, high altitude	L L48	180	4	Vette
1991	-	CKF	305	LB9	F	205	TPI	Firebird/Monte
1972	-	CKG	307	manual trans.	-	130	2	F A X
1972	-	CKH	307	Powerglide	-	130	2	F A X
-	-	-	-	-	-	-	-	Apollo/Ventura
1973	-	CKH	350	m/t, 4 spd, NB2	L48	175	4	F A X/Chevelle
-	-	-	-	-	-	-	-	Monte
1974	-	CKH	350	m/t ,3 & 4 spd, NB2	L48	160	4	F A X
1973	-	CKJ	350	tur hydro trans.	L65	-	4	A B F/Bel Air
-	-	-	-	-	-	-	-	Kingswd
1972	-	CKK	350	manual trans.	L48	175	4	A F X/Monte
1973	-	CKK	350	t/h, NB2	L65	-	2	B A X
1973	-	CKL	350	tur hydro, Calif	-	-	-	F A B
1975	-	CKL	262	-	-	-	-	Nova/Chevelle
-	-	-	-	-	-	-	-	Monte
1976	77	CKM	350	a/t, LM1	L	170	4	F A B X
1972	-	CKP	400	tur hydro trans.	-	170	2	Caprice
1973	-	CKR	350	tur hydro, Calif	B	-	-	Nova
1977	-	CKR	350	a/t, LM1	L	170	4	F A B X/Nova
1972	-	CKS	350	4 spd trans.	LT1	255	4	Z28
1973	-	CKS	350	tur hydro, Calif	-	145	2	F A B
1977	-	CKS	350	a/t, LM1	L	170	4	F
1972	-	CKT	350	tur hydramatic	LT1	255	4	Z28
1973	-	CKU	350	t/h	L48	175	4	Camaro
1974	-	CKU	350	T350	-	185	4	Camaro
1976	-	CKU	350	a/t	LM1	165	4	B
1972	-	CKW	350	4 spd trans.	K	200	4	Vette
1973	-	CKW	350	t/h	L65	145	2	F X
1976	-	CKW	350	m/t	L L48	180	4	Vette
1972	-	CKX	350	tur hydro trans.	K	200	4	Vette
1973	-	CKX	350	t/h, NB2	L65	145	2	Camaro
1976	77	CKX	350	a/t	L L48	180	4	Vette
1972	-	CKY	350	four spd trans.	L LT1	255	4	Vette/1200
1973	-	CKY	350	m/t, 4 spd NB2	L65	145	2	Camaro
1972	-	CKZ	350	LT-1, H.D. 4 spd	L LT1	255	4	Vette
1973	-	CKZ	350	4 spd trans.	J L48	190	4	Vette
1974	-	CKZ	350	4 spd trans.	J L48	195	4	Vette
1977	-	CKZ	350	L48	L	180	4	Vette
1960	-	CL	283	m/t	-	270	4	truck/1100
1962	-	CL	283	m/t, 3 spd, a/c	-	-	-	full size

first year	last year	stamp RPO	cid	application	VIN	h/p	bbls	body styles
1963	-	CL	283	m/t, a/c	-	-	-	cars
1973	-	CLA	350	tur hydro. 400	J L48	190	4	Vette
1974	-	CLA	350	tur hydro. 400	J L48	195	4	Vette
1977	-	CLA	350	a/t	L L48	180	4	Vette
1973	-	CLB	350	m/t, 4 spd, NB2	J L48	190	4	Vette
1974	-	CLB	350	m/t, 4 spd, NB2	J L48	195	4	Vette
1977	-	CLB	350	m/t, high altitude	L L48	180	4	Vette
1973	-	CLC	350	t/h, 4 spd, NB2	J L48	190	4	Vette
1974	-	CLC	350	t/h, 4 spd, NB2	J L48	195	4	Vette
1977	-	CLC	350	a/t, Calif	L L48	180	4	Vette
1973	74	CLD	350	tur hydro 400	T L82	250	4	Vette
1977	-	CLD	350	m/t, high altitude	X L82	210	4	Vette
1976	-	CLF	350	L65	V	145	2	A B
1977	-	CLF	350	a/t, Calif	X L82	210	4	Vette
1973	74	CLH	350	t/h trans., NB2	T L82	250	4	Vette/Camaro
1976	-	CLH	350	LM1	L	165	4	full size
1991	-	CLH	305	LB9	F	205	TPI	Firebird
1973	74	CLJ	350	m/t, 4 spd	Z28	245	4	Z-28/Kingswd
1991	-	CLJ	305	LB9	F	205	TPI	Firebird
1970	-	CLK	400	tur 350	-	265	2	full size
1971	-	CLK	400	tur hydro trans.	-	255	4	B
1973	-	CLK	350	Z-28	-	245	4	Camaro
1974	-	CLK	350	tur hydro trans.	-	185	4	Chevelle/Kingswd
1977	78	CLK	350	LM1	L	170	4	B
1973	-	CLL	350	t/h trans,Calif	Z28	245	4	Camaro
1977	-	CLL	350	LM1	L	170	4	B
1973	-	CLM	350	4 spd,Calif	Z28	245	4	Camaro
1976	78	CLM	350	a/t	L L48	185	4	Vette/Monte
1971	-	CLP	400	tur hydro trans.	-	255	4	B/Monte
1973	74	CLR	350	4 spd trans.	T L82	250	4	Vette
1978	-	CLR	350	a/t, Calif	L L48	175	4	Vette/Monte
1973	74	CLS	350	m/t, Calif	T L82	250	4	Vette
1976	-	CLS	350	a/t, high altitude	L L48	175	4	Vette
1973	-	CLT	350	tur hydro, Calif	L65	165	2	A B F/1200
1973	-	CLU	350	tur hydro, Calif	L65	165	2	A B F/Monte
1973	-	CLW	350	tur hydro, Calif	L65	165	2	A B F
1991	-	CLW	305	LB9	F	205	TPI	Firebird/Monte
1973	-	CLX	350	t/h, NB2	L65	-	2	full size
1960	-	CM	283	a/c	-	-	4	full size
1960	-	CM	283	m/t	-	230	4	truck/1100
1972	-	CMA	307	tur hydro, Calif	-	130	2	A F X
1974	-	CMA	350	tur hydro trans.	-	-	2	A B F X
1972	-	CMB	350	tur hydro, Calif	L65	165	2	A F X
1975	-	CMB	350	-	-	155	4	F
1991	-	CMB	350	L98, a/t	8	240	TPI	Firebird
-	-	-	-	-	-	-	-	Chevelle/Monte
1974	-	CMC	350	manual trans.	-	-	2	A F X
1980	-	CMC	305	LG4	H	155	4	G
1974	-	CMD	350	tur 350, taxi	-	-	2	full size
1980	-	CMD	305	LG4	H	155	4	G
1972	-	CMH	350	4spd, Calif	L65	165	2	Camaro
1974	76	CMH	350	tur hydro	-	-	4	A B F
1980	-	CMH	305	automatic trans.	H	-	-	full size
1974	76	CMJ	350	t400 police	-	-	4	full size
1980	-	CMJ	305	automatic trans.	H	-	-	full size/Camaro

first year	last year	stamp RPO	cid	application	VIN	h/p	bbls	body styles
1974	-	CMK	350	t400 NB2 pol/taxi		-	4	full size
1975	-	CML	350	-	-	155	4	Camaro
1976	-	CML	350	LM1	L	165	4	F X
1980	-	CML	305	LG4	H	155	4	Camaro
1980	-	CML	350	LM1	L	190	4	Z-28
1975	76	CMM	350	LM1	-	165	4	A B F
1975	77	CMN	350	LM1	L	165	4	A B F
1980	-	CMN	305	LG4	H	155	4	G
1991	-	CMP	350	L98, a/t	8	240	TPI	Firebird
1974	-	CMR	350	tur hydro trans.	-	145	2	A
1978	-	CMR	350	m/t	L82 4	220	4	Vette/Z-28
1980	-	CMR	305	auto trans.	H LG4	155	4	full size
1974	-	CMS	350	m/t, 4 spd	-	185	4	Camaro
1978	-	CMS	350	a/t	L82 4	220	4	Vette
1980	-	CMS	305	auto trans.	H LG4	155	4	full size
1974	-	CMT	350	t400	L82	245	4	Camaro/Chevy II
1978	-	CMT	350	LM1	L	170	4	B
1980	-	CMT	305	auto trans.	H LG4	155	4	full size/Chevy II
1975	-	CMU	350	145	-	-	2	A F X
1975	-	CMX	350	145	-	-	2	full size
1975	-	CMY	350	145	-	-	2	F X B
1970	-	CNA	302	manual trans.	-	290	4	Nova/Kingswd
1982	-	CNA	350	Police LM1	L	185	4	B
1970	-	CNB	302	tur hydramatic	-	290	4	Nova
1982	-	CNB	350	Police LM1	L	185	4	B
1970	-	CNC	307	manual trans.	-	200	2	A F X
1970	-	CND	307	manual 4 spd	-	200	2	A F X
1970	-	CND	350	manual trans.	-	250	2	B
1970	-	CNE	307	Powerglide	-	200	2	A F X
1970	-	CNF	307	tur 350 trans.	-	200	2	A F X
1982	-	CNF	350	Police LM1	L	185	4	B
1970	-	CNG	307	m/t	-	200	2	El Cam/Chevy II
1970	-	CNH	307	Powerglide	-	200	2	El Cam/Chevy II
1982	-	CNH	350	Police LM1	L	185	4	B/Bel Air Kingswd
-	-	-	-	-	-	-	-	Kingswd
1970	-	CNI	350	manual trans.	-	250	2	A F X
1970	-	CNJ	350	manual trans.	-	300	4	A F X/Bel Air Kingswd
-	-	-	-	-	-	-	-	Kingswd
1970	-	CNK	350	Powerglide	-	300	4	A F X/Bel Air Kingswd
-	-	-	-	-	-	-	-	Kingswd
1970	-	CNM	350	Powerglide	-	250	2	A F X/Bel Air Kingswd
-	-	-	-	-	-	-	-	Kingswd
1970	-	CNN	350	tur 350	-	250	2	A F X
1970	-	CNP	350	4 spd, pol/taxi	-	250	2	Caprice/Bel Air Kingswd
-	-	-	-	-	-	-	-	Kingswd
1971	-	CNQ	350	manual trans.	-	300	4	full size
1970	-	CNR	350	tur hydro trans	-	300	4	Caprice/Bel Air Kingswd
-	-	-	-	-	-	-	-	Kingswd
1970	-	CNS	350	Pwrglide, pol/taxi	-	300	4	Caprice/Bel Air Kingswd
-	-	-	-	-	-	-	-	Kingswd
1970	-	CNT	350	t/h trns, pol/taxi	-	300	4	Caprice/Bel Air Kingswd
-	-	-	-	-	-	-	-	Kingswd
1978	-	CNT	350	auto trans.	L	-	-	full size
1970	71	CNU	350	Powerglide trans.	-	250	2	full size
1970	-	CNV	350	tur hydro trans.	-	250	2	Caprice

first year	last year	stamp RPO	cid	application	VIN	h/p	bbls	body styles
1970	-	CNW	350	Pwrglide, pol/taxi	-	250	2	Caprice
1970	-	CNX	350	t/h trns, pol/taxi	-	250	2	Caprice
1976	77	CPA	305	vins; 76:Q, 77:U	LG3	145	2	F X
1980	-	CPA	267	L39	J	120	2	G
1976	77	CPC	305	vins; 76:Q, 77:U	LG3	145	2	F X
1980	-	CPC	267	auto trans.	J L39	120	2	G
1980	-	CPD	267	J L39	-	120	2	Camaro
1980	-	CPH	267	auto trans.	J L39	120	2	full size
1976	-	CPJ	305	LG3	Q	140	2	F X
1978	-	CPJ	305	LG3	U	145	2	X
1977	-	CPK	305	LG3	U	145	2	Monza
1977	-	CPL	305	LG3	U	145	2	Monza
1980	-	CPL	267	L39	J	120	2	full size
1977	78	CPM	305	LG3	U	145	2	B X
1980	-	CPM	267	L39	J	120	2	G
1977	-	CPR	305	LG3	U	145	2	B
1980	-	CPR	267	L39	J	120	2	G
1977	-	CPS	305	LG3	U	145	2	X
1977	-	CPT	305	LG3	U	145	2	X
1977	-	CPU	305	LG3	U	145	2	Monza
1977	-	CPX	305	LG3	U	145	2	Monza
1977	-	CPY	305	LG3	U	145	2	F A X
1978	-	CPZ	305	LG3	U	145	2	G
1958	61	CQ	283	m/t, 3 spd	-	230	4	Vette
1958	61	CR	283	m/t, 3 spd	-	250	FI	Vette
1975	-	CR2	350	-	-	-	-	Chevelle
1977	-	CRA	305	LG3	U	145	2	A
1982	-	CRA	305	LG4	H	145	4	F B G/Chevelle
-	-	-	-	-	-	-	-	Monte
1982	-	CRA	305	Roch E4ME carb.	H LG4	145	4	F G B
1977	-	CRB	305	LG3	U	145	2	B
1975	-	CRC	350	-	-	-	-	F A X/Chevy II
1977	-	CRC	305	LG3	U	145	2	Monza
1972	-	CRD	350	tur hydro, A.I.R.	L65	165	2	Camaro/Bel Air
-	-	-	-	-	-	-	-	Kingswd
1975	-	CRD	350	-	-	-	-	F A X/Chevelle
-	-	-	-	-	-	-	-	Monte
1977	-	CRD	305	LG3	U	145	2	Monza
1970	-	CRE	350	tur 350	-	300	4	A F X
1975	-	CRF	350	-	-	-	-	B
1977	-	CRF	305	LG3	U	145	2	A
1972	-	CRG	350	man trans, A.I.R.	L65	165	2	Camaro
1970	-	CRH	400	-	-	265	2	A
1978	-	CRH	305	LG3	U	145	2	G
1975	-	CRJ	350	m/t, 4 spd	J L48	165	4	Vette
1972	-	CRK	350	t/h A.I.R.	L48	200	4	Nova
1975	-	CRK	350	tur 400	J L48	165	4	Vette
1972	-	CRL	350	m/t, A.I.R.	L48	200	4	Nova/Monte
1975	-	CRL	350	h/p, 4 spd	T L82	205	4	Vette
1977	-	CRL	305	LG3	U	145	2	Starfire
1975	-	CRM	350	tur 400, h/p	T L82	205	4	Vette
1977	-	CRM	305	LG3	U	145	2	Starfire
1975	-	CRR	350	-	-	-	-	Camaro
1972	-	CRS	350	a/c, tur 400, A.I.R.	LT1	255	4	Vette
1972	-	CRS	350	a/t, a/c	L LT1	255	4	Vette

first year	last year	stamp RPO	cid	application	VIN	h/p	bbls	body styles
1975	-	CRS	350	-	-	-	-	F B
1982	-	CRS	267	E2ME carb. exc Cal	J	-	2	Malibu
1970	-	CRT	350	solid cam	LT1	360	4	A
1972	-	CRT	350	4 sp]d, A.I.R.	L LT1	255	4	Vette
1972	-	CRT	350	LT1	-	255	4	Vette
1975	-	CRT	350	-	-	-	-	F X
1976	-	CRT	350	-	-	165	4	Vette
1977	-	CRT	305	LG3	U	145	2	Starfire
1975	-	CRU	350	-	-	-	-	A B F X
1978	-	CRU	305	LG3	U	145	2	G
1975	-	CRW	350	-	-	-	-	full size
1978	-	CRW	305	LG3	U	145	2	G
1975	-	CRX	350	-	-	155	4	A B
1975	-	CRX	350	-	-	145	2	F X
1978	-	CRX	305	LG3	U	145	2	G
1975	-	CRY	350	-	-	-	-	full size/Bel Air
-	-	-	-	-	-	-	-	Kingswd
1978	-	CRY	305	LG3	U	145	2	G
1975	-	CRZ	350	-	-	-	-	F B X
1978	-	CRZ	305	LG3	U	145	2	G
1958	61	CS	283	m/t, 3sp, hi lift cam	-	290	FI	Vette
1973	-	CSA	400	tur hydro trans.	LE2 U	175	2	B
1976	-	CSA	400	LT4	U	175	4	A/Bel Air
-	-	-	-	-	-	-	-	Kingswd
1973	-	CSB	400	tur hydro trans.	LE2 U	175	2	Caprice
1976	-	CSB	400	LT4	U	175	4	A
1973	-	CSC	400	t/h trans., Calif	LE2 U	175	2	Caprice
1973	-	CSD	400	t/h trans., Calif	LE2 U	175	2	Caprice
1976	-	CSF	400	LT4	U LT4	175	4	A B
1972	-	CSH	350	tur hydro, pol/tax	-	165	2	A B/Bel Air
-	-	-	-	-	-	-	-	Kingswd
1975	-	CSH	400	LT4	U LT4	175	4	A B
1972	-	CSJ	350	manual trans.	-	165	2	B/Bel Air
-	-	-	-	-	-	-	-	Kingswd
1976	-	CSJ	400	a/t	LT4	175	2	B
1973	-	CSK	400	tur hydro trans.	LE2 U	175	2	B
1973	-	CSL	400	t/h, NB2	LE2 U	175	-	full size
1973	-	CSM	400	t/h trans., Calif	LE2 U	175	2	Caprice
1975	76	CSM	400	LT4	U LT4	175	4	Sprint
1975	-	CSR	400	LT4	U LT4	175	4	B
1975	-	CSS	400	LT4	U LT4	175	4	B
1975	-	CST	400	LT4	U LT4	175	4	B
1974	-	CSU	400	t350	U LT4	175	4	Chevelle
1974	-	CSU	400	t400 NB2	U LT4	175	2	full size
1974	-	CSW	400	a/t	U LT4	175	2	B
1974	-	CSW	400	t400	U LT4	175	2	full size
1976	-	CSW	400	LT4	U LT4	175	4	A B
1974	-	CSX	400	t350	U LT4	175	4	A B/Kingswd
1976	-	CSX	400	LT4	U LT4	175	4	A B
1958	61	CT	283	m/t, 3 spd	-	245	8	Vette
1972	-	CTA	400	tur hydramatic	LE2 U	175	2	B
1974	-	CTA	400	a/t	U LT4	175	2	A B
1978	-	CTA	305	LG3	U	145	2	Monza
1970	-	CTB	350	high perf, 4 spd	LT1	350	4	F X A
1972	-	CTB	400	man trans., A.I.R.	-	-	4	Caprice

first year	last year	stamp RPO	cid	application	VIN	h/p	bbls	body styles
1974	-	CTB	400	t/h trns, pol/taxi	-	175	2	Caprice
1975	-	CTB	400	a/t	-	175	4	A
1978	-	CTB	305	LG3	U	145	2	Monza
1970	-	CTC	350	high perf, tur 400	-	320	4	A/Bel Air
-	-	-	-	-	-	-	-	Kingswd
1970	-	CTC	350	LT1	-	360	4	F X
1974	-	CTC	400	t/h trans., Calif	-	175	4	A B
1978	-	CTC	305	LG3	U	145	2	Monza
1974	-	CTD	400	tur hydro trans.	-	175	4	Caprice
1978	-	CTD	305	LG3	U	145	2	Monza/Bel Air
-	-	-	-	-	-	-	-	Kingswd
1978	-	CTF	305	LG3	U	145	2	Monza
1978	-	CTH	305	LG3	U	145	2	F X
1974	-	CTJ	400	tur hydro trans.	-	175	4	B/Bel Air
-	-	-	-	-	-	-	-	Kingswd
1978	-	CTJ	305	LG3	U	145	2	Nova
1972	-	CTK	307	tur hydramatic	-	130	2	A F X
1974	-	CTK	400	t/h, pol/taxi, Calif	-	-	4	Caprice
1978	-	CTK	305	LG3	U	145	2	F X
1970	-	CTL	350	4 spd trans.	-	300	4	Vette
1972	-	CTL	350	tur hydramatic	L65	165	2	A F X
1975	76	CTL	400	LT4	U	175	4	B A
1978	-	CTL	305	LG3, a/t	U	145	2	B
1970	-	CTM	350	tur 400	-	300	4	Vette
1975	76	CTM	400	LT4	U	175	4	B
1978	-	CTM	305	LG3	U	145	2	G
1970	-	CTN	350	high perf, a/c, m/t	-	350	4	Vette
1970	-	CTO	350	h/p, a/c, m/t	-	350	4	Vette
1970	-	CTP	350	h/p, t/ign., m/t	-	350	4	Vette
1970	-	CTQ	350	h/p, t/ig, a/c, m/t	-	350	4	Vette
1970	-	CTR	350	spec hi perf, m/t	LT1	370	4	Vette
1975	-	CTR	400	LT4	U	175	4	B A
1978	-	CTR	305	LG3	U	145	2	G
1975	-	CTS	400	LT4	U	175	4	B
1970	-	CTU	350	H.E.I., sp hiper, m/t	LT1	370	4	Vette
1975	76	CTU	400	LT4	U	175	4	A B
1970	-	CTV	350	s h/p, m/t, t/ign.	LT1	370	4	Vette
1975	76	CTW	400	LT4	U	175	4	B
1978	-	CTW	305	LG3	U	145	2	G
1975	76	CTX	400	LT4	U	175	4	A B
1978	-	CTX	305	LG3	U	145	2	G
1976	-	CTY	400	LT4	U	175	4	B
1976	-	CTZ	400	LT4	U	175	4	B
1958	61	CU	283	m/t, 3sp, hi lift cam	-	270	8	Vette
1975	-	CUA	350	m/t, 4 spd	J L48	165	4	Vette
1980	-	CUA	305	LG4	H	155	4	B
1988	-	CUA	350	L98, a/t	8	225	TPI	Firebird
1975	-	CUB	350	4 spd trans.	J L48	165	4	Vette
1977	-	CUB	350	LM1	L	170	4	B
1980	-	CUB	305	LG4	H	155	4	B
1977	-	CUC	350	LM1	L	170	4	B
1980	-	CUC	305	LG4	H	155	4	B
1975	-	CUD	350	h/p, 4 spd	T L82	205	4	Vette
1977	-	CUD	350	LM1	L	170	4	B
1980	-	CUD	305	LG4	H	155	4	B

first year	last year	stamp RPO	cid	application	VIN	h/p	bbls	body styles
1976	-	CUF	350	LM1	L	165	4	A
1978	-	CUF	350	LM1	L	170	4	B
1980	-	CUF	305	LG4	H	155	4	B
1975	-	CUH	350	LM1	L	165	4	F X
1975	-	CUJ	350	LM1	L	165	4	F X
1975	-	CUL	350	LM1	L	165	4	Camaro
1975	-	CUM	350	LM1	L	165	4	F X
1978	-	CUM	350	LM1	L	170	4	B X
1978	-	CUR	350	LM1	L	170	4	B X
1975	-	CUS	350	LM1	L	165	4	A F X
1978	-	CUS	350	LM1	L	170	4	B X
1975	-	CUT	350	m/t, 4 spd	T L82	205	4	Vette
1978	-	CUT	350	a/t	L L48	185	4	Vette
1958	-	CY	283	m/t ,4 spd	-	-	FI	full size/Sunbird
1958	-	CZ	283	m/t ,4sp, hi lift cam	-	-	FI	full size
1975	-	CZA	262	LV1	G	110	2	Monza/Ventura
1989	-	CZA	350	export, al. heads	L98 8	240	TPI	Vette
1975	-	CZB	262	LV1	G	110	2	Monza/Ventura
1975	-	CZC	262	LV1	G	110	2	Monza
1975	-	CZD	262	LV1	G	110	2	Monza
1975	-	CZF	262	LV1	G	110	2	X
1975	-	CZG	262	LV1	G	110	2	Monza/Apollo
-	-	-	-	-	-	-	-	Ventura
1975	-	CZH	262	LV1	G	110	2	Nova
1975	-	CZJ	262	LV1	G	110	2	Nova
1975	-	CZK	262	LV1	G	110	2	Nova
1977	-	CZK	305	-	U	145	2	Camaro
1975	-	CZL	262	LV1	G	110	2	Nova
1977	-	CZL	305	-	U	145	2	Camaro
1975	-	CZM	262	LV1	G	110	2	Nova
1982	-	CZS	305	Roch E4ME carb.	H LG4	145	4	Firebird/Monte
1975	76	CZT	262	LV1	G	110	2	Monza
1982	-	CZT	305	Roch E4ME carb.	H LG4	145	4	Firebird
1975	76	CZU	262	LV1	G	110	2	Monza
1982	-	CZU	305	Roch E4ME carb.	H	145	4	Firebird
1975	-	CZW	262	LV1	G	110	2	Monza
1970	-	CZX	400	manual trans.	-	265	2	full size
1982	-	CZX	305	Roch E4ME carb.	H LG4	145	4	Firebird
1958	59	D	283	Powerglide	-	185	2	cars & truck
1960	64	D	283	Powerglide	-	170	2	truck & cars
1987	-	D34	305	LB9	F	190	TPI	Firebird
1986	-	D4C	305	LB9	F	190	TPI	Firebird
1986	-	D4K	305	LB9	F	190	TPI	Firebird
1987	-	D4W	305	LB9	F	190	TPI	Firebird
1981	-	D5A	350	Roch E4ME carb.	L LM1	190	4	Camaro
1981	-	D5B	350	Roch E4ME carb.	L LM1	190	4	Camaro/B F
1983	-	D5B	305	Roch E4ME carb.	H LG4	145	4	F B G
1983	-	D5C	305	Roch E4ME carb.	H LG4	145	4	F B G
1983	-	D5D	305	Roch E4ME carb.	H LG4	145	4	F B G
1983	-	D5F	305	Roch E4ME carb.	H LG4	145	4	F B G
1983	-	D5H	305	Roch E4ME carb.	H LG4	145	4	F B G
1983	-	D5N	350	T.B.I.	6	200	-	police/Malibu
1983	-	D5R	305	Roch E4ME carb.	H LG4	145	4	Pontiac/Malibu
1981	-	D6A	305	Roch E4ME carb.	H LG4	145	4	B G
1981	-	D6B	305	Roch E4ME carb.	H LG4	145	4	F B

first year	last year	stamp RPO	cid	application	VIN	h/p	bbls	body styles
1981	-	D6C	305	Roch E4ME carb.	H LG4	145	4	F B
1981	-	D6D	305	Roch M4ME carb.	H LG4	145	4	B F
1981	-	D8A	267	Roch E2ME carb.	J L39	120	2	B G
1981	-	D8B	267	Roch E2ME carb.	J L39	120	2	Monte
1981	-	D8C	267	Roch E2ME carb.	J L39	120	2	Monte
1981	-	D8D	267	Roch E2ME carb.	J L39	120	2	full size
1981	-	D8F	267	Roch E2ME carb.	J L39	120	2	full size
1981	-	D8H	267	E2ME carb ex Calif	J L39	120	2	Camaro
1980	-	D9B	305	Roch M4ME carb.	H LG4	145	4	Camaro
1965	67	DA	283	man trans., 3 spd	-	195	2	A
1968	69	DA	307	man trans., 3 spd	-	200	2	A F X
1978	-	DAA	305	LG3	U	145	2	B
1978	-	DAB	305	LG3	U	145	2	B
1978	-	DAF	305	LG3	U	145	2	G
1958	61	DB	283	Powerglide	-	230	4	truck/1271
1965	67	DB	283	man trans., 4 spd	-	195	-	A
1968	-	DB	307	m/t, 4 spd	-	200	-	F X A
1969	-	DC	307	Powerglide	-	200	-	F X A
1969	-	DD	307	tur 350 trans.	-	200	-	F X A
1986	-	DD4	305	LG4	H	150	4	Firebird
1983	-	DDA	305	T.B.I.	S	-	-	Parisien
1983	-	DDA	305	LU5, twin T.B.I.	7	165	TBI	Z-28/T/A
1986	-	DDA	305	LB9, 190 hp	F	-	TPI	Firebird
1983	-	DDB	305	Roch E4ME carb.	H LG4	145	4	F B G
1983	-	DDC	305	Roch E4ME carb.	H LG4	145	4	F B G
1983	-	DDD	305	Roch E4ME carb.	H LG4	145	4	F B G
1983	-	DDF	305	Roch E4ME carb.	H LG4	145	4	F B G
1983	-	DDH	305	Roch E4ME carb.	H LG4	145	4	F B G
1986	-	DDH	305	LB9	F	190	TPI	Firebird/F B
1983	-	DDJ	305	Roch E4ME carb.	H LG4	145	4	F B G
1983	-	DDK	305	Roch E4ME carb.	H LG4	145	4	F B G
1983	-	DDM	305	Roch E4ME carb.	H LG4	145	4	F B
1983	-	DDN	305	Roch E4ME carb.	H LG4	145	4	F B G
1983	-	DDS	305	Roch E4ME carb.	H LG4	145	4	Pontiac
1986	-	DDT	305	LB9	F	190	TPI	Firebird
1983	-	DDW	305	Roch E4ME carb.	H LG4	145	4	Pontiac
1986	-	DDX	305	LB9	F	190	TPI	Firebird
1983	-	DDY	305	LU5, twin T.B.I.	7	165	TBI	Firebird
1983	-	DDZ	305	O.D. auto trans.	H	-	4	Parisien/Malibu
1958	59	DE	283	Powrglid, air susp	-	-	-	full size/Malibu
1962	67	DE	283	Powerglide, a/c	-	195	-	A X
1968	69	DE	307	man trans., 4 spd	-	200	2	A F X
1968	-	DF	307	Powerglide	-	-	-	Chevelle
1981	-	DFA	267	Roch E2ME carb.	J L39	120	2	Monte
1981	-	DFB	267	Roch E2ME carb.	J L39	120	2	Monte
1981	-	DFC	267	Roch E2ME carb.	J L39	120	2	Monte
1981	-	DFD	267	Roch E2ME carb.	J L39	120	2	full size
1981	-	DFF	267	Roch E2ME carb.	J L39	120	2	full size
1981	-	DFH	267	E2ME carb ex Calif	J L39	120	2	Camaro
1981	-	DFK	267	E2ME carb ex Calif	J L39	120	2	B F G
1987	-	DFL	305	LG4	H	150	4	Firebird
1986	-	DFR	305	L69, H.O.	G	165	4	Firebird
1986	-	DFS	305	L69, H.O.	G	165	4	Firebird
1986	-	DFT	305	LG4	H	150	4	Firebird
1986	-	DFU	305	LG4	H	150	4	Firebird

first year	last year	stamp RPO	cid	application	VIN	h/p	bbls	body styles
1958	61	DG	283	Powerglide	-	230	4	Vette
1965	67	DG	283	m/t, 3 spd	-	220	4	Chevelle/Malibu
1983	-	DGN	305	Roch E4ME carb.	H LG4	145	4	F G B
1958	59	DH	283	Powerglide	-	250	FI	Vette
1965	66	DH	283	Powerglide	-	220	4	Chevelle
1968	-	DH	307	Powerglide	-	-	-	full size
1981	-	DHA	305	Roch E4ME carb.	H LG4	155	4	B G
1981	-	DHB	305	Roch E4ME carb.	H LG4	155	4	B G/Malibu
1981	-	DHC	305	Roch E4ME carb.	H LG4	155	4	B G/Malibu
1981	-	DHD	305	Roch E4ME carb.	H LG4	155	4	full size
1981	-	DHF	305	Roch E4ME carb.	H LG4	155	4	full size
1981	-	DHH	305	Roch E4ME carb.	H LG4	155	4	full size
1981	-	DHJ	305	Roch M4ME carb.	H LG4	155	4	F B
1981	-	DHK	305	Roch M4ME carb.	H LG4	155	4	F B
1981	-	DHM	305	Roch E4ME carb.	H LG4	155	4	Monte
1981	-	DHN	305	Roch E4ME carb.	H LG4	155	4	Monte
1981	-	DHR	305	Roch E4ME carb.	H LG4	155	4	full size
1981	-	DHS	305	Roch E4ME carb.	H LG4	155	4	full size
1981	-	DHT	305	Roch E4ME carb.	H LG4	155	4	full size/1200
1981	-	DHU	305	O.D. auto trans.	H LG4	155	4	Parisien
1981	-	DHZ	305	Roch M4ME carb.	H LG4	155	4	F B
1966	67	DI	283	air inj. react, m/t	-	195	2	A
1958	61	DJ	283	Powerglide	-	245	8	Vette
1966	67	DJ	283	Powerglide, A.I.R.	-	195	-	A
1959	-	DK	283	Powerglide	-	185	2	B/truck
1960	-	DK	283	Powerglide	-	170	2	truck/1100
1962	63	DK	283	Powerglide, a/c	-	-	-	full size
1966	67	DK	283	m/t, 4 spd, A.I.R.	-	195	-	Chevelle
1968	-	DK	307	tur 400	-	200	-	full size
1981	-	DKB	305	Roch M4ME carb.	H LG4	155	4	F B G
1986	-	DKB	350	m/t	L98 8	230	TPI	Vette
1986	-	DKC	350	a/t	L98 8	230	TPI	Vette
1986	-	DKD	350	m/t, oil cooler	L98 8	230	TPI	Vette
1981	-	DKF	305	Roch M4ME carb.	H LG4	155	4	F B G
1986	-	DKF	350	a/t, oil cooler	L98 8	230	TPI	Vette
1986	-	DKH	350	a/t, alum heads	L98 8	230	TPI	Vette
1981	-	DKJ	305	Roch M4ME carb.	H LG4	155	4	F B G
1986	-	DKJ	350	L98, a/t	8	230	TPI	Firebird
1986	-	DKK	350	L98, a/t	8	230	TPI	Firebird
1959	-	DL	283	glide, air susp., a/c	-	-	-	full size
1966	-	DL	283	A.I.R.	-	-	4	Chevelle
1959	61	DM	283	Powerglide, a/c	-	230	4	full size
1966	-	DM	283	A.I.R., glide	-	-	4	Chevelle
1979	-	DMA	267	L39	J	120	2	G
1981	-	DMA	350	Roch E4ME carb.	L LM1	190	4	Camaro
1979	-	DMB	267	L39	J	120	2	G
1981	-	DMB	350	Roch E4ME carb.	L LM1	190	4	Camaro
1979	-	DMC	267	L39	J	120	2	G
1981	-	DMC	350	Roch E4ME carb.	L	-	4	Camaro
1979	-	DMD	267	L39	J	120	2	G
1981	-	DMD	350	Roch E4ME carb.	L	-	4	Camaro
1979	-	DMF	267	L39	J	120	2	G
1981	-	DMF	350	Roch E4ME carb.	L	-	4	Camaro
1979	-	DMH	267	L39	J	120	2	G
1981	-	DMH	350	Roch E4ME carb.	L	-	4	Camaro

first year	last year	stamp RPO	cid	application	VIN	h/p	bbls	body styles
1979	-	DMM	267	L39	J	120	2	G
1979	-	DMR	267	L39	J	120	2	G
1959	-	DN	283	Powerglide	-	-	FI	fullsize
1967	-	DN	283	m/t, H.D. clutch	-	195	2	Chevelle
1968	-	DN	307	m/t, H.D. clutch	-	200	-	Chevelle
1979	-	DN2	305	LG3	G	135	2	Firebird
1979	-	DNA	305	LG3	G	130	2	Monza
1979	-	DNB	305	LG3	G	130	2	Monza
1979	-	DNC	305	LG3	G	130	2	Monza
1979	-	DND	305	LG3	G	130	2	Monza
1979	-	DNF	305	LG3	G	135	2	Firebird
1979	-	DNG	305	LG3	G	130	2	G
1979	-	DNH	305	LG3	G	130	2	Camaro
1979	-	DNJ	305	LG3	G	130	2	Firebird
1979	-	DNK	305	LG3	G	130	2	F
1979	-	DNL	305	LG3	G	130	2	full size
1979	-	DNM	305	LG3	G	130	2	full size
1979	-	DNR	305	LG3	G	130	2	full size
1979	-	DNS	305	LG4	H	160	4	G
1979	-	DNT	305	LG4	H	160	4	G
1979	-	DNU	305	LG4	H	160	4	G
1979	-	DNW	305	LG4	H	160	4	G
1979	-	DNX	305	LG4	H	160	4	G
1979	-	DNY	305	LG4	H	160	4	G
1979	-	DNZ	305	LG3	G	130	2	-
1968	-	DO	307	manual trans.	-	200	-	full size
1959	-	DP	283	Powerglide	-	250	FI	cars & truck
1968	-	DP	307	m/t, 4 spd, SS	-	200	-	full size
1968	-	DQ	307	-	-	200	2	B
1968	-	DR	307	-	-	200	2	B
1979	-	DRA	350	auto trans.	L LM1	170	4	full size
1983	-	DRA	305	O.D. auto trans.	H LG4	155	4	Parisien
1979	-	DRB	350	auto trans.	L LM1	170	4	full size
1979	-	DRC	350	auto trans.	L LM1	170	4	Camaro
1979	-	DRD	350	auto trans.	L LM1	170	4	Camaro
1979	-	DRF	350	auto trans.	L LM1	170	4	Camaro
1979	-	DRH	350	auto trans.	L LM1	170	4	F B
1979	-	DRJ	350	auto trans.	L LM1	170	4	F B
1979	-	DRK	350	auto trans.	L LM1	170	4	full size
1979	-	DRL	350	auto trans.	L LM1	170	4	full size
1979	-	DRW	350	auto trans.	L LM1	170	4	F
1979	-	DRY	350	auto trans.	L LM1	170	4	F B X G
1979	-	DRZ	350	auto trans.	L LM1	170	4	full size
1968	-	DS	307	tur hydramatic	-	-	-	full size
1983	-	DSC	305	O.D. auto trans.	H	-	4	Parisien
1979	-	DTA	305	a/t	H LG4	160	4	G
1979	-	DTB	305	a/t	H LG4	160	4	-
1979	-	DTC	305	a/t	G LG3	130	2	police
1979	-	DTD	305	a/t	G LG3	130	2	B
1979	-	DTF	305	a/t	H LG4	160	4	G
1979	-	DTH	305	a/t Police/taxi	H LG4	160	4	G
1979	-	DTJ	305	a/t Police/taxi	H LG4	160	4	G
1979	-	DTK	305	m/t	G LG3	130	2	G
1979	-	DTL	305	a/t	G LG3	130	2	Monza
1979	-	DTM	305	m/t	G LG3	130	2	F X

first year	last year	stamp RPO	cid	application	VIN	h/p	bbls	body styles
1979	-	DTR	305	a/t	G LG3	130	2	F
1979	-	DTS	305	a/t	H LG4	160	4	G
1979	-	DTU	305	a/t	H LG4	160	4	G
1979	-	DTX	305	a/t	H LG4	160	4	G
1979	-	DTY	305	auto trans.	G LG3	130	2	full size
1979	-	DTZ	305	auto trans.	G LG3	130	2	full size
1983	-	DUA	305	T.B.I.	S	-	-	Parisien
1983	-	DUA	305	LU5, twin T. B.I.	7	165	TBI	Z-28/T/A
1979	-	DUB	350	auto trans.	L LM1	170	4	full size
1979	-	DUC	350	auto trans.	L LM1	170	4	full size
1983	-	DUC	350	a/t	6	200	4	police/special
1979	-	DUD	350	auto trans.	L LM1	170	4	police/high perf.
1979	-	DUF	350	auto trans.	L LM1	170	4	G
1979	-	DUH	350	auto trans.	L LM1	170	4	G
1979	-	DUJ	350	auto trans.	L LM1	165	4	G
1983	-	DUK	305	LU5, twin T.B.I.	7	165	TBI	Firebird
1983	-	DUK	305	O.D. auto trans.	H LG4	160	4	Parisien
1983	-	DVA	305	O.D. auto trans.	H LG4	160	4	Parisien
1979	-	DWA	305	O.D. auto trans.	H LG4	160	4	G
1979	-	DWB	305	O.D. auto trans.	H LG4	160	4	G
1983	-	DWT	305	LU5, twin T.B.I.	7	165	TBI	Firebird
1979	-	DXA	305	auto trans.	G LG3	130	2	full size
1968	-	DZ	302	Z-28, late prod	Z28	290	4	F
1969	-	DZ	302	m/t, 4 spd	Z28	290	4	F
1957	59	E	283	manual trans.	-	185	2	Vette/truck
1960	62	E	283	turglide	-	170	2	B Y/truck
1957	-	EA	283	-	-	-	8	full size
1965	67	EA	327	manual trans.	-	250	-	A X
1957	-	EB	283	hi lift cam	-	-	8	full size
1958	60	EB	283	turglide	-	230	4	truck/1271
1965	67	EB	327	high performance	-	300	-	Chevelle
1957	59	EC	283	turglide	-	-	FI	B/truck
1965	66	EC	327	Special high perf.	-	300	4	Chevelle
1966	67	EC	327	A.I.R., glide	-	275	4	Chevelle/1200
1958	59	ED	283	turglide, air susp.	-	-	-	full size
1965	-	ED	327	transistor ign.	-	-	-	Chevelle
1967	68	ED	327	m/t, h.d. clutch	-	275	4	Chevelle
1965	67	EE	327	Powerglide	-	250	4	Chevelle
1968	-	EE	327	Powerglide	-	275	4	A X
1969	-	EE	350	Powerglide	-	255	-	El Cam
1957	59	EF	283	m/t, 3 spd	-	220	4	Vette
1958	59	EF	283	turglide, air susp.	-	-	4	full size/1200
1965	-	EF	327	Powerglide, hi perf.	-	300	4	Chevelle
1957	-	EG	265	2 4b,hi-lft cam,m/t	-	270	8	Vette
1959	-	EG	283	turglide, a/c	-	-	-	full size
1960	-	EG	283	turglide	-	170	2	truck/1100
1957	-	EH	265	twin 4 barrel, m/t	-	245	8	Vette
1959	-	EH	283	turg,air susp., a/c	-	-	-	full size
1968	-	EH	327	manual trans.	-	250	4	El Cam
1968	-	EI	327	Powerglide	-	250	4	Chevelle
1968	-	EI	327	Powerglide	-	275	4	El Cam
1957	-	EJ	283	-	-	-	FI	full size
1959	-	EJ	283	turglide, a/c	-	-	4	full size
1959	60	EJ	283	turglide	-	230	4	truck/1100
1968	-	EJ	327	m/t, h.d. clutch	-	275	4	Chevelle/3200

first year	last year	stamp RPO	cid	application	VIN	h/p	bbls	body styles
1957	-	EK	283	hi lift cam	-	-	FI	full size
1959	-	EK	283	turg, air susp., a/c	-	-	4	full size
1957	-	EL	283	m/t, 3 sp, h/l cam	-	283	FI	Vette
1957	-	EM	283	m/t, 3 spd	-	250	FI	Vette
1968	-	EO	327	m/t, h.d. clutch	-	275	4	Chevelle
1967	68	EP	327	spec. hi perf., m/t	-	325	4	A X
1967	-	EQ	327	m/t, h.d. clutch	-	275	4	Chevelle/Camaro
1967	-	ER	327	s h/p, A.I.R., H.D. c	-	325	4	Chevelle
1967	68	ES	327	sp hi perf, H.D. clu	-	325	4	Chevelle
1955	56	F	265	Powerglide	-	-	2	car
1957	-	F	283	Powerglide	-	-	2	cars & Vette
1956	-	FA	265	m/t	-	155	2	truck/3100
1957	-	FA	283	Powerglide, a/c	-	-	-	car
1969	-	FA	327	manual trans.	-	235	2	full size
1955	56	FB	265	Power Pack, glide	-	155	4	car & truck
1969	-	FB	327	Powerglide	-	235	2	full size
1955	-	FC	265	Powerglide, a/c	-	-	-	car
1957	-	FC	283	Powerglide	-	-	4	car
1969	-	FC	327	tur hydro trans.	-	235	2	B F
1955	56	FD	265	glide, 2 exh ,a/c	-	180	4	car
1957	-	FD	283	Powerglide	-	-	8	car
1957	-	FE	283	Powerglide, a/c	-	220	4	cars & truck
1955	-	FE	265	m/t	-	145	2	truck/3600
1955	-	FEA	265	m/t	-	145	2	truck/3600
1957	-	FEA	265	m/t	-	245	8	truck/1500
1955	-	FEB	265	m/t	-	145	2	truck/3800
1957	-	FEB	283	m/t	-	270	8	truck/1500
1957	-	FEC	283	m/t, O.D.	-	220	2	truck/1500
1957	-	FEJ	283	m/t	-	250	FI	truck/1500
1957	-	FEK	283	m/t	-	283	FI	truck/1500
1955	56	FF	265	a/t	-	162	2	truck/1500
1957	-	FF	283	Powerglide	-	185	2	truck/1500
1957	-	FFA	283	Powerglide	-	185	2	truck/1500
1955	-	FFB	265	a/t	-	180	4	truck/1500
1956	-	FFB	265	a/t	-	205	4	truck/1500
1955	56	FFC	265	a/t	-	162	2	truck/1500
1957	-	FFC	283	Powerglide	-	220	4	truck/1500
1955	-	FFD	265	a/t	-	180	4	truck/1500
1956	-	FFD	265	a/t	-	205	4	truck/1500
1957	-	FFD	283	Powerglide	-	245	8	truck/1500
1957	-	FFE	283	Powerglide	-	220	4	truck/1500
1957	-	FFJ	283	Powerglide	-	250	FI	truck/1500
1955	-	FG	265	Powerglide	-	162	2	cars
1955	-	FG	265	Powerglide	-	195	4	Vette
1955	-	FG	265	m/t	-	162	2	truck/1500
1956	-	FG	265	Powerglide	-	225	4	Vette
1956	-	FG	265	m/t	-	162	2	truck/1500
1957	-	FG	283	glide, 2 4b, a/t	-	245	8	Vette
1957	-	FG	283	turglide	-	185	2	truck/1500
1969	-	FG	327	-	-	-	-	police/full size
1955	-	FGC	265	m/t, O.D.	-	162	2	truck/1500
1956	-	FGC	265	m/t, O.D.	-	205	4	truck/1500
1957	-	FGC	283	turglide	-	220	4	truck/1500
1955	-	FGD	265	m/t	-	180	4	truck/1500
1957	-	FGD	283	turglide	-	245	4	truck/1500

first year	last year	stamp RPO	cid	application	VIN	h/p	bbls	body styles
1955	-	FGE	265	m/t, O.D.	-	180	4	truck/1500
1956	-	FGE	265	m/t, O.D.	-	205	4	truck/1500/Camaro
1955	56	FGF	265	m/t	-	162	2	truck/1500
1957	-	FGF	283	turglide	-	250	FI	truck/1500
1955	-	FGG	265	m/t	-	180	4	truck/1500
1955	-	FGJ	265	m/t	-	162	2	truck/1500
1956	-	FGJ	265	m/t	-	180	4	truck/1500
1955	56	FGK	265	m/t	-	162	2	truck/1500-3800
1955	-	FGL	265	m/t	-	180	4	truck/1500-3800
1956	-	FGL	265	m/t	-	205	4	truck/1500 & 3200
1955	-	FGM	265	m/t	-	180	4	truck/1500
1956	-	FGM	265	m/t	-	205	4	truck/1500
1957	-	FH	283	Powerglide	-	220	4	Vette
1969	-	FH	327	tur hydro trans.	-	235	2	B F
1957	-	FJ	283	Powerglide, a/t	-	250	FI	cars & Vette
1969	-	FJ	327	m/t	-	210	2	B F/Vette
1957	-	FK	265	Powerglide	-	-	FI	Vette
1969	-	FK	327	Powerglide	-	210	2	full size
1969	-	FL	327	tur 350	-	210	2	full size
1957	-	FLA	265	m/t	-	162	2	truck/3100/police
1957	-	FLB	265	H.D. m/t	-	162	2	truck/3100
1956	-	FM	265	m/t	-	155	2	truck/3100
1956	-	FMA	265	m/t	-	155	2	truck/3600
1956	-	FMB	265	m/t	-	155	2	truck/3800
1969	-	FY	327	m/t, taxi	-	-	-	full size
1969	-	FZ	327	Powerglide, taxi	-	-	-	full size
1955	56	G	265	man trans, 3 spd	-	-	-	cars
1957	-	G	283	turglide	-	-	2	full size
1965	67	GA	283	3 spd trans. std	-	195	2	full size
1969	-	GB	327	tur 400, taxi	-	195	2	full size
1955	57	GC	265	overdrive	-	-	-	-
1965	67	GC	283	m/t, 4 sp, H.D. chass	-	195	2	full size
1957	-	GD	283	turglide	-	-	8	car
1956	-	GE	265	o/d, Power Pack	-	205	-	car
1969	-	GE	350	Powerglide	-	-	-	full size
1955	56	GF	265	m/t, 3 spd, a/c	-	-	-	-
1957	-	GF	283	turglide	-		FI	car
1965	67	GF	283	Powerglide	-	195	2	full size
1955	56	GJ	265	H.D. clutch	-	-	-	-
1955	56	GK	265	H.D. clutch, a/c	-	-	-	car
1965	67	GK	283	a/c	-	195	4	full size
1955	56	GL	265	Power Pack, m/t	-	-	4	car
1965	66	GL	283	glide	-	-	4	full size
1955	56	GM	265	Pwr Pack, a/c, m/t	-	-	4	car
1955	56	GN	265	Pwr Pack, o/d, a/c	-	-	4	car
1967	-	GO	283	glide, A.I.R.	-	195	2	full size/Camaro
1955	56	GQ	265	o/d, a/c	-	-	-	car
1955	-	GR	265	m/t, 3 spd	-	195	4	Vette
1956	-	GR	265	m/t, 3 spd	-	225	8	Vette
1966	67	GS	283	4 spd, air cond.	-	195	2	full size/Camaro
1966	-	GT	283	A.I.R., glide	-	195	2	full size
1967	-	GU	283	m/t, H.D. clutch	-	240	8	cars/Vette/Camaro
1956	-	GV	265	Powerglide	-	210	4	Vette
1966	-	GW	283	-	-	-	4	full size
1966	-	GX	283	A.I.R.	-	-	4	full size/Camaro

first year	last year	stamp RPO	cid	application	VIN	h/p	bbls	body styles
1966	-	GZ	283	A.I.R., glide	-	-	4	full size
1965	68	HA	327	4 spd tran. std	-	275	4	full size/Camaro
1969	-	HA	350	manual trans.	-	300	4	A F X
1965	66	HB	327	std trans., hi perf.	-	300	4	full size
1967	-	HB	327	A.I.R.	-	275	4	full size/Camaro
1968	-	HB	327	H.D. clutch	-	275	4	full size
1969	-	HB	350	tur hydro trans.	-	300	4	A F X
1965	68	HC	327	Powerglide	-	275	4	full size
1969	-	HC	350	m/t	-	250	2	A F X
1965	-	HD	327	Powerglide, h/p	-	-	-	full size
1966	67	HD	327	a/c, spec high perf.	-	350	4	Vette
1969	-	HD	350	tur hydro trans.	-	250	2	A F X
1965	68	HE	327	m/t	-	300	4	Vette
1969	-	HE	350	Powerglide	-	300	4	A F X
1965	-	HF	327	h/p	-	300	4	Vette
1966	68	HF	327	Powerglide, A.I.R.	-	275	4	full size
1969	-	HF	350	Powerglide	-	275	2	A F X
1978	-	HF	350	LM1	L	170	4	Firebird
1965	-	HG	327	fuel inject, m/t	-	375	FI	Vette
1968	69	HG	327	Powerglide	-	250	2	full size
1969	-	HG	350	manual trans.	-	300	4	full size
1965	-	HH	327	s h/p, m/t	-	365	4	Vette
1966	67	HH	327	air inj. reactor	-	300	4	Vette
1969	-	HH	350	tur 400	-	300	4	full size
1965	-	HI	327	a/c, m/t	-	250	4	Vette
1968	-	HI	327	m/t	-	250	4	full size
1969	-	HI	350	-	-	250	2	full size/Phoenix
1965	-	HJ	327	h/p, a/c, m/t	-	300	4	Vette
1968	-	HJ	327	Powerglide	-	250	4	full size
1969	-	HJ	327	tur 400	-	250	2	full size
1969	-	HJ	350	tur 400	-	250	2	full size
1978	-	HJ	350	LM1	L	170	4	Firebird
1965	-	HK	327	s h/p, a/c, m/t	-	365	4	Vette
1968	69	HK	327	Powerglide	-	250	4	full size
1969	-	HK	350	Powerglide	-	300	4	full size
1965	-	HL	327	trans ign, m/t	-	365	4	Vette
1968	-	HL	327	m/t, H.D. clutch	-	250	4	full size
1969	-	HL	350	Powerglide	-	250	2	full size
1978	-	HL	350	LM1	L	170	4	Firebird
1965	-	HM	327	a/c, trans ign, m/t	-	365	4	Vette/Chevy II
1968	69	HM	327	tur hydramatic	-	250	4	full size
1969	-	HM	350	a/t	-	250	2	full size/Chevy II
1965	-	HN	327	t/ign., m/t	-	375	FI	Vette
1968	-	HN	327	Pwrglide, reg gas	-	-	4	full size/Chevy II
1969	-	HN	327	tur 350	-	-	-	full size
1969	-	HN	350	tur hydramatic	-	300	4	full size
1965	68	HO	327	Powerglide	-	300	4	Vette
1969	-	HO	350	-	-	300	4	B
1965	68	HP	327	Powerglide, h/p	-	300	4	Vette
1969	-	HP	350	m/t	-	300	4	A B F X
1965	-	HQ	327	Powerglide, a/c	-	250	4	Vette
1969	-	HQ	350	manual trans.	-	300	4	A F X
1965	67	HR	327	Pwrglide, h/p, a/c	-	300	4	Vette
1969	-	HR	350	Powerglide	-	255	4	A F X
1978	-	HR	350	LM1	L	170	4	Firebird

first year	last year	stamp RPO	cid	application	VIN	h/p	bbls	body styles
1969	-	HS	350	tur 350	-	255	4	A F X
1965	67	HT	327	s h/p, hyd lift, m/t	-	350	4	Vette
1969	-	HT	350	manual trans.	-	255	4	full size
1965	-	HU	327	h/p, hylft, a/c, m/t	-	350	4	Vette
1969	-	HU	350	Powerglide	-	255	4	full size
1965	-	HV	327	h/p, hylif, t/ig, m/t	-	350	4	Vette
1965	67	HW	327	s/hp, hl, ti, ac, m/t	-	350	4	Vette
1969	-	HW	350	hi perf eng, m/t	-	350	4	Vette
1969	-	HX	350	high perf, a/c, m/t	-	350	4	Vette
1969	-	HY	350	tur 350	-	300	4	B
1969	-	HY	350	m/t 4 spd	-	300	4	Vette
1969	-	HZ	350	tur 400	-	300	4	Vette
1969	-	IA	350	tur 400	-	255	4	full size
1966	68	ID	327	spec. high perf.	-	-	4	full size
1969	-	IL	350	man trans., taxi	-	-	2	full size
1969	-	IM	350	Powerglide, taxi	-	-	2	full size
1969	-	IN	350	tur 350, taxi	-	-	2	full size
1969	-	IP	350	tur 400, taxi	-	-	2	full size
1969	-	IQ	350	m/t, police, taxi	-	-	4	full size
1969	-	IR	350	m/t, police, taxi	-	-	4	full size
1969	-	IS	350	glide, taxi, pol.	-	-	4	full size
1969	-	IT	350	tur 350, taxi	-	-	4	full size
1969	-	IV	350	tur 400, taxi	-	-	4	full size
1969	-	IW	350	man trans., taxi	-	-	4	full size
1969	-	IX	350	glide, taxi, pol.	-	-	4	full size
1969	-	IY	350	tur 350, taxi	-	-	4	full size
1969	-	IZ	350	tur 400, taxi	-	-	4	full size
1964	-	J	283	man trans., 3 spd	-	195	2	A B
1964	-	JA	283	man trans., 4 spd	-	195	2	Chevelle
1964	-	JD	283	Powerglide	-	195	2	Chevelle
1964	-	JG	283	Powerglide	-	220	4	Chevelle
1964	-	JH	283	man trans., 3 spd	-	220	4	Chevelle
1964	-	JQ	327	man trans.	-	250	4	Chevelle
1964	-	JR	327	m/t, high perf.	-	300	4	Chevelle
1964	-	JS	327	m/t, spec. hi perf.	-	-	-	Chevelle
1964	-	JT	327	m/t, trans ign	-	250	4	Chevelle
1967	-	KE	327	m/t, 4 spd	-	275	4	full size
1966	67	KH	327	s h/p, A.I.R., a/c	-	350	4	Vette
1967	-	KL	327	tur 350	-	275	4	full size
1967	-	KM	327	a/t, A.I.R.	-	275	4	full size
1958	64	M	283	m/t	-	160	2	trucks
1958	62	MA	283	H.D. m/t	-	160	2	trucks
1963	64	MA	283	Powerglide	-	175	2	trucks
1967	68	MA	327	manual trans.	-	210	2	Camaro
1958	-	MB	283	m/t	-	160	2	trucks
1967	-	MB	327	a/c, A.I.R.	-	210	2	Camaro
1968	-	MB	307	manual trans.	-	200	2	Nova
1968	-	MC	307	-	-	200	2	Nova
1978	-	MC	350	LM1	L	170	4	LeMans
1967	-	MD	283	4 spd trans.	-	-	2	Camaro
1968	-	MD	307	-	-	200	2	Nova
1967	68	ME	327	Powerglide	-	210	2	Camaro
1967	-	MF	327	Powerglide, A.I.R.	-	-	2	Camaro
1967	-	MJ	283	Powerglide	-	-	2	Camaro
1967	68	MK	327	manual trans	-	275	4	F X

first year	last year	stamp RPO	cid	application	VIN	h/p	bbls	body styles
1967	-	ML	327	air cond.	-	275	4	F X
1968	-	ML	327	s h/p	-	325	4	Chevy II
1967	-	MM	327	Powerglide	-	275	4	Camaro
1968	-	MM	327	Powerglide	-	275	4	Chevy II/K-20
1967	-	MN	327	Powerglide, A.I.R.	-	275	4	Camaro
1968	-	MN	350	-	-	295	4	Nova
1968	-	MO	302	m/t ,4 spd	Z28	290	4	Camaro
1967	-	MP	283	A.I.R.	-	-	4	Camaro
1967	-	MP	302	Z-28, w/A.I.R.	-	290	4	Camaro
1967	68	MS	350	m/t	-	295	4	F X
1967	-	MT	350	A.I.R.	-	295	4	Camaro/Chevy II
1967	68	MU	350	Powerglide	-	295	4	F X
1967	-	MV	350	glide, A.I.R.	-	295	4	Camaro
1964	-	MX	283	m/t	-	175	2	trucks
1964	-	MY	283	Powerglide	-	175	2	trucks
1978	-	O3N	305	LG3	U	135	2	Firebird
1978	-	O3T	350	LM1	L	170	4	Firebird
1965	66	PB	283	glide, a/c	-	-	4	Chevy II
1965	67	PD	283	m/t	-	-	-	Chevy II
1965	66	PE	283	-	-	195	2	Chevy II
1965	67	PF	283	a/c	-	-	-	Chevy II
1965	67	PF	283	air conditioning	-	-	-	Nova
1965	67	PG	283	a/c	-	-	4	Chevy II
1978	-	PH	305	LG3	U	145	2	Pontiac
1965	66	PK	283	Powerglide	-	-	4	Chevy II
1965	67	PL	283	m/t, 4 speed	-	195	2	Chevy II
1965	67	PM	283	m/t, 4 speed, a/c	-	195	2	Chevy II
1965	67	PN	283	Powerglide	-	195	2	Chevy II
1965	66	PO	283	Powerglide	-	-	4	Chevy II
1965	67	PP	283	Powerglide, a/c	-	195	2	Chevy II
1965	67	PQ	283	a/c, Powerglide	-	195	2	Chevy II
1966	-	PS	283	a/c, 4 spd, A.I.R.	-	195	2	Chevy II
1966	67	PU	283	Pwrglide, a/c, EM	-	195	2	Chevy II
1979	-	PX4	305	a/t, LG3	G	150	2	Firebird
1979	-	PX6	305	a/t, LG3	G	150	2	Firebird
1979	-	PXP	305	a/t, LG3	G	150	2	Firebird
1979	-	PXR	305	a/t, LG3	G	150	2	Firebird
1978	-	PZ	305	LG3	U	145	2	Pontiac
1966	-	QA	283	glide, A.I.R., a/c	-	-	-	Chevy II
1962	-	QB	327	-	-	-	8	Vette
1966	-	QB	283	a/c	-	-	4	Chevy II
1966	-	QC	283	A.I.R.	-	-	4	Chevy II
1966	-	QE	283	glide, A.I.R., a/c	-	-	4	Chevy II
1966	-	QF	283	A.I.R., a/c, 4 spd	-	-	4	Chevy II
1962	64	R	327	m/t	-	-	-	full size
1962	63	RA	327	m/t, a/c	-	-	-	full size
1962	64	RB	327	h/p, m/t	-	-	-	full size
1962	64	RC	327	m/t	-	250	4	Vette
1962	64	RD	327	m/t, high perf.	-	300	4	Vette
1962	64	RE	327	m/t, spec. hi perf.	-	340	4	Vette
1962	64	RF	327	manual trans.	-	360	FI	Vette
1963	-	RK	327	m/t, hi perf, a/c	-	-	4	cars
1964	-	RP	327	m/t, a/c	-	250	4	Vette
1964	-	RQ	327	m/t ,a/c, hi perf	-	300	4	Vette
1964	-	RR	327	m/t, a/c, s hi perf	-	365	4	Vette

first year	last year	stamp RPO	cid	application	VIN	h/p	bbls	body styles
1964	-	RT	327	m/t, t/ign.	-	365	4	Vette
1964	-	RU	327	m/t, a/c, trans ign	-	365	4	Vette
1978	-	RU	305	LG3	-	145	2	LeMans
1964	-	RX	327	m/t, trans ign	-	375	FI	Vette
1962	64	S	327	Powerglide	-	-	-	full size
1962	63	SA	327	Powerglide, a/c	-	-	-	full size
1962	64	SB	327	h/p, Powerglide	-	300	4	full size
1962	64	SC	327	Powerglide	-	250	4	Vette
1962	64	SD	327	glide, s hi perf.	-	350	4	Vette
1984	-	SDA	305	Roch E4ME carb.	H LG4	150	4	F B G
1987	-	SDB	305	Roch E4ME carb.	H LG4	150	4	Firebird
1987	-	SDD	305	LB9	F	190	TPI	Firebird
1984	-	SDH	305	Roch E4ME carb.	H LG4	150	4	F B G
1984	-	SDJ	305	Roch E4ME carb.	H LG4	150	4	F B G
1987	-	SDK	305	LB9	F	190	TPI	Firebird
1984	-	SDN	305	Roch E4ME carb.	H LG4	150	4	F B G
1984	-	SDR	305	Roch E4ME carb.	H LG4	150	4	F B G
1984	-	SDU	305	Roch E4ME carb.	H LG4	150	4	F B G/Z-28/T/A
1987	-	SFD	305	LB9	F	190	TPI	Firbd/Z-28/T/A/B
1987	-	SFS	305	LB9	F	190	TPI	Firbd/Z-28/T/A/B
1963	-	SG	327	glide, h/p, a/c	-	300	4	cars/Z-28/T/A/B
1964	-	SK	327	Powerglide, a/c	-	250	4	Vette
1964	-	SL	327	glide, a/c, hi perf.	-	300	4	Vette
1987	-	SNA	350	L98, a/t	8	225	TPI	Firebird
1987	-	SNJ	350	L98, a/t	8	225	TPI	Firebird
1964	-	SR	327	Powerglide	-	250	-	Chevelle/3200
1987	-	SRL	305	LB9	F	190	TPI	Firebird
1964	-	SS	327	Pwrglide, hi perf.	-	300	4	Chevelle
1984	-	SUF	305	L69, H.O.	G	190	4	Firebird
1984	-	SUF	305	HO E4ME carb	G L69	190	4	Monte SS
1984	-	SUH	305	HO E4ME carb	G L69	190	4	Monte SS
1984	-	SUJ	305	HO E4ME carb	G L69	190	4	Monte SS
1984	-	SXA	305	HO E4ME carb	G L69	190	4	Monte SS
1985	-	T9N	305	Roch E4ME carb.	H	-	4	F B
1985	-	T9P	305	Roch E4ME carb.	H	-	4	F B
1985	-	T9R	305	Roch E4ME carb.	H	-	4	F B
1985	-	T9S	305	Roch E4ME carb.	H	-	4	F B
1956	-	TA	265	m/t	-	155	2	truck/3100
1956	-	TAA	265	m/t	-	155	2	truck/3600
1971	-	TAA	350	convcab, van, bus	-	255	4	C-10 to 3500
1956	-	TAB	265	m/t	-	155	2	truck 3800
1971	-	TAB	350	convcab, van, bus	-	255	4	C-10 to 3500
1972	-	TAD	307	convcab, m/t	-	135	2	K-10 & 20
1970	71	TAH	307	cnv&fwd cabs, a/t	-	200	2	C-20 & 2500
1972	-	TAH	307	cnv&fwd cabs, a/t	-	135	2	C-10 to 2500
1970	-	TAI	307	Powerglide	-	200	2	C-10
1970	-	TAI	307	cnvfwd cabs, glide	-	200	2	C-10 & 1500
1970	71	TAJ	307	cnvfwd cabs, glide	-	200	2	C-10
1972	-	TAJ	307	conv. cab, t350	-	135	2	K-10 & 20 & 3200
1970	-	TAK	307	conv. cab, t350	-	200	2	C-10 & 1500
1972	-	TAK	307	van & bus	-	135	2	C 10
1970	-	TAL	307	convcab, a/t	-	200	2	C-20 to 3500
1972	-	TAL	307	van & bus	-	135	2	C 10
1970	-	TAM	307	m/t	-	200	2	C-20
1970	-	TAN	307	convcab, m/t, 3 spd	-	200	2	K-20 & 2500

first year	last year	stamp RPO	cid	application	VIN	h/p	bbls	body styles
1970	-	TAO	307	convcab, a/t	-	200	2	K-10 & 1500
1970	-	TAP	307	convcab, a/t	-	200	2	K-20 & 2500
1970	-	TAR	307	convcab, m/t	-	200	2	C-20 to 3500
1970	-	TAS	307	convcab, m/t	-	200	2	C-10 & 1500
1970	-	TAT	307	convcab, m/t, 3 spd	-	200	2	K-10 & 1500
1970	-	TAU	350	m/t	-	255	4	C-10
1970	-	TAV	350	m/t, 3 spd	-	255	4	C-20
1970	-	TAW	307	m/t, 3 spd	-	200	2	K-20
1970	71	TAX	350	convfwd cabs, a/t	-	255	4	C-10 to 3500
1972	-	TAX	350	m/t	-	175	4	C-10
1970	-	TAY	350	convcab, t350	-	255	4	K-10 to 2500
1972	-	TAY	350	m/t	-	175	4	C-20
1970	-	TAZ	350	convfwd cab, glide	-	215	2	C-10 & 20
1956	-	TB	265	a/t	-	155	2	truck/3100
1956	-	TBA	265	a/t	-	155	2	truck/3600
1970	-	TBA	350	convfwd cabs, t350	-	215	2	C-10, 20, 30
1971	-	TBA	350	convfwd cabs, m/t	-	255	4	C-10 to 3500
1979	-	TBA	350	convcab, m/t, fed	L LS9	165	4	C-10 & 1500
1956	-	TBB	265	a/t	-	155	2	truck/3800
1970	-	TBB	350	cv/fd cab, m/t 3sp	-	255	4	C-10 to 3500
1979	-	TBB	350	convcab,m/t, fed	L LS9	165	4	C-10 to 2500
1970	71	TBC	350	convfwd cabs, a/t	-	255	4	C-10 to 3500
1970	-	TBC	350	m/t, 3 spd	-	255	4	K-10 & 20
1979	-	TBC	350	conv. cab, m/t,f ed	L LS9	165	4	C-10 to 2500
1970	71	TBD	350	convfwd cab, m/t	-	255	4	C-10, 20, 30
1971	-	TBD	350	conv. & fwd cabs	-	255	4	K-10 to 2500
1979	-	TBD	350	conv. cab,m/t, fed	L LS9	165	4	K-10 to 2500
1970	-	TBE	307	m/t, 3 spd	-	200	2	K-10
1970	71	TBF	350	convfwd cab, m/t	-	255	4	C-10, 20, 30
1979	-	TBF	350	convcab, a/t, fed	L LS9	165	4	K-10, 15, 20
1971	-	TBG	350	convcab, a/t	-	255	4	K-10 to 2500
1971	-	TBH	350	convcab, m/t	-	215	2	C-10, 20, 30
1979	-	TBH	350	bus & vans	L LS9	165	4	C-10 & 1500
1971	-	TBJ	350	Powerglide	-	250	4	trucks
1979	-	TBJ	350	conv., van, bus,m/t	L LS9	165	4	C-20 to 3500
1982	-	TBJ	305	conv., van, bus	H LE9	-	4	C-10 to 2500
1971	-	TBK	350	turhydro	-	250	4	trucks
1979	-	TBK	350	conv., van, bus, a/t	L LS9	165	4	C-20 to 3500
1982	-	TBK	305	conv., van, bus	H LE9	-	4	C-10 to 2500
1972	-	TBL	350	conv. cab, m/t	-	175	4	C-10 & 20
1979	-	TBL	350	conv., van, bus, m/t	L LS9	165	4	C-20 to 3500
1982	-	TBL	350	conv., van, bus	L LS9	165	4	C-10 to 3500
1970	71	TBM	307	conv., van, bus	-	200	2	C-10 & 1500
1979	-	TBM	350	conv., van, bus, a/t	L LS9	165	4	C-20 to 3500/Phoenix
1982	-	TBM	305	conv., van, bus	H LE9	-	4	C-10 to 2500
1970	71	TBN	307	conv., van, bus	-	200	2	C-10 & 1500
1979	-	TBR	350	C:mt, K:at, cnvcab	L LS9	165	4	C-10-20, K-15 & 25
1979	-	TBR	350	conv., van, bus, at, Cal	L LS9	155	4	C-10-2500, K-10/1500
1982	-	TBR	305	conv., van, bus cab	H LE9	-	4	C-10 to 2500
1970	71	TBS	307	van & bus	-	200	2	C-10, 15, 20
1979	-	TBS	350	mtC10/20 at C20/25	L LS9	155	4	C-10 to 2500
1982	-	TBS	305	conv., van, bus cab	H LE9	-	4	C-10 to 2500/Phoenix
1979	-	TBT	350	a/t, Calif	L LS9	155	4	C-10 to 1500
1982	-	TBT	305	conv., van, bus cab	H LE9	-	4	C-10 to 2500
1970	-	TBU	350	van & bus	-	255	4	C-10 & 20

first year	last year	stamp RPO	cid	application	VIN	h/p	bbls	body styles
1979	-	TBU	350	convcab, m/t	L LS9	155	4	K-10 to 2500
1982	-	TBU	305	conv., van, bus cab	H LE9	-	4	C-10 to 2500
1970	71	TBV	350	van & bus	-	255	4	C-10, 20, 2500 to 3800
1982	-	TBV	305	conv., van, bus cab	H LE9	-	4	C-10 - 2500 to 3800
1979	-	TBW	350	conv. cab, m/t	L LS9	155	4	K-10, 1500, 20 to 3800
1982	-	TBW	305	conv., van, bus cab	H LE9	-	4	C-10 to 2500
1970	71	TBX	350	van & bus	-	255	4	C-10, 20, 2500,3500,3200
1979	-	TBX	350	conv. cab, a/t	L LS9	155	4	K-10 to 2500
1970	-	TBY	350	van & bus	-	255	4	C-10 & 20
1979	-	TBY	350	conv. cab, a/t	L LS9	155	4	K-10 to 2500
1970	71	TBZ	350	van & bus	-	255	4	C-10, 20, 2500, 3500
1979	-	TBZ	350	van,bus, Cal, m/t	L LS9	155	4	C-10 to 2500
1982	-	TBZ	305	conv., van, bus cab	H LE9	-	4	C-10 to 2500
1973	-	TCA	307	conv. cab	-	130	2	C-20 to 3500
1982	-	TCA	305	conv., van,.bus cab	H LE9	-	4	C-10 to 2500
1973	-	TCB	307	conv. cab	-	130	2	C-20 to 3500
1982	-	TCB	305	conv., van,.bus cab	H LE9	-	4	C-10 to 2500
1973	-	TCC	307	conv. cab	-	130	2	C-20 to 3500/LeMans
1982	-	TCC	305	conv., van,.bus cab	H LE9	-	4	C-10 to 2500
1973	-	TCD	307	conv. cab	-	130	2	C-20 to 3500
1982	-	TCD	305	conv., van,.bus cab	H LE9	-	4	C-10 to 2500
1957	-	TCE	265	m/t	-	162	2	truck/1500
1982	-	TCF	305	conv., van,bus cab	H LE9	-	4	C-10 to 2500/LeMans
1973	-	TCH	307	conv. cab, m/t	-	115	2	C-10 & 1500/LeMans
1978	-	TCHC	350	L LM1	-	170	4	Camaro/LeMans
1978	-	TCHS	350	L LM1	-	170	4	Camaro/LeMans
1978	-	TCHT	350	L LM1	-	170	4	Camaro/LeMans
1978	-	TCHU	350	L LM1	-	170	4	Camaro
1973	-	TCJ	307	conv. cab	-	115	2	C-10 & 1500
1973	-	TCK	307	fwrd cab	-	130	2	C-20 to 3500
1973	-	TCL	307	fwrd cab	-	130	2	C-20 to 3500
1982	-	TCL	305	conv., van, bus cab	H LE9	-	4	C-10 to 2500
1973	-	TCM	307	fwrd cab	-	130	2	C-20 to 3500
1982	-	TCM	305	conv., van, bus cab	H LE9	-	4	C-10 to 2500
1973	-	TCR	307	fwrd cab	-	130	2	C-20 to 3500
1982	-	TCR	305	conv., van, bus cab	H LE9	-	4	C-10 to 2500
1973	-	TCS	307	fwrd cab	-	130	2	C-20 to 3500
1982	-	TCS	305	conv., van, bus cab	H LE9	-	4	C-10 to 2500
1973	-	TCT	307	van & bus	-	130	2	C-10 to 1500
1982	-	TCT	305	conv., van, bus cab	H LE9	-	4	C-10 to 2500
1973	-	TCU	307	van & bus	-	130	2	C-10 to 1500
1982	-	TCU	305	conv., van, bus cab	H LE9	-	4	C-10 to 2500
1973	-	TCW	307	van & bus	-	130	2	C-10 to 1500
1982	-	TCW	305	conv., van, bus cab	H LE9	-	4	C-10 to 2500
1973	-	TCX	307	conv. cab	-	115	2	C-10 to 1500
1982	-	TCX	305	conv., van, bus cab	H LE9	-	4	C-10 to 2500
1973	-	TCY	307	conv. cab	-	115	2	C-10 to 1500
1982	-	TCY	305	conv., van, bus cab	H LE9	-	4	C-10 to 2500
1972	-	TDA	307	conv. cab, m/t	-	135	2	C-10 & 20
1980	-	TDA	350	conv. cab, a/t	L LS9	155	4	C-10 & 15
1972	-	TDB	307	conv. cab, m/t	-	135	2	K-10 & 20
1980	-	TDB	350	conv. cab, m/t	L LS9	155	4	C-10 & 1500
1972	-	TDD	307	conv. cab, m/t	-	175	4	C-10 & 20

first year	last year	stamp RPO	cid	application	VIN	h/p	bbls	body styles
1980	-	TDD	350	conv. cab, m/t	L LS9	155	4	C-20 & 2500
1980	-	TDF	350	conv. cab, a/t	L LS9	155	4	C-20 & 2500
1972	-	TDG	350	conv. cab	-	175	4	K-10 & 20
1972	-	TDG	350	m/t	-	175	4	K-10 & 20
1972	-	TDH	350	conv. cab, m/t	-	175	4	C-10, 20, 30
1980	-	TDH	350	conv. cab, m/t	L LS9	155	4	C-20 & 2500
1972	-	TDJ	350	conv. cab, a/t	-	175	4	C-10 & 20
1980	-	TDJ	350	van & bus, a/t	L LS9	155	4	C-10 to 2500
1972	-	TDK	350	conv. cab, a/t	-	175	4	C-10, 20, 30, K-10
1980	-	TDK	350	van & bus, m/t	L LS9	155	4	C-20 & 2500
1972	-	TDL	307	conv. cab, a/t	-	135	2	C-10 & 20
1980	-	TDL	350	van & bus, a/t	L LS9	155	4	C-20 & 2500
1980	-	TDM	350	conv. cab, m/t	L LS9	155	4	C-20 & 2500
1972	-	TDP	307	conv. cab, a/t	-	135	2	K-10 & 20
1972	-	TDR	350	conv. cab, a/t	-	175	4	K-10 & 20
1980	-	TDR	350	conv. cab, a/t, Cal	L LS9	155	4	C-10 & 1500
1972	-	TDT	307	van & bus	-	135	2	C-10 & 1500
1980	-	TDT	350	conv. cab, a/t, Cal	L LS9	155	4	C-20 & 2500
1980	-	TDU	350	conv. cab, m/t	L LS9	155	4	K-10 & 1500
1972	-	TDW	350	van & bus	-	175	4	C-10 to 3500
1980	-	TDW	350	conv. cab, a/t	L LS9	155	4	K-10 & 15, C-20 & 25
1972	-	TDX	307	van & bus	-	135	2	C-10 & 1500
1972	-	TDY	350	van & bus	-	175	4	C-10 to 3500
1973	-	TDY	350	conv. cab	-	155	4	C-10 to 2500
1980	-	TDY	350	van/bus, Cal, a/t	L LS9	155	4	C-20 & 25
1955	-	TE	265	m/t	-	145	2	truck/3600
1957	-	TE	265	m/t	-	220	2	truck/1500
1955	-	TEA	265	m/t	-	145	2	truck/3600
1957	-	TEA	283	m/t	-	245	8	truck/1500
1955	-	TEB	265	m/t	-	145	2	truck/3800
1957	-	TEB	283	m/t	-	270	8	truck/1500
1957	-	TEC	283	m/t, O.D.	-	220	2	truck/1500
1957	-	TEJ	283	m/t	-	250	FI	truck/1500
1957	-	TEK	283	m/t	-	283	FI	truck/1500
1955	56	TF	265	a/t	-	162	2	truck/1500
1957	-	TF	283	Powerglide	-	185	2	truck/1500
1957	-	TFA	283	Powerglide	-	185	2	truck/1500
1972	-	TFA	350	van & bus	-	175	4	C-10, 20, 30
1980	-	TFA	350	conv. cab, m/t	L LS9	155	4	C-10 & 1500
1982	-	TFA	350	van & bus	L LS9	155	4	C-10 to 3500
1955	-	TFB	265	a/t	-	180	4	truck/1500
1956	-	TFB	265	a/t	-	205	4	truck/1500
1972	-	TFB	350	van & bus	-	175	4	C-10, 20, 30
1980	-	TFB	350	van & bus, m/t	L LS9	155	4	C-10 & 1500
1982	-	TFB	350	conv. cab	L LS9	155	4	C-10 to 2500
1955	56	TFC	265	a/t	-	162	2	truck/1500
1957	-	TFC	283	Powerglide	-	220	4	truck/1500
1982	-	TFC	350	conv., van & bus	L LS9	155	4	C-10 to 3500
1955	-	TFD	265	a/t	-	180	4	truck/1500
1956	-	TFD	265	a/t	-	205	4	truck/1500
1957	-	TFD	283	Powerglide	-	245	8	truck/1500
1972	-	TFD	350	conv.. cab, a/t	-	175	4	C-10 & 20
1982	-	TFD	350	conv., van & bus	L LS9	155	4	C-10 to 3500
1957	-	TFE	283	Powerglide	-	220	4	truck/1500
1982	-	TFF	350	conv., van & bus	L LS9	155	4	C-10 to 3500

113

first year	last year	stamp RPO	cid	application	VIN	h/p	bbls	body styles
1972	-	TFH	350	conv. cab, m/t	-	175	4	C & K: 10 & 20
1980	-	TFH	350	conv. cab, m/t	L LS9	155	-	C-20 to 3500
1957	-	TFJ	283	Powerglide	-	250	FI	truck/1500
1972	-	TFJ	350	conv. cab, a/t	-	175	4	C & K: 10 & 20
1979	-	TFJ	350	van, bus, a/t, Cal	L LS9	155	4	C-10 to 3500
1982	-	TFJ	350	conv., van & bus	L LS9	155	4	C-10 to 3500
1979	-	TFK	350	van, bus, m/t, Cal	L LS9	155	4	C-10 to 3500
1982	-	TFK	350	conv., van & bus	L LS9	155	4	C-20 to 3500
1979	-	TFL	350	van, bus, m/t, Cal	L LS9	155	4	C-10 to 3500
1982	-	TFL	350	conv., van & bus	L LS9	155	4	C-20 to 3500
1979	-	TFM	350	van, bus, a/t, Cal	L LS9	155	4	C-10 to 3500
1982	-	TFM	350	conv., van & bus	L LS9	155	4	C-20 to 3500
1979	-	TFR	350	fwd cab, Calif, a/t	L LS9	155	4	C-10 to 3500
1979	-	TFS	350	conv. cab, m/t	L LS9	155	4	C-20 & 2500
1982	-	TFS	350	conv., van & bus	L LS9	155	4	C-30 & 3500
1979	-	TFT	350	conv. cab,a/t	L LS9	155	4	C-10 to 3500
1979	-	TFU	350	conv. cab, m/t	L LS9	155	4	C-20 to 3500
1982	-	TFU	350	conv., van & bus	L LS9	155	4	C-30 & 3500
1979	-	TFW	350	conv. cab, a/t	L LS9	155	4	C-10 to 3500
1982	-	TFW	350	con, fd, van, bus cab	M LT9	-	4	C-30 & 3500
1979	-	TFX	350	conv. cab, m/t	L LS9	155	4	C-20 to 3500
1982	-	TFX	350	con, fd, van, bus cab	M LT9	-	4	C-30 & 3500
1979	-	TFY	350	conv. cab, m/t	L LS9	155	4	C-20 to 3500
1982	-	TFY	350	con, fd, van, bus cab	M LT9	-	4	C-30 & 3500
1979	-	TFZ	350	frwd. cab, a/t	L LS9	155	4	C-20 to 3500
1982	-	TFZ	350	con, fd, van, bus cab	M LT9	-	4	C-20 to 3500
1955	56	TG	265	m/t	-	162	2	truck/1500
1957	-	TG	283	turglide	-	185	2	truck/1500
1955	56	TGC	265	m/t, O.D.	-	162	2	truck/1500
1957	-	TGC	283	turglide	-	220	2	truck/1500
1955	-	TGD	265	m/t	-	180	4	truck/1500
1957	-	TGD	283	turglide	-	245	4	truck/1500
1955	-	TGE	265	m/t, O.D.	-	180	4	truck/1500
1956	-	TGE	265	m/t, O.D.	-	205	4	truck/1500
1955	56	TGF	265	m/t	-	162	2	truck/1500
1957	-	TGF	283	turglide	-	250	FI	truck/1500
1955	-	TGG	265	m/t	-	180	4	truck/1500
1982	-	TGH	350	conv., van & bus	L LS9	155	4	C-10 to 3500
1955	-	TGJ	265	m/t	-	162	2	truck/1500
1956	-	TGJ	265	m/t	-	180	4	truck/1500
1982	-	TGJ	350	conv., van & bus	L LS9	155	4	C-10 to 3500
1955	56	TGK	265	m/t	-	162	2	truck/1500
1982	-	TGK	350	conv., van & bus	L LS9	155	4	C-10 to 3500
1955	-	TGL	265	m/t	-	180	4	truck/1500
1956	-	TGL	265	m/t	-	205	4	truck/1500
1955	-	TGM	265	m/t	-	180	4	truck/1500
1956	-	TGM	265	m/t	-	205	4	truck/1500
1982	-	TGM	350	conv., van & bus	L LS9	155	4	C-10 to 3500
1956	-	TGN	265	m/t	-	205	4	truck/1500
1956	-	TGQ	265	m/t, O.D.	-	205	4	truck/1500
1978	-	TH	305	LG3	U	135	2	Firebird
1971	-	THA	307	conv. cab	-	200	2	C-10 & 1500
1971	-	THA	307	m/t	-	200	2	C-10
1977	-	THA	350	frwd cab	L LS9	165	4	C-30/3500/CF inj
1982	-	THA	350	con, fd, van, bus cab	M LT9	-	4	C-20 to 3500

first year	last year	stamp RPO	cid	application	VIN	h/p	bbls	body styles
1977	-	THB	350	frwd cab	L LS9	165	4	C-30 & 3500
1982	-	THB	350	con, fd, van, bus cab	M LT9	-	4	C-20 to 3500
1971	-	THC	307	conv. cab	-	200	2	C-10 & 1500
1971	-	THC	307	tur hydro	-	200	2	C-10
1982	-	THC	350	con, fd, van, bus cab	M LT9	-	4	C-20 to 3500
1971	-	THD	307	conv. cab	-	200	2	K-10 & 1500
1971	-	THD	307	m/t	-	200	2	K-10
1982	-	THD	350	con, fd, van, bus cab	M LT9	-	4	C-20 to 3500
1982	-	THF	350	con, fd, van, bus cab	M LT9	-	4	C-20 to 3500
1971	-	THG	307	conv. cab	-	200	2	K-10 & 1500
1971	-	THH	307	frwd cab	-	200	2	C-20 to 3500
1982	-	THH	350	con, fd, van, bus cab	M LT9	-	4	C-20 to 3500
1982	-	THJ	350	con, fd, van, bus cab	M LT9	-	4	C-20 to 3500
1971	-	THK	307	con, frwd cabs, a/t	-	200	2	C-20 & 2500
1971	-	THK	307	turhydro	-	200	2	C & K: 10 & 20
1982	-	THK	350	con, fd, van, bus cab	M LT9	-	4	C-20 to 3500
1971	-	THL	307	con, frwd cabs, a/t	-	200	2	C-30 & 3500
1982	-	THL	350	con, fd, van, bus cab	M LT9	-	4	C-20 to 3500
1982	-	THM	350	con, fd, van, bus cab	M LT9	-	4	C-20 to 3500
1971	-	THP	307	conv. cab, m/t	-	200	2	C-20 to 3500
1971	-	THR	307	conv. cab, m/t	-	200	2	K-20 & 2500
1982	-	THR	350	con, fd, van, bus cab	M LT9	-	4	C-20 to 3500
1971	-	THS	307	conv. cab, a/t	-	200	2	K-20 & 2500
1982	-	THS	350	con, fd, van, bus cab	M LT9	-	4	C-20 to 3500
1982	-	THT	350	con, fd, van, bus cab	M LT9	-	4	C-20 to 3500
1978	-	TJ	305	LG3	U	145	2	Firebird
1973	74	TJA	350	conv. cab	-	160	4	C-20 to 3500
1979	-	TJA	350	frwd cab, a/t	L LS9	165	4	C-30 & 3500
1973	74	TJB	350	conv. cab	-	160	4	C-10 to 2500
1979	-	TJB	350	frwd cab, a/t	L LS9	165	4	C-30 & 3500
1973	74	TJC	350	conv. cab	-	160	4	C-20 to 3500
1974	-	TJD	350	conv. cab	-	160	4	C-10 & 1500
1975	-	TJE	350	van & bus	-	145	2	C-10 & 1500
1975	-	TJG	350	conv. cab	-	145	2	C-10 & 1500
1973	-	TJH	350	conv. & frwd cabs	-	155	4	C-10 to 3500
1976	-	TJH	350	conv. cab	L LS9	165	4	C-10 & 1500
1973	-	TJJ	350	frwd cab	-	155	4	C-30 & 3500
1976	-	TJJ	350	van & bus	L LS9	165	4	C-10 & 1500
1973	-	TJK	350	frwd cab	-	155	4	C-20 to 3500
1976	77	TJK	350	conv. cab	L LS9	165	4	C-10 & 1500
1973	-	TJL	350	frwd cab	-	155	4	C-20 to 3500
1976	77	TJL	350	van & bus	L LS9	165	4	C-10 & 1500
1973	-	TJM	350	van & bus	-	155	4	C-10 to 3500
1974	-	TJM	350	van & bus	-	160	4	C-10 to 3500
1975	-	TJN	350	conv. cab	-	145	2	C-10 & 1500
1972	-	TJP	307	conv. cab, a/t	-	135	2	C-20
1972	-	TJR	307	conv. cab, m/t	-	135	2	C-20 & 30
1973	-	TJR	350	van & bus	-	155	4	C-30 & 3500
1977	-	TJR	350	conv. cab	L LS9	165	4	C-10 & 1500
1972	-	TJS	307	conv. cab, a/t	-	135	2	K-20
1973	-	TJS	350	van & bus	-	155	4	C-10 to 3500
1977	-	TJS	350	van & bus	L LS9	165	4	C-10 to 3500
1979	-	TJS	350	conv. cab, a/t	L LS9	165	4	C-10 & 1500
1972	-	TJT	307	conv. cab, m/t	-	135	2	K-20
1973	-	TJT	350	van & bus	-	155	4	C-30 & 3500

first year	last year	stamp RPO	cid	application	VIN	h/p	bbls	body styles
1979	-	TJT	350	conv. cab, a/t	L LS9	165	4	C-20 & 2500
1973	-	TJU	350	van & bus	-	155	4	C-10 to 3500
1974	-	TJU	350	van & bus	-	160	4	C-10 to 3500
1972	-	TJW	307	fwrd cab	-	135	2	C-20 & 30
1973	-	TJW	350	van & bus	-	155	4	C-10 to 3500
1974	-	TJW	350	van & bus	-	160	4	C-10 to 3500
1980	-	TJW	350	conv. cab, a/t	M LT9	-	4	C-20 to 3500
1972	-	TJX	307	fwrd cab	-	135	2	C-20 & 30
1973	-	TJX	350	conv. cab	-	155	4	C-10 to 3500
1978	-	TJX	350	conv. cab	L LS9	165	4	C-10 & 1500
1973	-	TJY	350	conv. cab	-	155	4	C-10 to 2500
1974	-	TJY	350	conv. cab	-	160	4	C-10 to 2500
1978	-	TJY	350	conv. cab	L LS9	165	4	C-10 & 1500
1973	-	TJZ	350	conv. cab	-	155	4	C-10 to 2500
1978	-	TK	305	LG3	U	145	2	Firebird
1976	-	TKA	350	conv. cab	L LS9	165	4	C-10 & 1500
1978	80	TKA	350	conv. cab, m/t	L LS9	165	4	C-10 & 1500
1976	77	TKB	350	conv. cab	L LS9	165	4	C-10 & 1500
1979	-	TKB	350	conv. cab, m/t	L LS9	165	4	C-30 & 3500
1976	77	TKC	350	van & bus	L LS9	165	4	C-10 & 1500
1979	-	TKC	350	conv. cab, a/t	L LS9	165	4	C-30 & 3500
1976	77	TKD	350	van & bus	L LS9	165	4	C-10 & 1500
1980	-	TKD	350	conv. cab, m/t	L LS9	165	4	C-10 & 1500
1975	-	TKE	350	van & bus	L LS9	165	4	C-10 & 1500
1975	76	TKF	350	van & bus	V LF5	145	2	C-10 & 1500
1978	-	TKF	350	van & bus	L LS9	165	4	C-10 & 1500
1975	76	TKG	350	van & bus	V LF5	145	2	C-10 & 1500
1976	-	TKH	350	conv. cab	L LS9	165	4	C-10 & 1500
1978	-	TKH	350	van & bus	L LS9	165	4	C-10 & 1500
1980	-	TKH	350	con. cab, m/t, Cal	L LS9	165	4	K-10 & 1500, C 2500
1978	-	TKK	350	conv. cab	L LS9	165	4	C-20 to 3500
1980	-	TKK	350	conv. cab, a/t	L LS9	165	4	K-10 & 1500
1978	-	TKL	350	conv. cab	L LS9	165	4	C-20 to 3500
1978	-	TKL	400	conv. cab	R LF4	-	4	K-10 & 1500
1980	-	TKL	350	conv. cab, a/t	L LS9	165	4	C-10 & 1500
1974	-	TKM	350	fd cab, 11Klb axle	-	160	4	C-30 & 3500
1978	-	TKM	350	van & bus	L LS9	165	4	C-30 & 3500
1980	-	TKM	350	conv. cab, a/t	L LS9	165	4	C-10 & 1500
1975	-	TKN	350	conv. cab	-	160	4	C-10 & 1500
1974	-	TKR	350	van & bus	-	160	4	C-10 to 2500
1978	-	TKR	350	van & bus	L LS9	165	4	C-30 & 3500
1980	-	TKR	350	conv. cab, a/t	L LS9	165	4	C-20 & 2500
1974	-	TKS	350	van & bus	-	160	4	C-10 to 2500
1978	-	TKS	350	fwrd cab	L LS9	165	4	C-30 & 3500
1980	-	TKS	350	conv. cab, a/t	L LS9	165	4	K-20 & 2500
1974	-	TKT	350	conv. cab	-	160	4	C-10 & 1500
1978	-	TKT	350	fwrd cab	L LS9	165	4	C-20 to 3500
1980	-	TKT	350	conv. cab, a/t	L LS9	165	4	K-10 & 1500
1974	-	TKU	350	conv. cab	-	160	4	C-10 to 2500
1978	-	TKU	350	fwrd cab	L LS9	165	4	C-30 & 3500
1980	-	TKU	350	van, bus, a/t, Cal	L LS9	165	4	C-20 & 2500
1974	-	TKW	350	van & bus	-	160	4	C-10 to 2500
1978	-	TKW	350	fwrd cab	L LS9	165	4	C-20 to 3500
1974	-	TKX	350	van & bus	-	160	4	C-30 & 3500
1978	-	TKX	350	fwrd cab	L LS9	165	4	C-20 to 3500

first year	last year	stamp RPO	cid	application	VIN	h/p	bbls	body styles
1974	-	TKY	350	conv. cab	-	160	4	C-20 to 3500
1978	-	TKY	350	fwrd cab	L LS9	165	4	C-30 & 3500
1980	-	TKY	350	conv. cab, m/t	L LS9	165	4	C-10 to 2500
f1978	-	TKZ	350	fwrd cab	L LS9	165	4	C-30 & 3500
1980	-	TKZ	350	conv. cab	L LS9	165	4	K-10 & 1500
1957	-	TL	265	m/t	-	162	2	truck/3100
1957	-	TLA	265	H.D. m/t	-	162	2	truck/3100
1978	-	TLA	400	conv. cab	R LF4	175	4	K-10 to 2500
1957	-	TLB	265	m/t	-	162	2	truck/3100
1972	-	TLB	307	m/t	-	135	2	C-10
1978	-	TLB	400	conv. cab	R LF4	175	4	K-10 to 2500
1980	-	TLB	400	van & bus, a/t	R LF4	175	4	C-20 & 2500
1978	-	TLC	400	conv. cab	R LF4	175	4	K-30 & 3500
1980	-	TLC	400	van & bus, a/t	R LF4	175	4	C-20 & 2500
1972	-	TLD	350	fwrd cab	-	155	4	C-30
1975	76	TLD	400	van & bus	U LF4	175	4	C-30 & 3500
1977	-	TLD	400	van & bus	R LF4	175	4	C-30 & 3500
1979	-	TLD	400	conv. cab, a/t	R LF4	175	4	K-10 to 2500
1978	-	TLF	400	van & bus	R LF4	175	4	C-30 & 3500
1975	76	TLH	400	van & bus	U LF4	175	4	C-30 & 3500
1977	-	TLH	400	van & bus	R LF4	175	4	C-30 & 3500
1979	-	TLH	400	conv. cab, a/t	R LF4	175	4	K-10 to 2500
1978	-	TLJ	400	conv. cab	R LF4	175	4	K-20 to 3500
1980	-	TLK	400	van, bus, a/t, Cal	R LF4	170	4	C-20 & 2500
1976	-	TLL	400	conv. cab	U LF4	175	4	K-20 & 2500
1977	-	TLL	400	conv. cab	R LF4	175	4	K-20 to 3500
1979	-	TLL	400	van & bus, a/t	R LF4	175	4	C-20 to 3500
1976	-	TLM	400	conv. cab	U LF4	175	4	K-20 & 2500
1977	-	TLM	400	conv. cab	R LF4	175	4	K-20 to 3500
1979	-	TLM	400	van & bus, a/t	R LF4	175	4	C-20 to 3500
1975	76	TLR	400	conv. cab	U LF4	175	4	K-10 to 2500
1977	-	TLR	400	conv. cab	R LF4	175	4	K-10 to 2500
1979	-	TLR	400	con. cab, a/t, Cal	R LF4	170	4	K-10 to 2500
1975	76	TLS	400	conv. cab	U LF4	175	4	K-10 to 2500
1977	-	TLS	400	conv. cab	R LF4	175	4	K-10 to 2500
1979	-	TLS	400	con. cab, a/t, Cal	R LF4	170	4	K-10 to 2500
1975	76	TLT	400	van & bus	U LF4	175	4	C-20 to 3500
1977	-	TLT	400	van & bus	R LF4	175	4	C-20 to 3500
1979	-	TLT	400	van, bus, a/t, Cal	R LF4	170	4	C-20 to 3500
1975	76	TLU	400	van & bus	U LF4	175	4	C-20 to 3500
1977	-	TLU	400	van & bus	R LF4	175	4	C-20 to 3500
1979	-	TLU	400	conv. cab, a/t	R LF4	175	4	K-30 & 3500
1972	-	TLW	350	fwrd cab	-	175	4	C-20 & 30
1978	-	TLW	400	van & bus	R LF4	175	4	C-20 to 3500
1980	-	TLW	400	van, bus, a/t, Cal	R LF4	170	4	C-20 & 2500
1972	-	TLX	350	fwrd cab	-	175	4	C-20 & 30
1978	-	TLX	400	van & bus	R LF4	175	4	C-20 to 3500
1980	-	TLX	400	conv. cab, a/t	X LE4	175	4	K-20 to 3500
1978	-	TLY	400	van & bus	R LF4	175	4	C-30 & 3500
1980	-	TLY	400	van, bus, a/t, Cal	X LE4	175	4	C-30 & 3500
1978	-	TLZ	400	van & bus	R LF4	175	4	C-20 to 3500
1956	-	TM	265	m/t	-	155	2	truck/3100
1978	-	TM	305	LG3	U	145	2	LeMans
1956	-	TMA	265	m/t	-	155	2	truck/3600
1974	-	TMA	350	fwrd cab	-	160	4	C-20 & 2500

first year	last year	stamp RPO	cid	application	VIN	h/p	bbls	body styles
1980	-	TMA	350	con. cab, m/t, Cal	M LT9	-	4	C-20 to 3500
1970	-	TMB	350	tilt cab	-	215	2	C-50
1970	-	TMB	350	tilt cab	-	255	4	C 5500
1971	-	TMB	307	van & bus	-	200	2	C-10, 20 & 30
1974	-	TMB	350	fwrd cab	-	160	4	C-30 & 3500
1974	-	TMC	350	fd cab: mtr home	-	160	4	C-30 & 3500
1979	-	TMC	350	con. cab, hi alt, a/t	L LS9	175	4	C-10 & 1500
1974	-	TMD	350	fwrd cab	-	160	4	C-20 to 3500
1977	-	TMD	350	con/school bus	-	160	4	C-60 & 6000
1979	-	TMD	350	van,bus, hi alt, a/t	L LS9	175	4	C-10 & 1500
1975	-	TME	350	conv. cab	-	160	4	C-10 & 1500
1975	-	TMF	350	van & bus	-	160	4	C-10 & 1500
1979	-	TMF	350	conv. cab, m/t	L LS9	175	4	C-10 & 1500
1975	-	TMG	350	van & bus	-	160	4	C-10 & 1500
1979	-	TMH	350	conv. cab, m/t	L LS9	175	4	C-10 & 1500
1970	-	TMJ	350	con, fd, van, bus	-	215	2	C-10, 20, 30
1970	-	TMJ	350	turhydro	-	255	4	C-10 to 30
1980	-	TMJ	350	van, bus, m/t, Cal	M LT9	170	4	C-30 & 3500
1974	-	TMK	350	van & bus	-	145	2	C-10 & 1500
1980	-	TMK	350	van, bus, m/t, Cal	M LT9	170	4	C-30 & 3500
1974	-	TML	350	van & bus	-	145	2	C-10 & 1500
1980	-	TML	350	van, bus, m/t, Cal	M LT9	170	4	C-30 & 3500
1974	-	TMM	350	conv. cab	-	145	2	C-10 & 1500
1980	-	TMM	350	conv. cab, a/t, Cal	M LT9	170	4	C-20 to 3500
1980	-	TMR	350	van, bus, a/t, Cal	M LT9	170	4	C-30 & 3500
1980	-	TMS	350	fwrd cab, a/t, Cal	M LT9	170	4	C-30 & 3500
1974	77	TMT	350	conv. cab	-	160	2	C-50 & 5000
1980	-	TMT	350	fwrd cab, a/t, Cal	M LT9	170	4	C-30 & 3500
1974	76	TMU	350	con, /school bus	-	160	2	C-60 & 6000
1980	-	TMU	350	conv. cab, m/t	L LS9	175	4	C-20 & 2500
1974	77	TMW	350	con, /school bus	-	160	2	C-50, 60, 5000, 6000
1974	77	TMX	350	con, /school bus	-	160	2	C-60 & 6000
1974	75	TMY	350	con, /school bus	-	160	2	C-60 & 6000
1974	75	TMZ	350	con, /school bus	-	160	2	C-60 & 6000
1970	-	TNS	307	fwrd cab	-	200	2	C 2500 & 3500
1970	-	TNT	350	con/fd cabs, glide	-	255	4	C-10 to 2500
1971	-	TPB	307	van & bus	-	200	2	C 1500
1971	-	TPC	307	van & bus	-	200	2	C 1500
1978	-	TR	305	LG3	U	145	2	LeMans
1972	-	TRA	307	conv. cab, m/t	-	135	2	C-10 & 20
1973	-	TRC	350	fwrd cab	-	155	4	C-30 & 3500
1972	-	TRD	350	van & bus	-	175	4	C-30 & 3500
1972	-	TRG	350	van & bus	-	175	4	C-30
1972	-	TRH	350	conv. cab, m/t	-	175	4	C-20 & 30
1972	-	TRJ	350	conv. cab, a/t	-	175	4	C-20 & 30
1972	-	TRK	350	conv. cab, m/t	-	175	4	K-20
1973	-	TRK	350	conv. & fwrd cabs	-	155	4	C-20 to 3500
1972	-	TRL	350	conv. cab, a/t	-	175	4	K-20
1974	-	TRM	350	conv. cab	-	145	2	C-10 & 1500
1973	-	TRR	350	fwrd cab	-	155	4	C-30 & 3500
1979	-	TRR	350	con. cab, hi alt, a/t	L LS9	160	4	C-10 to 2500
1972	-	TRS	350	van & bus	-	175	4	C 3500
1979	-	TRS	350	con. cab, hi alt, a/t	L LS9	160	4	C-20 & 2500
1979	-	TRZ	350	van, bus, hi alt, m/t	L LS9	160	4	C-20 & 2500
1978	-	TS	305	LG3	U	145	2	Grand Prix

first year	last year	stamp RPO	cid	application	VIN	h/p	bbls	body styles
1982	-	TSC	350	con, van, bus cabs	L LS9	160	4	C-10 to 3500
1982	-	TSD	350	con, van, bus cabs	L LS9	160	4	C-10 to 3500
1982	-	TSF	350	con, van, bus cabs	L LS9	160	4	C-10 to 3500
1982	-	TSH	350	con, van, bus cabs	L LS9	160	4	C-10 to 3500
1972	-	TSJ	307	tur hydro	-	135	2	K-20
1982	-	TSJ	350	con, van, bus cabs	L LS9	160	4	C-10 to 3500
1982	-	TSK	350	con, van, bus cabs	L LS9	160	4	C-10 to 3500
1972	-	TSP	307	tur hydro	-	135	2	C-10 & 20
1972	-	TSR	307	m/t	-	135	2	K-10 & 20
1972	-	TSS	307	m/t	-	135	2	C-10 & 20
1978	-	TT	305	LG3	U	145	2	Grand Prix
1982	-	TTA	350	con, fd, van, bus	M LT9	160	4	C-20 to 3500
1980	-	TTB	400	con. cab, a/t, Cal	X LT4	175	4	C-20 to 3500
1982	-	TTB	350	con, fd, van, bus	M LT9	160	4	C-20 to 3500
1980	-	TTC	400	con. cab, a/t, Cal	X LT4	175	4	C-30 & 3500
1982	-	TTC	350	con, fd, van, bus	M LT9	160	4	C-20 to 3500
1982	-	TTD	350	con, fd, van, bus	M LT9	160	4	C-20 to 3500
1979	-	TTJ	400	van & bus, a/t	X LT4	175	4	C-30 & 3500
1979	-	TTM	400	van, bus, a/t, Cal	X LT4	175	4	C-20 to 3500
1970	-	TTO	350	conv. cab	-	215	2	C-40
1970	-	TTO	350	conv. cab	-	255	4	C 4500
1970	-	TTP	350	conv. cab	-	215	2	C-50
1970	-	TTP	350	con/school bus	-	255	4	C 5500
1970	-	TTQ	350	conv. cab	-	215	2	C-50
1970	-	TTQ	350	con/school bus	-	255	4	C 5500
1970	-	TTR	350	conv. cab	-	215	2	C-50
1970	-	TTR	350	conv. cab	-	255	4	C 5500
1979	-	TTR	400	conv. cab	R LF4	185	4	K-10 to 2500
1970	-	TTS	350	conv. cab	-	215	2	C-50
1970	-	TTS	350	conv. cab	-	255	4	C 5500
1970	-	TTT	350	conv. cab	-	215	2	C-40
1970	-	TTU	350	conv. cab	-	215	2	C-50
1970	-	TTV	350	conv. cab	-	215	2	C-50
1978	-	TU	305	LG3	U	145	2	Grand Prix
1978	-	TW	305	LG3	U	145	2	Grand Prix
1974	77	TWA	350	con/school bus	-	160	2	C-60 & 6000
1974	77	TWB	350	tilt cab	-	160	2	C-60 & 6000
1974	77	TWC	350	tilt cab	-	160	2	C-60 & 6000
1974	-	TWD	350	con. cab, LPgas eng	-	160	2	C-60 & 6000
1977	-	TWD	350	conv. cab	L LS9	165	4	C-10 & 1500
1976	77	TWF	350	conv. cab	L LS9	165	4	C-10 & 1500
1976	77	TWJ	350	conv. cab	L LS9	165	4	C-10 & 1500
1978	-	TWJ	350	conv. cab	L LS9	165	4	C-10 & 1500
1976	77	TWK	350	van & bus	L LS9	165	4	C-10 & 1500
1978	-	TWK	350	conv. cab	L LS9	165	4	C-10 & 1500
1977	-	TWT	350	fwrd cab	L LS9	165	4	C-30 & 3500
1977	-	TWU	350	fwrd cab	L LS9	165	4	C-30 & 3500
1977	-	TWV	350	fwrd cab	L LS9	165	4	C-30 & 3500
1978	-	TWW	350	fwrd cab	L LS9	165	4	C-30 & 3500
1978	-	TWX	350	fwrd cab	L LS9	165	4	C-30 & 3500
1978	-	TWY	350	conv. cab	L LS9	165	4	C-20 & 2500
1978	-	TWZ	350	conv. cab	L LS9	165	4	K-10 to 2500
1978	-	TX	305	LG3	U	145	2	Grand Prix
1975	77	TXA	350	conv. cab	L LS9	165	4	C-20 to 3500
1975	77	TXB	350	conv. cab	L LS9	165	4	C-20 to 3500

first year	last year	stamp RPO	cid	application	VIN	h/p	bbls	body styles
1975	77	TXC	350	conv. cab	L LS9	165	4	C-20 to 3500
1975	77	TXD	350	conv. cab	L LS9	165	4	C-20 to 3500
1975	77	TXH	350	van & bus	L LS9	165	4	C-30 & 3500
1975	77	TXJ	350	van & bus	L LS9	165	4	C-30 & 3500
1975	77	TXK	350	van & bus	L LS9	165	4	C-30 & 3500
1975	77	TXL	350	van & bus	L LS9	165	4	C-30 & 3500
1975	77	TXM	350	fwrd cab	L LS9	165	4	C-20 to 3500
1975	77	TXR	350	fwrd cab	L LS9	165	4	C-20 to 3500
1975	77	TXS	350	fwrd cab	L LS9	165	4	C-20 to 3500
1975	77	TXT	350	fwrd cab	L LS9	165	4	C-20 to 3500
1975	-	TXU	350	fd cab: mtr home	-	160	4	C-30 & 3500
1977	-	TXU	350	fd cab: mtr home	L LS9	165	4	C-30 & 3500
1975	-	TXW	350	fd cab: mtr home	-	160	4	C-30 & 3500
1977	-	TXW	350	fd cab: mtr home	L LS9	165	4	C-30 & 3500
1975	-	TXX	350	fd cab: mtr home	-	160	4	C-30 & 3500
1977	-	TXX	350	fd cab: mtr home	L LS9	165	4	C-30 & 3500
1975	-	TXY	350	fd cab: mtr home	-	160	4	C-30 & 3500
1977	-	TXY	350	fd cab: mtr home	L LS9	165	4	C-30 & 3500
1978	-	TXZ	350	fwrd cab	L LS9	165	4	C-30 & 3500
1978	-	TY	305	LG3	U	145	2	Grand Prix
1975	76	TYA	350	van & bus	V LF5	145	2	C-10 & 1500
1978	-	TYA	350	van & bus	L LS9	165	4	C-20 to 3500
1980	-	TYA	305	van & bus, m/t	G LG9	140	2	C-10 & 1500
1978	-	TYB	350	conv. cab	L LS9	165	4	C-10 & 1500
1980	-	TYB	305	van & bus, a/t	G LG9	140	2	C-10 & 1500
1975	76	TYC	350	conv. cab	V LF5	145	2	C-10 & 1500
1978	-	TYC	350	van & bus	L LS9	165	4	C-20 to 3500
1975	-	TYD	350	conv. cab	-	160	4	C-10 & 1500
1978	-	TYD	350	van & bus	L LS9	165	4	C-20 to 3500
1978	-	TYF	350	conv. cab	L LS9	165	4	C-10 & 1500
1978	-	TYH	350	conv. cab	L LS9	165	4	C-10 & 1500
1975	-	TYJ	350	van & bus	-	160	4	C-10 & 1500
1978	-	TYJ	350	conv. cab	L LS9	165	4	C-10 & 1500
1978	-	TYK	350	conv. cab	L LS9	165	4	C-10 & 1500
1978	-	TYL	350	conv. cab	L LS9	165	4	C-30 & 3500
1978	-	TYM	350	conv. cab	L LS9	165	4	C-30 & 3500
1975	77	TYR	350	van & bus	L LS9	165	4	C-20 to 3500
1979	-	TYR	305	conv. cab, m/t	U LG9	140	2	C-20 to 3500
1975	77	TYS	350	van & bus	L LS9	165	4	C-20 to 3500
1979	-	TYS	305	conv. cab, a/t	U LG9	140	2	C-10 to 2500
1975	77	TYT	350	van & bus	L LS9	165	4	C-20 to 3500
1975	77	TYU	350	van & bus	L LS9	165	4	C-20 to 3500
1975	77	TYW	350	conv. cab	L LS9	165	4	C-10 to 2500
1975	77	TYX	350	conv. cab	L LS9	165	4	C-10 to 2500
1975	77	TYY	350	conv. cab	L LS9	165	4	C-10 to 2500
1975	77	TYZ	350	conv. cab	L LS9	165	4	C-10 to 2500
1978	-	TZ	305	LG3	U	145	2	LeMans
1975	-	TZA	350	conv. cab	-	160	4	C-10 & 1500
1978	-	TZA	350	van & bus	L LS9	165	4	C-10 & 1500
1975	-	TZB	350	van & bus	-	160	4	C-10 & 1500
1978	-	TZB	350	van & bus	L LS9	165	4	C-10 to 3500
1975	-	TZC	350	conv. cab	-	160	4	C-10 & 1500
1978	-	TZC	350	van & bus	L LS9	165	4	C-10 to 3500
1978	-	TZD	350	van & bus	L LS9	165	4	C-20 to 3500
1975	-	TZF	350	van & bus	-	160	4	C-10 & 1500

first year	last year	stamp RPO	cid	application	VIN	h/p	bbls	body styles
1978	-	TZF	350	van & bus	L LS9	165	4	C-20 to 3500
1975	-	TZH	350	van & bus	-	160	4	C-10 & 1500
1978	-	TZH	350	van & bus	L LS9	165	4	C-20 to 3500
1975	-	TZJ	350	conv. cab	-	160	4	C-10 & 1500
1975	-	TZK	350	conv. cab	-	160	4	C-10 & 1500
1978	-	TZK	350	van & bus	L LS9	165	4	C-30 & 3500
1975	-	TZL	350	van & bus	-	160	4	C-10 & 1500
1978	-	TZL	350	van & bus	L LS9	165	4	C-30 & 3500
1975	-	TZM	350	van & bus	-	160	4	C-10 & 1500
1978	-	TZR	350	fwrd cab	L LS9	165	4	C-20 & 2500
1978	-	TZS	350	conv. cab	L LS9	165	4	K-10 to 2500
1978	-	TZT	350	conv. cab	L LS9	165	4	K-10 to 2500
1978	-	TZU	350	conv. cab	L LS9	165	4	K-10 to 2500
1978	-	TZW	350	conv. cab	L LS9	165	4	K-10 to 2500
1969	-	UA	307	m/t	-	200	2	trucks
1981	-	UAA	305	conv. cab, m/t	G LG9	140	2	C-10 & 1500
1981	-	UAB	305	conv. cab, a/t	G LG9	140	2	C-10 & 1500
1981	-	UAC	305	conv. cab, m/t	G LG9	140	2	C-10 & 1500
1981	-	UAD	305	conv. cab, a/t	G LG9	140	2	C-10 & 1500
1981	-	UAF	305	van & bus, m/t	G LG9	140	2	C-10 to 2500
1981	-	UAH	305	van & bus, a/t	G LG9	140	2	C-10 to 2500
1981	-	UAJ	305	conv. cab, m/t	G LG9	140	2	C-10 & 1500
1981	-	UAK	305	conv. cab, a/t	G LG9	140	2	C-10 & 1500
1981	-	UAT	305	con. cab, m/t, A.I.R.	H LE9	150	4	K-10 & 1500
1981	-	UAU	305	con. cab, m/t, A.I.R.	H LE9	150	4	C-20 & 2500
1981	-	UAW	305	con. cab, a/t, A.I.R.	H LE9	150	4	K-10 & 1500
1981	-	UAX	305	van & bus, m/t	H LE9	150	4	C-10 to 2500
1981	-	UAY	305	van & bus, a/t	H LE9	150	4	C-10 to 2500
1981	-	UAZ	305	conv. cab, A.I.R.	G LG9	140	2	C-10 & 1500
1969	-	UB	307	m/t	-	200	2	trucks
1983	-	UBA	305	van, bus, a/t, Cal	F LF3	145	4	C-10 to 2500
1983	-	UBB	305	con. cab, m/t, A.I.R.	F LF3	145	4	C-10 & 1500
1983	-	UBC	305	con. cab, a/t, A.I.R.	F LF3	145	4	C-10 & 1500
1983	-	UBD	305	con. cab, a/t, A.I.R.	F LF3	145	4	C-20 & 2500
1969	-	UC	307	Powerglide	-	200	2	C-10 to 25
1983	-	UCA	305	conv. cab	H LE9	150	4	C-10 to 2500
1983	-	UCB	305	conv. cab	H LE9	150	4	C-10 to 2500
1983	-	UCC	305	conv. cab	H LE9	150	4	C-10 to 2500
1983	-	UCD	305	conv. cab	H LE9	150	4	C-10 to 2500
1983	-	UCF	305	conv. cab	H LE9	150	4	C-10 to 2500
1983	-	UCH	305	conv. cab	H LE9	150	4	C-10 to 2500
1983	-	UCJ	305	conv. cab	H LE9	150	4	C-10 to 2500
1983	-	UCK	305	conv. cab	H LE9	150	4	C-10 to 2500
1983	-	UCM	305	conv. cab	H LE9	150	4	C-10 to 2500
1983	-	UCN	305	conv. cab	H LE9	150	4	C-10 to 2500
1983	-	UCR	305	conv. cab	H LE9	150	4	C-10 to 2500
1983	-	UCT	305	conv. cab	H LE9	150	4	C-10 to 2500
1983	-	UCU	305	conv. cab	H LE9	150	4	C-10 to 2500
1969	-	UD	307	Powerglide, A.I.R.	-	200	2	C-20 & 25
1983	-	UDA	305	conv. cab	F LE3	150	4	C-10 to 2500
1983	-	UDB	305	conv. cab	F LE3	150	4	C-10 to 2500
1983	-	UDC	305	conv. cab	H LE9	150	4	C-10 to 2500
1983	-	UDD	305	conv. cab	H LE9	150	4	C-10 to 2500
1983	-	UDF	305	conv. cab	H LE9	150	4	C-10 to 2500
1983	-	UDH	305	conv. cab	H LE9	150	4	C-10 to 2500

first year	last year	stamp RPO	cid	application	VIN	h/p	bbls	body styles
1983	-	UDJ	305	conv. cab	H LE9	150	4	C-10 to 2500
1983	-	UDK	305	conv. cab	H LE9	150	4	C-10 to 2500
1983	-	UDM	305	conv. cab	H LE9	150	4	C-10 to 2500
1983	-	UDN	305	conv. cab	H LE9	150	4	C-10 to 2500
1983	-	UDR	305	conv. cab	H LE9	150	4	C-10 to 2500
1983	-	UDS	305	conv. cab	H LE9	150	4	C-10 to 2500
1983	-	UDT	305	conv. cab	H LE9	150	4	C-10 to 2500
1983	-	UDU	305	conv. cab	H LE9	150	4	C-10 to 2500
1969	-	UE	307	tur hydro, A.I.R.	-	200	2	C-20 to 35
1969	-	UF	307	tur hydro	-	200	2	K-20 & 25
1980	-	UFA	350	van, bus, a/t, Cal	L LS9	165	4	C-10 & 1500
1980	-	UFB	350	van, bus, m/t, Cal	M LT9	165	4	C-30 & 3500
1980	-	UFC	350	van, bus, a/t, Cal	M LT9	165	4	C-30 & 3500
1980	-	UFD	350	van, bus, m/t, Cal	M LT9	165	4	C-20 to 3500
1980	-	UFF	350	van, bus, a/t, Cal	M LT9	165	4	C-20 to 3500
1980	-	UFH	350	van, bus, m/t, Cal	M LT9	165	4	C-30 & 3500
1980	-	UFJ	350	fwrd cab, a/t	M LT9	165	4	C-30 & 3500
1980	-	UFK	350	fwrd cab, a/t	M LT9	165	4	C-30 & 3500
1980	-	UFR	350	fwrd cab, a/t, Cal	M LT9	165	4	C-30 & 3500
1980	-	UFS	350	fwrd cab, a/t	M LT9	165	4	C-30 & 3500
1980	-	UFT	350	conv. cab, m/t	P LF5	150	2	C-30 & 3500
1980	-	UFU	350	conv. cab, a/t	P LF5	150	2	C-30 & 3500
1969	-	UG	307	-	-	200	2	van 10 to 25
1969	-	UH	307	-	-	200	2	van 15 to 25
1981	-	UHA	350	con. cab, m/t, A.I.R.	L LS9	165	4	K-10 & 1500
1981	-	UHB	350	con. cab, a/t, A.I.R.	L LS9	165	4	K-10 & 1500
1981	-	UHC	350	con. cab, m/t, A.I.R.	L LS9	165	4	K-20 & 2500
1981	-	UHD	350	con. cab, a/t, A.I.R.	L LS9	165	4	K-20 & 2500
1981	-	UHF	350	van & bus, m/t	L LS9	165	4	C-10 & 1500
1981	-	UHH	350	van & bus, m/t	L LS9	165	4	C-20 & 2500
1981	-	UHJ	350	van & bus, a/t	L LS9	165	4	C-10 to 2500
1981	-	UHK	350	con, a/t, A.I.R., Cal	L LS9	165	4	C-10 & 1500
1981	-	UHL	350	con. cab, A.I.R., Cal	L LS9	165	4	K-10 & 1500
1981	-	UHM	350	con, a/t, A.I.R., Cal	L LS9	165	4	K-10 & 1500
1981	-	UHR	350	conv. cab, A.I.R.	L LS9	165	4	C-20 & 2500
1981	-	UHS	350	con, a/t, A.I.R., Cal	L LS9	165	4	C-20 & 2500
1981	-	UHT	350	van, bus, a/t, Cal	L LS9	165	4	C-10 & 1500
1981	-	UHU	350	van, bus, a/t, Cal	L LS9	165	4	C-20 & 2500
1981	-	UHW	350	con cab, m/t , A.I.R.	M LT9	165	4	C-20 to 3500
1981	-	UHX	350	con cab, a/t, A.I.R.	M LT9	165	4	C-20 to 3500
1981	-	UHY	350	con, m/t, A.I.R., Cal	M LT9	165	4	C-20 to 3500
1981	-	UHZ	350	con, a/t, A.I.R., Cal	M LT9	165	4	C-20 to 3500
1969	-	UI	307	-	-	200	2	van 10 to 25
1969	-	UJ	307	-	-	200	2	van 10 & 20
1981	-	UJA	350	van & bus, m/t	M LT9	165	4	C-30 & 3500
1981	-	UJB	350	van & bus, a/t	M LT9	165	4	C-30 & 3500
1981	-	UJC	350	van, bus, m/t, Cal	M LT9	165	4	C-30 & 3500
1981	-	UJD	350	van, bus, a/t, Cal	M LT9	165	4	C-30 & 3500
1981	-	UJF	350	fwrd cab, m/t	M LT9	165	4	C-20 to 3500
1981	-	UJH	350	fwrd cab, a/t	M LT9	165	4	C-20 to 3500
1981	-	UJJ	350	fd cab, m/t, Calif	M LT9	165	4	C-30 & 3500
1981	-	UJK	350	fd cab, a/t, Calif	M LT9	165	4	C-30 & 3500
1981	-	UJL	350	fwrd cab, m/t	M LT9	165	4	C-20 to 3500
1981	-	UJM	350	fwrd cab, a/t	M LT9	165	4	C-20 to 3500
1981	-	UJR	350	fd cab, m/t, Calif	M LT9	165	4	C-30 & 3500

first year	last year	stamp RPO	cid	application	VIN	h/p	bbls	body styles
1981	-	UJS	350	fd cab, a/t, Calif	M LT9	165	4	C-30 & 3500
1981	-	UJT	350	fwrd cab, m/t	M LT9	165	4	C-30 & 3500
1981	-	UJU	350	con. cab, m/t, A.I.R.	L LS9	165	4	C-10 & 1500
1981	-	UJW	350	con. cab, a/t, A.I.R.	L LS9	165	4	C-10 & 1500
1969	-	UK	307	-	-	200	2	van 20
1981	-	UKA	350	con. cab, m/t, A.I.R.	P LF5	150	2	C-30 & 3500,159.5WB
1981	-	UKB	350	con .cab, a/t, A.I.R.	P LF5	150	2	C-30 & 3500,159.5WB
1969	-	UL	307	-	-	200	2	van 10 to 25
1969	-	UM	307	tur hydro	-	200	2	C-10
1969	-	UN	307	-	-	200	2	C-10 to 35
1969	-	UO	307	m/t	-	200	4	K-10 to 25
1969	-	UP	307	m/t	-	200	2	K-20 & 25
1969	-	UQ	307	tur hydro	-	200	4	K-10 to 25
1983	-	URA	350	conv. cab	L LS9	165	4	C-10 to 3500
1983	-	URB	350	conv. cab	L LS9	165	4	C-10 to 3500
1983	-	URC	350	conv. cab	L LS9	165	4	C-10 to 3500
1983	-	URD	350	conv. cab	L LS9	165	4	C-10 to 3500
1983	-	URF	350	conv. cab	L LS9	165	4	C-10 to 3500
1983	-	URH	350	conv. cab	L LS9	165	4	C-10 to 3500
1983	-	URJ	350	conv. cab	L LS9	165	4	C-10 to 3500
1983	-	URK	350	conv. cab	L LS9	165	4	C-10 to 3500
1983	-	URM	350	conv. cab	L LS9	165	4	C-10 to 3500
1983	-	URN	350	conv. cab	L LS9	165	4	C-10 to 3500
1979	-	US	305	LG4	H	160	4	Cutlass
1983	-	USA	350	conv. cab	M LT9	165	4	C-20 to 3500
1983	-	USB	350	conv. cab	M LT9	165	4	C-20 to 3500
1983	-	USC	350	conv. cab	M LT9	165	4	C-20 to 3500
1983	-	USD	350	conv. cab	M LT9	165	4	C-20 to 3500
1983	-	USF	350	conv. cab	M LT9	165	4	C-20 to 3500
1983	-	USH	350	conv. cab	M LT9	165	4	C-20 to 3500
1983	-	USJ	350	conv. cab	M LT9	165	4	C-20 to 3500
1983	-	USK	350	conv. cab	M LT9	165	4	C-20 to 3500
1983	-	USM	350	conv. cab	M LT9	165	4	C-20 to 3500
1983	-	USN	350	conv. cab	M LT9	165	4	C-20 to 3500
1983	-	USR	350	conv. cab	M LT9	165	4	C-20 to 3500
1983	-	USS	350	conv. cab	M LT9	165	4	C-20 to 3500
1983	-	UST	350	conv. cab	M LT9	165	4	C-20 to 3500
1983	-	USU	350	conv. cab	M LT9	165	4	C-20 to 3500
1983	-	USW	350	conv. cab	M LT9	165	4	C-20 to 3500
1983	-	USX	350	conv. cab	M LT9	165	4	C-20 to 3500
1983	-	USY	350	conv. cab	M LT9	165	4	C-20 to 3500
1983	-	USZ	350	conv. cab	M LT9	165	4	C-20 to 3500
1969	-	UT	307	m/t	-	200	4	K-10 & 20
1979	-	UT	305	LG4	H	160	4	Cutlass
1977	79	UTA	305	conv. cab, m/t	U LG9	145	2	C-10 & 1500
1977	79	UTB	305	conv. cab, a/t	U LG9	145	2	C-10 & 1500
1977	79	UTC	305	van & bus, m/t	U LG9	145	2	C-10 & 1500
1977	79	UTD	305	van & bus, a/t	U LG9	145	2	C-10 & 1500
1977	80	UTF	305	conv. cab, m/t	U LG9	145	2	C-10 to 2500
1977	80	UTH	305	conv. cab, a/t	U LG9	145	2	C-10 to 2500
1980	-	UTJ	305	conv. cab, m/t	G LG9	145	2	C-10 & 1500
1980	-	UTL	305	conv. cab, a/t	G LG9	145	2	C-10 & 1500
1978	-	UTR	305	conv. cab	U LG9	145	2	C-10 & 1500
1978	-	UTS	305	conv. cab	U LG9	145	2	C-10 & 1500
1978	-	UTT	305	van & bus	U LG9	145	2	C-10 & 1500

first year	last year	stamp RPO	cid	application	VIN	h/p	bbls	body styles
978	-	UTU	305	van & bus	U LG9	145	2	C-10 & 1500
1978	-	UTW	305	conv. cab	U LG9	145	2	C-10 to 2500
1978	-	UTX	305	conv. cab	U LG9	145	2	C-10 to 2500
1969	-	UU	307	m/t	-	200	2	C-20
1983	-	UUB	350	conv. cab	L LS9	165	4	C-10 to 3500
1983	-	UUC	350	conv. cab	L LS9	165	4	C-10 to 3500
1983	-	UUD	350	conv. cab	L LS9	165	4	C-10 to 3500
1983	-	UUF	350	conv. cab	L LS9	165	4	C-10 to 3500
1983	-	UUH	350	conv. cab	L LS9	165	4	C-10 to 3500
1983	-	UUJ	350	conv. cab	L LS9	165	4	C-10 to 3500
1969	-	UV	307	m/t	-	200	2	K-20
1969	-	UW	307	m/t	-	200	2	K-20
1979	-	UYR	305	conv. cab, m/t	G LG9	145	2	C-10 to 2500
1979	-	UYS	305	conv. cab, a/t	G LG9	145	2	C-10 to 2500
1981	-	UZA	350	con cab, m/t, exp	L LS9	165	4	C-10 & 1500
1981	-	UZB	350	con cab, a/t, exp	L LS9	165	4	C-10 & 1500
1981	-	UZC	350	con cab, m/t, exp	L LS9	165	4	K-10 & 1500
1981	-	UZD	350	con cab, a/t, exp	L LS9	165	4	K-10 & 1500
1969	-	VB	350	m/t	-	255	4	C-10 & 20
1972	-	VJZ	350	m/t	-	175	4	C-10 & 20
1969	-	VR	350	m/t, 3 spd	-	255	4	C-20 & 30
1969	-	VS	350	m/t, 3 spd	-	255	4	K-20
1965	67	WA	283	m/t	-	175	2	C-10 to 35
1968	-	WA	307	m/t	-	200	2	C-10 to 25
1969	-	WA	350	-	-	255	4	C-20 to 35
1967	-	WB	283	m/t	-	175	2	K-10 to 25
1968	-	WB	307	m/t	-	200	2	C-20 to 35
1967	-	WC	283	tur hydro	-	175	2	C-20 to 35
1968	-	WC	307	m/t, 3 spd	-	200	2	C-10 to 35
1967	-	WD	283	-	-	175	2	van 10 to 25
1968	-	WD	307	-	-	200	2	van 10 to 25
1965	67	WE	283	m/t	-	175	2	C-10 to 25
1968	-	WE	307	Powerglide	-	200	2	C-10
1966	67	WF	283	m/t, A.I.R.	-	175	2	C-10, 15, 20
1968	-	WF	307	m/t	-	200	2	C-20 & 25
1969	-	WF	350	-	-	215	2	C-50
1967	-	WG	283	m/t	-	175	2	C-10 to 30
1968	-	WG	307	m/t	-	200	2	C-20 & 30
1966	67	WH	283	Powerglide, A.I.R.	-	175	2	C-10 to 25
1968	-	WH	307	m/t	-	200	2	K-20 & 25
1969	-	WH	350	m/t, A.I.R.	-	255	4	C-15, 25, 35
1967	-	WI	283	m/t	-	175	2	K-10 to 25
1968	-	WI	307	m/t	-	200	2	K-10 to 25
1969	-	WI	350	-	-	255	4	C 25 & 35
1969	-	WJ	350	Powerglide	-	255	4	C-10 to 35
1969	-	WK	350	tur hydro	-	255	4	C-10 to 35
1967	-	WL	283	-	-	175	2	van 10 to 25
1968	-	WL	307	-	-	200	2	van 15 to 25
1969	-	WL	350	Powerglide, A.I.R.	-	255	4	C-20 & 25
1967	-	WM	283	-	-	175	2	van 10 to 25
1968	-	WM	307	-	-	175	2	van 10 to 25
1969	-	WM	350	-	-	255	4	C-20 to 35
1968	-	WN	307	-	-	200	2	C-20 to 35
1969	-	WN	350	m/t, A.I.R.	-	255	4	K-10 to 25
1967	-	WO	283	m/t	-	175	2	K-10 & 20

first year	last year	stamp RPO	cid	application	VIN	h/p	bbls	body styles
1968	-	WO	307	m/t, 3 spd	-	200	2	C-10 to 30
1969	-	WO	350	m/t	-	255	4	K-20 & 25
1968	-	WP	307	-	-	200	2	C-20 to 35
1969	-	WP	350	tur hydro	-	255	4	K-10 to 25
1968	-	WQ	307	-	-	200	2	C-20 & 25
1969	-	WQ	350	turbohydro, A.I.R.	-	255	4	K-20 & 25
1967	-	WR	283	turbohydro, A.I.R.	-	175	2	C-10 to 25
1968	-	WR	307	m/t, 3 spd	-	200	2	C-20 to 35
1969	-	WR	350	Powerglide	-	255	4	C-20 & 30
1969	-	WS	350	turhydro	-	255	4	C-20 & 30
1969	-	WT	350	m/t	-	255	4	C-20 & 30
1967	-	WW	283	-	-	175	2	van 10 to 25
1968	-	WW	307	-	-	200	2	van 15 to 25
1969	-	WZ	350	m/t, 3 spd	-	255	4	C-10 & 20
1969	-	XA	350	m/t	-	255	4	C-10 to 35
1969	-	XB	350	m/t	-	255	4	C-20 to 35
1969	-	XC	350	Powerglide	-	255	4	C-10 to 25
1969	-	XD	350	turhydro	-	255	4	C-10 to 35
1963	64	XE	327	universal service	-	-	-	cars
1969	-	XE	350	m/t	-	255	4	C-20 & 30
1969	-	XF	350	Powerglide	-	255	4	C-10 to 35
1969	-	XG	350	turbohydro	-	255	4	C-10, 20, 30
1969	-	XH	350	-	-	215	2	C-40
1969	-	XI	350	-	-	215	2	C-50 & 60
1969	-	XJ	350	-	-	215	2	C-50
1969	-	XK	350	-	-	215	2	T-50 & 60
1969	-	XN	350	-	-	215	2	C-60
1969	-	XO	350	turbohydro, A.I.R.	-	255	4	K-20
1969	-	XP	350	m/t, A.I.R.	-	255	4	C-10 to 30
1969	-	XS	350	-	-	215	2	C-40 & 50
1969	-	XU	350	-	-	215	2	C-50
1969	-	XV	350	-	-	215	2	T-50
1969	-	XW	350	m/t	-	255	4	K-10 to 25
1969	-	XX	350	m/t	-	255	4	K-20 & 25
1969	-	XY	350	turbohydro	-	255	4	K-10 to 25
1969	-	XZ	350	Powerglide, A.I.R.	-	255	4	C-20 & 25
1968	-	YA	327	-	-	240	4	C-20 to 35
1968	-	YB	327	Powerglide	-	220	4	C-10
1966	67	YC	327	m/t, A.I.R.	-	220	4	C-10 to 25
1968	-	YC	327	m/t, A.I.R.	-	240	4	C-10 to 25
1966	67	YD	327	Powerglide, A.I.R.	-	220	4	C-10 to 25
1968	-	YD	327	Powerglide, A.I.R.	-	240	4	C-10 to 25
1966	-	YH	327	hydramatic	-	220	4	C-30
1967	68	YH	327	Powerglide, A.I.R.	-	220	4	C-10 to 35
1967	-	YJ	327	turbohydro, A.I.R.	-	220	4	C-10 to 25
1968	-	YJ	327	turbohydro, A.I.R.	-	240	4	C-20 & 25
1968	-	YK	327	m/t, 3 spd	-	240	4	C-10 to 35
1968	-	YL	327	m/t	-	240	4	K-20 & 25
1967	-	YM	327	m/t	-	220	4	K-10 to 25
1968	-	YM	327	m/t	-	240	4	C-20 to 35
1966	67	YR	327	Powerglide	-	220	4	C-10 to 25
1968	-	YR	327	Powerglide	-	240	4	C-20 & 25
1966	67	YS	327	m/t	-	220	4	C-10 to 35
1968	-	YS	327	m/t, 3 spd	-	220	4	C-20 to 35
1968	-	YT	327	Powerglide	-	220	4	K-10 & 20

first year	last year	stamp RPO	cid	application	VIN	h/p	bbls	body styles
1968	-	YU	327	m/t, 3 spd	-	220	4	K-20
1968	-	YV	327	m/t	-	220	4	C-10
1967	68	YX	327	m/t	-	220	4	K-10 to 25
1965	67	ZA	327	m/t	-	275	4	Nova
1969	-	ZA	350	m/t, A.I.R.	-	255	4	C-10, 20, 30
1979	-	ZAA	350	m/t, L48	8	195	4	Vette
1992	-	ZAA	350	ZR1, ohc, 32v, m/t	J LT5	375	MPFI	Vette
1979	-	ZAB	350	a/t, L48, fed.	8	195	4	Vette
1979	-	ZAC	350	L48, Calif	8	195	4	Vette
1992	-	ZAC	350	rev cooling, a/t	LT1 P	300	TPI	Vette
1979	-	ZAD	350	L48, high altitude	8	195	4	Vette
1980	-	ZAK	350	a/t, L48	8	190	4	Vette
1980	-	ZAM	350	m/t, L48	8	190	4	Vette
1965	-	ZB	327	m/t, high perf.	-	300	4	Chevy II
1966	67	ZB	327	m/t, hi perf. A.I.R.	-	300	4	Chevy II
1969	-	ZB	350	m/t	-	255	4	C-20
1979	-	ZBA	350	m/t, L82	4	225	4	Vette
1982	-	ZBA	350	Cross-fire inject	L83 8	200	TTBI	Vette
1979	-	ZBB	350	a/t, L82	4	225	4	Vette
1980	-	ZBC	350	a/t, L82	6	230	4	Vette
1982	-	ZBC	350	Cross-fire inject	L83 8	200	TTBI	Vette
1980	-	ZBD	350	m/t, L82	6	230	4	Vette
1966	-	ZC	327	A.I.R., a/c	-	-	-	Chevy II
1969	-	ZC	350	m/t	-	255	4	C-20 & 30
1980	-	ZCA	305	a/t, LG4	H	180	4	Vette
1966	67	ZD	327	Powerglide, A.I.R.	-	275	4	Chevy II
1969	-	ZD	350	Powerglide	-	255	4	C-10
1981	-	ZDA	350	m/t	L81 6	190	4	Vette
1981	-	ZDB	350	a/t	L81 6	190	4	Vette
1981	-	ZDC	350	m/t	L81 6	190	4	Vette
1981	-	ZDD	350	m/t	L81 6	190	4	Vette
1985	-	ZDF	350	Tuned port inj, a/t	L98 8	230	TPI	Vette
1965	67	ZE	327	man trans., a/c	-	-	-	Chevy II
1969	-	ZE	350	m/t	-	255	4	C-20
1965	66	ZF	327	m/t, a/c, hi perf.	-	300	4	Chevy II
1969	-	ZF	350	turbohydro	-	255	4	C-10 & 20
1969	-	ZF	350	m/t	-	255	4	K-10
1984	-	ZFC	350	Tuned prt inj, a/t	L83 8	205	TPI	Vette
1984	-	ZFD	350	Tuned prt inj, m/t	L83 8	205	TPI	Vette
1984	-	ZFF	350	Tuned prt inj, a/t	L83 8	205	TPI	Vette
1984	-	ZFM	350	Tuned prt inj, m/t	L83 8	205	TPI	Vette
1982	-	ZFN	350	Tuned prt inj, a/t	L83 8	200	TPI	Vette
1984	-	ZFN	350	Tuned prt inj, a/t	L83 8	205	TPI	Vette
1966	67	ZG	327	A.I.R.spec hi perf.	-	325	4	Chevy II
1969	-	ZG	350	m/t, 3 spd	-	255	4	K-10 & 20
1966	66	ZH	327	sp hi per, EM, a/c	-	325	4	Chevy II
1969	-	ZH	350	m/t, 3 spd	-	255	4	K-20
1966	67	ZI	327	special high perf.	-	325	4	Chevy II
1966	67	ZJ	327	spec high perf, a/c	-	325	4	Chevy II
1969	-	ZJ	350	turbohydro	-	255	4	K-10 & 20
1985	-	ZJB	350	Tuned prt inj,m/t	L98 8	230	TPI	Vette
1985	-	ZJC	350	Tuned prt inj,exp	L98 8	230	TPI	Vette
1986	-	ZJH	350	a/t, alum heads	L98 8	235	TPI	Vette
1985	-	ZJJ	350	Tuned prt inj, a/t	L98 8	230	TPI	Vette

first year	last year	stamp RPO	cid	application	VIN	h/p	bbls	body styles
1985	-	ZJK	350	Tuned prt inj, m/t	L98 8	230	TPI	Vette
1987	-	ZJN	350	a/t, alum heads	L98 8	240	TPI	Vette
1987	-	ZJR	350	m/t, alum heads	L98 8	240	TPI	Vette
1986	-	ZJS	350	a/t, alhds, oil cool	L98 8	235	TPI	Vette
1986	-	ZJW	350	m/t, alhds, oil cool	L98 8	235	TPI	Vette
1965	67	ZK	327	Powerglide	-	275	4	Chevy II
1986	-	ZKA	350	m/t, alum heads	L98 8	235	TPI	Vette
1986	-	ZKD	350	a/t, alum heads	L98 8	235	TPI	Vette
1965	66	ZL	327	Pwerglide, hi perf.	-	300	4	Chevy II
1987	-	ZLA	350	a/t, alhds, oil cool	L98 8	240	TPI	Vette
1987	-	ZLB	350	export, al. heads	L98 8	240	TPI	Vette
1987	-	ZLC	350	m/t, alhds, oil cool	L98 8	240	TPI	Vette
1965	67	ZM	327	Powerglide, a/c	-	275	4	Chevy II
1988	-	ZMA	350	a/t, alum heads	L98 8	240	TPI	Vette
1988	-	ZMC	350	a/t, alhds, oil cool	L98 8	240	TPI	Vette
1988	-	ZMD	350	m/t, alhds, oil cool	L98 8	240	TPI	Vette
1965	66	ZN	327	glide, a/c, hi perf.	-	300	4	Chevy II
1968	-	ZO	307	m/t	-	200	2	C-10
1968	-	ZP	307	m/t	-	200	2	K-10 & 20
1968	-	ZQ	307	m/t	-	200	4	K-20
1989	-	ZRA	350	m/t, alhds, oil cool	L98 8	240	TPI	Vette
1989	-	ZRB	350	a/t, alum heads	L98 8	240	TPI	Vette
1989	-	ZRC	350	a/t, alhds, oil cool	L98 8	240	TPI	Vette
1990	-	ZRJ	350	ZR1, ohc, 32v, m/t	J LT5	380	MPFI	Vette
1968	-	ZS	307	m/t	-	200	2	C-20
1990	-	ZSA	350	a/t, alum heads	L98 8	250	TPI	Vette
1990	-	ZSB	350	m/t, alum heads	L98 8	250	TPI	Vette
1990	-	ZSC	350	a/t, alhds, oil cool	L98 8	250	TPI	Vette
1991	-	ZTA	350	a/t, alum heads	L98 8	245	TPI	Vette
1991	-	ZTB	350	m/t, alhds, oil cool	L98 8	245	TPI	Vette
1991	-	ZTC	350	a/t, alhds, oil cool	L98 8	245	TPI	Vette
1991	-	ZTD	350	ZR1, ohc, 32v, m/t	J LT5	375	MPFI	Vette
1991	-	ZTH	350	ZR1, ohc, 32v, m/t	J LT5	375	MPFI	Vette
1991	-	ZTJ	350	ZR1, ohc, 32v, m/t	J LT5	375	MPFI	Vette
1991	-	ZTK	350	ZR1, ohc, 32v, m/t	J LT5	375	MPFI	Vette
1992	-	ZUA	350	rev cooling, a/t	LT1 P	300	TPI	Vette
1992	-	ZUB	350	rev cooling, m/t	LT1 P	300	TPI	Vette
1993	-	ZVA	350	rev cooling, a/t	LT1 P	300	TPI	Vette
1993	-	ZVB	350	rev cooling, m/t	LT1 P	300	TPI	Vette
1993	-	ZVC	350	ZR1, ohc, 32v, m/t	J LT5	375	MPFI	Vette
1968	-	ZX	307	m/t, 3 spd	-	200	2	K-10 & 20
1968	-	ZY	307	m/t, 3 spd	-	200	2	K-20

Index